British Queer Cinema

British Queer Cinema draws together a diverse range of innovative new essays that explore, for the first time, the provocative history of lesbian, gay and queer representation in British cinema.

From the early years of 'Pre-Gay' film, through to the social upheaval of post-war 'permissiveness', Gay Liberation and the 'post-AIDS' queer generation, contributors examine the shifting and complex nature of queer identity, desire and spectatorship across a number of classical and contemporary British popular film genres and traditions.

Through case studies of key works such as *The Killing of Sister George*, *Prick Up Your Ears* and *Beautiful Thing*; a reappraisal of the films of Anthony Asquith, Terence Davies and Derek Jarman; to the 'queerness' of the heritage film, the homoerotic 'New Wave', or the star performances of Dirk Bogarde, Beryl Reid and Stephen Fry, this timely collection maps the relationship between contemporary queer sexuality and its socio-historical, national and critical contexts.

Contributors: Raymond Armstrong, Stephen Bourne, Glyn Davis, Alexander Doty, Jim Ellis, Robin Griffiths, Keith Howes, Ros Jennings, Kenneth MacKinnon, Andy Medhurst, Andrew Moor, Ani Ritchie, Lizzie Thynne, Michael Williams and Gregory Woods.

Robin Griffiths is Senior Lecturer in Film Studies at the University of Gloucestershire. He is the author of *New Queer Cinema: Beyond the Celluloid Closet* (2006) and editor of *Queer Cinema in Europe* (2006).

British Popular Cinema
Series Editors: Steve Chibnall and I. Q. Hunter
DeMontfort University, Leicester

At a time when there is a growing popular and scholarly interest in British film, with new sources of funding and notable successes in world markets, this series explores the largely submerged history of the UK's cinema of entertainment.

The series rediscovers and evaluates not only individual films but whole genres, such as science fiction and the crime film, that have been ignored by a past generation of critics. Dismissed for decades as aberrations in the national cinema and anaemic imitations of American originals, these films are now being celebrated in some quarters as important contributions to our cinematic heritage.

The emergence of cult genre movies from the apparently respectable lineage of British film emphasises the gap between traditional academic criticism and a new alliance between revisionist film theorists and extra-mural (but well-informed) cinema enthusiasts who wish to take the study of British film in unexpected directions. This series offers the opportunity for both established cineastes and new writers to examine long-neglected areas of British film production or to develop new approaches to more familiar territory. The books will enhance our understanding of how ideas and representations in films relate to changing gender and class relations in post-war Britain, and their accessible writing style will make these insights available to a much wider readership.

British Crime Cinema
Edited by Steve Chibnall and Robert Murphy

British Science Fiction Cinema
Edited by I. Q. Hunter

British Horror Cinema
Edited by Julian Petley and Steve Chibnall

British Historical Cinema
Edited by Claire Monk and Amy Sargeant

British Queer Cinema
Edited by Robin Griffiths

British Queer Cinema

Edited by Robin Griffiths

Routledge
Taylor & Francis Group

LONDON AND NEW YORK

First published 2006
by Routledge
2 Park Square, Milton Park, Abingdon, Oxon OX14 4RN

Simultaneously published in the USA and Canada
by Routledge
270 Madison Ave, New York, NY 10016

Routledge is an imprint of the Taylor & Francis Group

Typeset in Perpetua by
Keystroke, Jacaranda Lodge, Wolverhampton
Printed and bound in Great Britain by
The Cromwell Press, Trowbridge, Wiltshire

British Library Cataloguing in Publication Data
A catalogue record for this book is available from the British Library

Library of Congress Cataloging in Publication Data
Britsh queer cinema / edited by Robin Griffiths.
    p. cm. – (British popular cinema)
  Includes bibliographical references and index.
1. Homosexuality in motion pictures. 2. Gays in motion pictures. 3. Motion
pictures–Great Britain. I. Griffiths, Robin. II. Series.
  PN1995.9.H55B75 2005
  791.43′653–dc22   2005027729

ISBN10: 0–415–30778–3 (hbk)
ISBN10: 0–415–30779–1 (pbk)

ISBN13: 9–78–0–415–30778–9 (hbk)
ISBN13: 9–78–0–415–30779–6 (pbk)

Contents

List of illustrations   vii
Notes on contributors   ix
Acknowledgements   xiii

Introduction: Queer Britannia – a century of *sinema*   1
ROBIN GRIFFITHS

1 **In search of nebulous nancies: Looking for queers in
   pre-gay British film**   21
   ANDY MEDHURST

2 **Behind the masks: Anthony Asquith and
   Brian Desmond Hurst**   35
   STEPHEN BOURNE

3 **An instrument with a flaming sword: Conservative
   queerness in *A Canterbury Tale***   47
   ALEXANDER DOTY

4 **Are there stars out tonight?**   61
   KEITH HOWES

5 **Sad and angry: Queers in 1960s British cinema**   71
   ROBIN GRIFFITHS

 6 'A comic monster of revue': Beryl Reid, *Sister George*
    and the performance of dykery   91
    LIZZIE THYNNE

 7 'Come and have a bathe!': Landscaping the queer utopia   105
    MICHAEL WILLIAMS

 8 Intermingling under controlled conditions: The queerness
    of *Prick Up Your Ears*   121
    KENNETH MACKINNON

 9 Terence Davies and the *Unheimlich* home movie   133
    JIM ELLIS

10 More jiggery than pokery: Derek Jarman's *Edward II*   145
    RAYMOND ARMSTRONG

11 Beyond the pale: The politics of Neil Jordan's
    The Crying Game   157
    ANDREW MOOR

12 'It's my nature': AIDS narratives and the moral
    re-branding of queerness in the mid-1990s   171
    GREGORY WOODS

13 *Beautiful Thing*: British queer cinema, positive
    unoriginality and the everyday   183
    ROS JENNINGS

14 Taming Oscar Wilde: Queerness, heritage and stardom   195
    GLYN DAVIS

15 An interview with Lisa Gornick: Reflections on a
    'first draft' film about love and its labels   207
    ANI RITCHIE

    Selective filmography   215
    Index   241

Illustrations

0.1   Jordan as 'Amyl Nitrate' in Derek Jarman's *Jubilee* (1977)   2
0.2   Charles Hawtrey and Kenneth Williams in *Carry on Constable* (1960)   7
0.3   Michael Praed as 'the Queen' in *Nine Dead Gay Guys* (2002)   17
1.1   Original British poster for Basil Dearden's *Victim* (1961)   22
1.2   Michael Ward   25
1.3   Kenneth Griffith as Jimmy Ellis in *High Treason* (1951)   30
2.1   Anthony Asquith   36
3.1   Eric Portman and Sheila Sim in *A Canterbury Tale* (1944)   48
3.2   Dennis Price and Eric Portman on the road to Canterbury   53
4.1   Rupert Everett as Guy Bennett in *Another Country* (1984)   62
4.2   Dirk Bogarde in *Once a Jolly Swagman* (1948)   65
5.1   Michéle Breton, Anita Pallenberg and Mick Jagger in *Performance*
      (1970)   72
5.2   Murray Melvin as 'sad young man' Geoffrey in *A Taste of Honey*
      (1961)   79
5.3   Richard Harris joins 'the Club' in *This Sporting Life* (1963)   82
5.4   Ken Robertson in Ron Peck and Paul Hallam's *Nighthawks* (1978)   86
6.1   Beryl Reid as predatory soap star June Buckridge in *The Killing
      of Sister George* (1968)   92
6.2   June and girlfriend Childie (Susannah York) at the Gateways Club   96
6.3   Mrs Croft (Coral Browne) seduces Childie   99
7.1   James Wilby and Hugh Grant in *Maurice* (1987)   108
7.2   Ben Silverstone and Brad Gorton in *Get Real* (1998)   114
8.1   Daniel Day-Lewis and Gordon Warnecke in *My Beautiful Laundrette*
      (1985)   123
8.2   Gary Oldman as Joe Orton in *Prick Up Your Ears* (1987)   125
9.1   Pete Postlethwaite in *Distant Voices, Still Lives* (1988)   135
9.2   Leigh McCormack as Bud in *The Long Day Closes* (1992)   140
10.1 Edward (Steven Waddington) and Gaveston (Andrew Tiernan)
      in Derek Jarman's *Edward II* (1991)   146

11.1   Stephen Rea and Jaye Davidson in *The Crying Game* (1992)   158
11.2   Dil (Jaye Davidson) meets *femme-fatale* Jude (Miranda Richardson)   166
12.1   Jane Asher and Tim Woodward in *Closing Numbers* (1993)   175
13.1   Glen Berry and Scott Neal in *Beautiful Thing* (1996)   185
13.2   Sandra (Linda Henry) and Leah (Tameka Empson) show their
       support as Jamie and Ste publicly proclaim their love   191
14.1   Stephen Fry as Oscar Wilde in *Wilde* (1997)   203
15.1   Lisa Gornick and Raquel Cassidy in *Do I Love You?* (2003)   208

Notes on contributors

Raymond Armstrong teaches Film Studies at Queen's University, Belfast. He is a graduate of the Ulster Polytechnic (BA 1980) and the University of Ulster (PhD 1988). From 1992–2001, he worked as a lecturer in Humanities at the University of Ulster, Jordanstown, where he taught Literature, Drama and Film Studies. He is the author of *Kafka and Pinter: Shadow-Boxing* (Macmillan/St Martin's Press, 1999).

Stephen Bourne is the author of *Brief Encounters: Lesbians and Gays in British Cinema 1930–71* (Cassell, 1996) and *Black in the British Frame*, his award-winning history of black British film and television, published in a revised, updated edition by Continuum (2001). He has also contributed to Methuen's *The Encyclopedia of British Film* (2003) as well as Routledge's *Who's Who in Gay and Lesbian History* (2001) and *British Historical Cinema* (2002). He has completed an MPhil on gay representation in British television drama at De Montfort University, and in 2005 published *Elisabeth Welch: Soft Lights and Sweet Music* (Scarecrow Press) and *Speak of Me As I Am: The Black Presence in Southwark Since 1600* (London Borough of Southwark).

Glyn Davis is a lecturer in Screen Studies at the University of Bristol. He is the co-editor, with Kay Dickinson, of *Teen TV: Genre, Consumption, Identity* (BFI, 2004) and is a contributor to an edited collection on *Post-Punk Cinema* (Edinburgh University Press, 2005).

Alexander Doty is a Professor in the English Department at Lehigh University in Bethlehem, Pennsylvania. He has written *Making Things Perfectly Queer: Interpreting Mass Culture* (University of Minnesota Press, 1993) and *Flaming Classics: Queering the Film Canon* (Routledge, 2000), and has co-edited *Out in Culture: Gay, Lesbian, and Queer Essays on Popular Culture* (Duke University Press, 1995). At present, he is working on a book on the films of Powell and Pressburger, as well as on a certain-to-be-unproduced play.

Jim Ellis is an Associate Professor at the University of Calgary, where he teaches Film and Renaissance Literature. He is the author of *Sexuality and Citizenship:*

Metamorphosis in Elizabethan Erotic Verse (University of Toronto Press, 2003) and numerous articles on British cinema. He is currently at work on a study of the films of Derek Jarman.

Robin Griffiths is Senior Lecturer in Film Studies at the University of Gloucestershire. He is author of *New Queer Cinema: Beyond the Celluloid Closet* (Wallflower Press, 2006) and editor of *Queer Cinema in Europe* (Intellect Books, 2006). He is currently working on AHRC funded research into the critical history of *Cinema and Sexuality* for the Open University Press.

Keith Howes was Features Editor of *London Gay News* 1976–79 and co-editor of *British Film Year* 1985. He is author of *Broadcasting It: An Encyclopedia of Homosexuality on Film, Radio and TV* (Cassell, 1993) and *Outspoken: Keith Howes's Gay News Interviews* (Cassell, 1995). He is a contributor to *Who's Who in Gay and Lesbian History* (Routledge, 2001).

Ros Jennings is Director of Research for Arts & Humanities at the University of Gloucestershire. She has researched and published widely in both Australian Studies and Film and Television Studies (including audience/reception studies). Recent work includes articles on Ana Kokkinos' film *Head On* and the pedagogic authority of teaching Australian Studies in a British context.

Kenneth MacKinnon gained a First Class MA in Classics from Edinburgh University in 1965, the postgraduate degree of B.Litt. (in ancient Greek) from Oxford in 1969, before being awarded a Diploma in Film Studies from the BFI/University of London, in 1978. Much of his university career was spent as subject tutor of Classical Civilisation, before Film Studies was introduced to the curriculum in 1984. During his years as Film Studies subject tutor and Professor at what is now London Metropolitan University, he has had seven books on aspects of film published, including *Uneasy Pleasures* (Cygnus Arts, 1998), *Love, Tears and the Male Spectator* (Fairleigh Dickinson University Press, 2002) and *Representing Men* (Hodder Arnold, 2003), as well as two books of translations of modern Greek drama, and many articles on both Classics and Film Studies.

Andy Medhurst teaches about television, film, popular culture and sexuality at the University of Sussex. He has been writing about those (and other) topics since 1982, a statistic which has suddenly made him feel rather ancient.

Andrew Moor lectures in Film and Literature at the University of Wales, Bangor. His chief research areas are British cinema (particularly Powell and Pressburger) and sexuality, and he has contributed essays on Derek Jarman, Anton Walbrook and Powell and Pressburger. He is currently co-editing (with Graeme Harper) a volume on medicine and cinema for Wallflower Press, and is completing a monograph on Powell and Pressburger for I. B. Tauris.

Ani Ritchie is Lecturer in Media with Cultural Studies at Southampton Institute. Her teaching interests lie primarily in the areas of queer and feminist film theory, and more generally on the representations of queer sexuality. She is currently working on her PhD, which explores the representation of lesbian sex on film with a particular focus on the negotiation of sexual identity amongst young lesbian audiences.

Lizzie Thynne is Senior Lecturer in Media and Cultural Studies at Sussex University. She has made programmes for Channel Four and ITV as well as video work for galleries and festivals, and is currently producing a film on the surrealist photographer, Claude Cahun. She has published on lesbian representation and women's employment in television.

Michael Williams lectures in Film Studies at the University of Southampton. He has published several articles on Ivor Novello, Britain's leading matinée-idol of the 1920s, and his monograph *Ivor Novello: Screen Idol*, a contextual star study, was published by the BFI in 2003. He has also published on Noel Coward and has forthcoming articles on the heritage film in *Screen Method: Comparative Readings in Screen Studies* (Wallflower Press); Belgian filmmaker Bavo Defurne in *Queer Cinema in Europe* (Intellect Books) and film adaptations of *The Talented Mr Ripley* in the *Journal of Romance Studies*.

Gregory Woods is Professor of Gay & Lesbian Studies at the Nottingham Trent University. His was the first such appointment in the UK. He is the author of *Articulate Flesh: Male Homo-eroticism and Modern Poetry* (1987) and *A History of Gay Literature: The Male Tradition* (1998), both from Yale University Press. Until 2002, Woods was on the board of directors of East Midland Arts. He is also on the board of the Theory, Culture and Society Centre, and chairs the board of the trAce Online Writing Centre. His poetry, highly regarded by such writers as Stephen Spender and Thom Gunn, is published by Carcanet Press. His most recent collection was *The District Commissioner's Dreams* (2002). Woods is a fellow of the English Association.

Acknowledgements

I would like to begin by thanking the Series Editors, Steve Chibnall and Ian Hunter, for their great enthusiasm and encouragement in commissioning this timely contribution to the *British Popular Cinema* series. Likewise, I would like to thank everyone at Routledge, particularly Rebecca Barden, Lesley Riddle and Aileen Irwin for all their invaluable advice, support and patience throughout the lengthy editing process.

Special thanks also go to Richard Dyer, Sarah Street and Yvonne Tasker for recommending potential contributors, Stephen Bourne for kindly granting me access to his personal collection of film stills and Laila Torsun at the BFI Stills Collection for all her help.

I would also like to acknowledge the support of the School of Art, Media and Design at the University of Gloucestershire, for granting me research leave in order to complete this project.

Every effort has been made to obtain permission to reproduce copyright material in this volume. If any oversight has been made in the publication of this book, I apologise in advance, and welcome copyright holders to inform me of any unintentional errors and/or omissions.

This book is dedicated to the memory of cinema's greatest British 'queer' – Derek Jarman (1942–94).

Robin Griffiths
May, 2005

Introduction

Queer Britannia – a century of *sinema*

Robin Griffiths

In the revised introduction to his esteemed *The British Cinema Book*, Robert Murphy proclaims that 'the study of British cinema has never been so widespread' (2001:1). And granted, the last ten years or so have witnessed a veritable renaissance in research and new writing on British film, particularly from within the UK. But as the editors of another key anthology in the field – *British Cinema: Past and Present* – note, the principal dilemma that commonly emerges in most studies of the subject is exactly 'how we should conceptualise British cinema or what it means to talk about British cinema' (Ashby and Higson, 2000:14). For although there is no question that recent and more established academic debates have proved invaluable for the fertile advancement of 'British Cinema Studies', it is arguable that they have also, more problematically, prescribed rather exclusive and preferred models of how this 'conceptualisation' or 'discussion' should be articulated. Film historians such as Andrew Higson and Jeffrey Richards[1] have expressed the need for a re-framing of critical positions on British film – envisaging a much more pluralist methodology that is representative of the rich diversity of historical production and reception in the UK – but the one position that still remains 'unknown' and 'amorphous' (to cite Alan Lovell and Peter Wollen's seminal descriptions of the 'state' of British cinema in 1969) is sexuality, particularly sexuality beyond the 'hetero-normative'.[2]

Whilst alluding to a revisionist bent, academic film criticism in the UK has, on the whole, remained decidedly heterocentrist in terms of the types of film texts and critical perspectives that comprise this rather selective discursive canon. For despite some expression of concern about 'the scarcity of scholarship discussing British cinema in terms of race, ethnicity and multi-culturalism' (Ashby and Higson, 2000: 15), continual omission with regards to lesbian, gay or more recently *queer* scholarship remains discretely unaddressed (including the other volumes in this *British Popular Cinema* series). With very few exceptions, 'this vast pink and lavender arena', as Keith Howes vividly observes, 'has mostly escaped the attentions of the orthodox critic and historian',[3] but as the contributors to this landmark collection ably demonstrate, 'queers' have historically played a pivotal role in both

Figure 0.1   'Queer Britannia': cinema beyond the 'hetero-normative' (Derek Jarman's
          Jubilee [1977]).

Source: Cinegate Ltd.

creatively shaping and politically challenging issues of textual production and
reception in the UK over the years – from both inside and 'out' of the industry.

   In contrast to the other volumes in this series, however, *British Queer Cinema* is
unable to straightforwardly 'focus on a hitherto little-known or neglected genre of
British cinema' (Monk and Sargeant, 2002: 1). As the first (of hopefully many) to
consider *British* queer cinema in its own right, the contributors to this book broach

the subject from a variety of perspectives, and address a much wider range of thematic and generic concerns. But given that little formative critical work exists for considering the specificities of queer cinema from within a British context, and due to the broad spectrum that such a fluid methodological framework should encompass, this collection can in no way hope to present a definitive model for surveying queer 'representation' in British cinema. Rather it is concerned, more appropriately, with carving out a critical space for *queerly* rethinking common assumptions around particular British cinematic texts, pleasures and viewing positions, and the socio-cultural and historical frameworks through which they have been consistently addressed and evaluated. The history of *queerness* in British *sinema* consequently represents a history of erasure and marginality, a struggle over meaning and interpretation, and a questioning of the very 'nature' of desire and identity on the screen.

However, as is problematic with studies of 'national' cinemas, attempts at constructing categorical notions of 'identity' in British film have been persistently burdened with accusations of misrepresentation and exclusion, for 'there is no core identity to British cinema – it is far too diverse, far too rich to be reduced to a fixed essence' (Higson, 1996: 2). This is a problem that is equally troubling in any attempt at defining an essential or reducible form of lesbian, gay or queer identity on the British screen, even when it moves beyond the usual suspects that we have come to expect (i.e. the stereotypical preponderance of screaming queens, menacing bull dykes and suicidal loners). The title 'British *Queer* Cinema' as an inclusive slant for this collection is therefore, on many levels, a highly contentious yet challenging proposition. For if it has proved so difficult to reach any critical consensus on what exactly 'British' cinema and identity are – past or present – then the sandwiching of the term 'queer' makes for an even more 'slippery' ménage à trois.

The British films, directors and actors queerly investigated in the contents of this volume are therefore in no way definitive or exhaustive; but their inclusion here is primarily on the grounds that they either directly address and/or seek to represent 'lesbian', 'gay', 'bisexual' or 'transgender' themes and/or identities (e.g. *Beautiful Thing, The Killing of Sister George, Closing Numbers, The Crying Game*, etc.), or in some sense or another lend themselves to – or even openly solicit – queer modes of interpretation: via textual mechanisms that seemingly resist 'hetero-normative' assimilation, or through extra-textual perceptions of the alleged orientations of the actors/directors/writers, etc. connected with their production (from readings of Powell and Pressburger's *A Canterbury Tale*, the British New Wave cycle or the Heritage film, to a re-appraisal of the films of Anthony Asquith and Terence Davies, or the apparently 'straight' performances of Michael Ward, Dirk Bogarde and Beryl Reid). Collectively, they comprise an 'alternative' celluloid archive that has warranted very special appreciative attention and investment from queer audiences throughout the twentieth century, thereby underscoring the breadth of queerness that exists within British cinema across a diverse range of genres and historical periods.

Even though the term *queer* was purportedly 'reclaimed' by North American cultural theorists in the early 1990s – seemingly evacuated of its historically pejorative semantic specificity and re-configured to represent a productive rethinking of discourses around gender and sexuality – its reception within British academic circles has, in comparison, elicited much more suspicion of embracing this apparently unproblematic resignification. Still mired in the final death throes of post-Thatcherite conservatism, with its institutionalised homophobia, AIDS hysteria and politically sanctioned discrimination (the notorious 'Section 28'), Britain in the late 1980s and early 1990s was hardly the 'gay-friendly' place to warrant such apolitical disregard for the implications of the word. For the generations of British lesbians and gay men who have struggled through decades of homophobic abuse and discrimination, 'queer' has socio-historical resonance that is not so easily ignored. My usage of the term in this context then, is not to deny the irrevocable significance of the past it still evokes; but as other editors of similarly themed anthologies have argued, its most basic and productive function is more as an inclusive means of drawing together – though not unproblematically – those disparate sexual identities, viewpoints and cultural artefacts that resist easy assimilation to the 'norm'.

The mainstream globalisation of 'Queer Theory' has been perceived by many of its critics to be both detached from the realities of the history of gay liberation, and politically indifferent towards the lives and experiences of the very queers it seeks to address.[4] But although it may, at first sight, be suggestive of a problematic break with traditionalist lesbian and gay socio-political models, it more properly marks a continuum, since as Annamarie Jagose rightly clarifies, 'Queer theory's debunking of stable sexes, genders and sexualities develops out of a specifically lesbian and gay reworking of the poststructuralist figuring of identity as a constellation of multiple and unstable positions' (1996: 3). And so, contrary to being perceived as a uniquely contemporary critical development, its actual radical efficacy as an ontological model thus lies in the fact that it is 'already imbricated in and informing existing knowledges of sexuality' (4). Queer theory is not, therefore, an assumed extension of, or departure from, 'lesbian and gay studies' per se, but is more significantly a means of conceptualising the abstract, genealogically fluid conditions through which these 'studies' and 'identities' have evolved (including, of course, those concerning heterosexuality). For to declare oneself as 'queer' not only enables an opportunity to re-define ourselves against 'the norm' – however that manifests itself in relation to both homo- and hetero-sexuality – but also allows for a querying (or *queering*) of the stability of such notions of 'normality', and the validity of the accepted epistemology of sexuality itself.

Political tensions aside, however, some of the most productively deployed queer critiques have emerged in relation to film studies. Even Dennis Altman, one of queer theory's most outspoken detractors, acknowledges its usefulness in rethinking issues around identity and representation in cinema. For Altman, British films such as Neil Jordan's *The Crying Game* (1992) and Sally Potter's *Orlando* (1993) 'can be described as "queer"' because they radically 'unsettle assumptions and preconceptions about sexuality and gender and their inter-relationship'.[5] *The Crying Game* in particular, as Andrew Moor argues in his contribution to this collection (Chapter 11), epitomises these very 'crises of category in the realm of sex and gender' that – as is quite common to British queer cinema – are consistently inter-connected to socio-cultural crises of nationhood, class, race and ethnicity which queer theory can both articulate and exploit; interrogating the preconditions for such configurations and their affects 'as part of its rhetorical strategy to deconstruct traditional ways of seeing'.

In parallel with the rise of queer theory as an institutionalised academic discipline, a newly legitimised 'Queer Film Studies' has similarly positioned itself at the 'cutting edge' of new and progressive debates within the field. And since queer theory's *modus operandi* is not only to limn the performative complexities of gender and sexual identity, but also the wider historical conditions and cultural practices that characterise and propagate our understandings of them, the defining and representative role of cinema plays an important part in the process – for as Richard Dyer has already established, 'no social group can afford to ignore the importance of cinema . . . [for it] has acted as a repository of images of how people are and how they should be, images that are both produced by and help to produce the general thought and feeling of our culture' (*Gays and Film*, 1977: 1). But as is frustrating about the emergent heterocentric bias to discourses around British cinema, the diverse canon that currently comprises queer film studies has similarly tended to ignore the contribution that British film has made – and continues to make – to the field which this volume seeks to begin to lay the formative groundwork for redress.

Gay film historians from Dyer (1977, 1990, 2002), to Vito Russo (1981) and, more recently, Brett Farmer (2000) have quite effectively illustrated how the cinematic medium (and the multifarious practices of film spectatorship) plays a vital role in the formulation and covert articulation of queer identity and desire:

> cinema has long been a forum for the circulation of sexual meanings and pleasures. With its congregation of bodies in close, darkened spaces; its simulation of patently voyeuristic structures; and its lush supply of erotic visual spectacles, cinema has, from the beginning, been marked as a profoundly sexualised form.
>
> (Farmer, 2000: 25)

But since marginalised and 'deviant' forms of identity, sexuality and pleasure in British cinema have long been historically and narratively precluded – for economic as well as legal or moral reasons – Britain's queer audiences have had to activate their own very unique forms of cultural identification, that are either mobilised around particularly significant narrative themes and scenarios (from public school sublimation to war-time homosociality), or coloured by the tacit extra-textual nuances that surround the directors, writers and stars involved (from the loaded linguistic inflections of Noel Coward and Kenneth Williams to the 'cottaging' scandals of Alec Guinness and John Gielgud). The fantasy realms of cinema have thus proved to be especially fertile for subversive re-imagining, and have allowed for the appropriative cultivation of liminal modes of spectatorship that disavow the recuperative hetero-normalising impetus of the popular mainstream.

As Andy Medhurst argues in Chapter 1, the pioneering queer spectators of British cinema were repeatedly forced to 'teas[e] a text apart', in order to reveal the fundamental 'wanton speculativeness' of narrative meaning in film. And yet as Alexander Doty has earlier insisted (2000: 2), these commonly labelled 'queer readings' of mainstream film should not in any way be seen as 'alternative' or 'against the grain' in relation to dominant heteronormative interpretive regimes – thereby safely colluding with and maintaining oppositional 'normalising' hierarchies – but should actually be regarded as no less legitimate than their 'straight' equivalents:

> for me, any text is already potentially queer [. . .] we should drop the idea of 'queering' something, as it implies taking a thing that is straight and doing something to it. I'd like to see queer discourses and practices as being less about co-opting and 'making' things queer and more about discussing how things are, or might be understood as, queer.

From this standpoint, the intimate 'man-to-man' scenarios of the early films of gay directors James Whale and Anthony Asquith, for example, or the ambivalent 'performances' of Mary Morris and Michael Redgrave; the flamboyant artificiality of the Gainsborough melodramas and the subversive campery of the Ealing comedies or *Carry On* films – to propose to 'unpack' but a few – start to look decidedly *queer*. In fact, classic British cinema, with its wonderful history of faux 'close your eyes and think of England' *stiff-upper-lip-ness*, burlesque masquerade and sublimated desires, is in many ways quintessentially queer by the very nature of its ironies and excesses. So by re-viewing these cinematic texts for their underlying instabilities, fissures and ambiguities – commonly perceived by queer theorists as the 'symptomatic' signs of queerness – an opportunity is enabled for revisiting the very cultural narratives that have persistently sought to exclude us, but, ironically, are synonymously contingent upon our presence: 'Infamy! Infamy! They've all got it in-for-me!'

By situating these works chronologically in their socio-historical context, this anthology is shaped via two overlapping yet distinctive methodological approaches:

Figure 0.2 'Symptomatic signs of queerness'? Charles Hawtrey and Kenneth Williams in
    Carry On Constable (1960).

Source: BFI stills, posters and designs (courtesy of Stephen Bourne).

firstly, a determination to re-envisage the apparently 'repressed' past of classic
British cinema during the first half of the twentieth century (a time in which
'deviant' identity seemingly existed beyond the frame, and safely out of view); and
secondly, a perhaps even more critical re-assessment of the seemingly 'liberated'
post-war British screen (and emergent attempts to negotiate the variable degrees
of lesbian, gay and queer 'representation' and desire that have evolved in the
popular mainstream since).

    For queer audiences, the cultural history of British popular narrative cinema may
have involved a subversive re-viewing of recurrent themes, characters, context
and biography in order to 'read between the lines' of a film's preferred heteronormative meanings, but as the chapters that comprise the first part of this
collection effectively demonstrate, early British cinema was in fact positively
'flaming'. However, as Medhurst finds in his search for 'nebulous nancies', it is
impossible to realistically attempt any 'systematic' or 'testable' survey of how
queers were represented in what he terms as 'pre-Gay' British cinema (i.e. prior
to the word's re-configuration within the public imagination as a deviant identity-
formation). For queers rarely occupied a central narrative position in the popular

mainstream, unless their sexuality was safely locked away in an off-screen dressing room closet, or textually coded as some 'other' form of malevolent threat to (hetero-) narrative stability. The real problem with such an undertaking then actually lies in determining exactly *who* British cinema's antecedent screen 'nancies' were, what specific 'signs' of queerness should we search for – beyond the stereotypical – and whether or not it's really possible to 'be sure of who you're looking at' in the first place?

In attempting to fix some boundaries for identifying such an elusive quarry, Medhurst sets his sights on those ephemeral figures who hover on the peripheries of most mainstream heterosexual narratives: 'almost always ludicrous, villainous, monstrous, shadowy, pained, paranoid, edgy, guilty, doomed, or mocked'. Figures that allusively embody 'something other, something dangerous, and something that could trouble the established patterns of British family life'. And even though the implicit sexuality of these characters has remained safely denied within such narratives, what is really crucial in any attempt at comprehending British cinema's early queers is the strategic significance of casting. Since as Keith Howes later reiterates in Chapter 4, actors such as Michael Ward, Kenneth Griffith, Alec Guiness and Michael Redgrave (or more recently, Simon Callow, Rupert Everett, Ian McKellen and Tilda Swinton), to name but a few, have repeatedly played roles that 'carry echoes of that on-screen or off-screen queerness into otherwise ostensibly straight situations'. These *performers'* contribution to British queer cinema has been less about playing specifically gay roles, and more subversively about playing rather ambiguously coded heterosexual characters whose 'every appearance challenges the humdrumness of Either/Or'. Their 'known' *les-bi-gay* sexuality has long been exploited in mainstream cinema as 'sissified shorthand' for that which the film itself refuses to acknowledge, thereby reducing all the 'sybaritic excess' and 'dandified perversity' of any coded threat to social and national stability into 'a single despised creature'. A strategy that is thus deployed as a narrative means of underscoring both the legitimacy and centrality of the naturalized heterocentric narrative and ideological preoccupations of the films in which they appear. But in spite of all this apparent narrative contempt, it also, ironically, enabled an emergent visibility in British cinema at the time that could – for its queer audiences – 'guide you to interesting places'.

Film historian Stephen Bourne, on the other hand, aims to set the record 'straight' regarding historically obscured perceptions of two of classic British cinema's most influential filmmakers, Anthony Asquith and Brian Desmond Hurst (Chapter 2). Bourne unmasks a long history of inaccurate and 'preferred' accounts of their films that have continually denied their subtle yet deliberate intervention in heteronormative discourses. Through a re-appraisal of such queerly inflected films as *Pygmalion* (1938), *The Browning Version* (1951), *The Importance of Being Earnest* (1952) and *The Black Tent* (1956), the extra-textual connotations of both filmmakers' close association with some of British cinema's biggest closeted gay icons (Dirk Bogarde,

Eric Portman, Michael Redgrave *et al.*), and their well-documented 'unconventional' private activities, Bourne reveals a much queerer historical account that has 'been constantly overlooked or marginalised in histories of British cinema'. Despite being hailed as two of the most important directors in the formative history of British film, the mischievous ways in which they covertly ridiculed the 'normalcy' of heterosexual romantic narratives, coupled with their blatant indifference towards their female characters and clearly erotic fascination with 'male-bonding', has remained largely ignored by 'orthodox' accounts of their *oeuvre*, when it demonstrates considerable bravery at a time in which the public revelation of such 'criminal' intent would result in quite devastating consequences for them both.

In contrast, however, to Bourne's more positive reclamation of Asquith and Hurst's films, Alexander Doty finds a far more troubling ideological deployment of queerness in Powell and Pressburger's classic 1944 war-time melodrama *A Canterbury Tale* (Chapter 3). In a continuation of his earlier study of their 'flaming classic' *The Red Shoes* (1948),[6] Doty illustrates how many of Powell and Pressburger's 'repressed heroes' were queerly coded. But contrary to the subversive potential that we have come to expect from such textually transmitted alterity, *A Canterbury Tale* mobilises a 'conservative queerness' that is paradoxically less accessible to progressive reader reclamation. For despite occupying an ambiguously liminal sexual position (in the sense that the film's prospective queers are not 'definitively represented as homosexual or heterosexual'), characters such as 'loony squire' Thomas Colpeper (Eric Portman), trainee 'organist' Peter Gibbs (Dennis Price) and butch 'old maid' Prudence Honeywood (Freda Jackson) are allowed a modicum of coded queer visibility in the film, but only in the de-sexualised 'service of a nation at war'. The radical challenge that queerness may pose in such a context is thus narratively contained and assimilated, so that it does not pose any real threat to the dominant hegemonic ideology of the time: 'the only good queer is one willing to sublimate his/her sexual desires and translate them into a desire to serve dominant culture'. However, as Doty concludes, there is some consolation in the ironic fact that the film synonymously aligns queerness with 'Ye Olde England virtues and values', thereby forcing the conservative audiences of the time to recognise that these 'deviants' have the same ideological beliefs as they do.

In most historical accounts of British narrative cinema, homosexuality is commonly regarded to have been largely invisible on the screen until the release of Basil Dearden's landmark post-war social problem film *Victim* in 1961. Featuring allegedly 'straight' screen icon Dirk Bogarde as a closeted gay middle-class lawyer who is blackmailed by a leather-clad youth, the film was unique for the time in that it foregrounded the contradictory nature of the law, the institutions of family and marriage, and the fragile concept of social 'normality'. However, as I discuss in Chapter 5, the film actually emerged as part of a much wider socio-cinematic queer 'wave' that reflected the shifting moral *Zeitgeist* of Britain in the 1950s and 1960s. From the alienated, homoerotic, sad and angry young men of the 'British

New Wave' to the undisputable sexual decadence of 'Swinging London', Britain's allegedly most progressive and 'exciting period' (Street, 1997: 81) was characterised by a reflexive and 'quite distinctive break with more established cinematic themes and traditions'. But as a number of critics from John Hill (1986) to Peter Hutchings (1997) have argued, the films of the period were rarely as 'radical' or even 'swinging' as initially promised, and were more commonly quite conservative in terms of their overarching gender and sexual politics, which in the end espouse (heteronormative) conformity as the only 'unproblematic' narrative resolution. However, what has been persistently overlooked in studies of this landmark period for British cinema is the significance of the queer sexuality of the three leading visionaries of the 'movement': Tony Richardson, Lindsay Anderson and John Schlesinger.

Not only did such socio-reflexive and homoerotically skewed films as *Look Back in Anger* (1958), *A Kind of Loving* (1962) and *This Sporting Life* (1963), for example, succeed in releasing post-war British cinema from the 'straight-jacket' of decades of middle-class conservatism, but they also, more interestingly, 'exhibited liminal conflicts between transgressive desire and social conformity that are not easily resolved in "hetero-normative" narrative or ideological terms'. Despite the fact that their directors' 'queerness' remained very much in the closet throughout, their consistent narrative pre-occupation with rejecting the social systems and values of 1950s and 1960s Britain not only reflected their own personal artistic and ideological agendas as 'radical' filmmakers, but also, more covertly, symbolised their 'dilemma of being queer in British society at the time'. And whilst their 'New Wave' films tended to be quite erotically focused on a commodified working-class heterosexual male – 'framed through an infatuated middle-class gaze' – and usually at the problematic expense of their female protagonists, in mapping the evolution of their work throughout the 1960s it becomes evident that they were also, more importantly, quite revolutionary in establishing a much wider cultural forum for debate concerning issues of social identity and marginality. Their visionary works both mirrored and influenced the changing perception of homosexuals and homosexuality in 1960s Britain, and laid the socio-cultural and representational foundations for the 'polymorphously perverse' explorations of sexuality that have emerged in a seemingly 'liberated' British cinema since.

However, the 1960s may have been a time in which an embryonic gay male identity slowly became 'identified as existing in all walks of life' (Hill, 1986: 92) and to some extent 'normalised', but lesbian identity on the other hand has, as Lizzie Thynne asserts in Chapter 6, been largely absent from public discourse. Since female homosexuality has been historically invisible within British law – due to Queen Victoria's alleged refusal to even acknowledge its existence – it has never received the same level of public debate that male homosexuality received in the wake of the de-criminalising impetus of Wolfenden: 'while liberal progressive opinion championed the cause of the male homosexual in the late fifties and early sixties, there was a tendency to assume that because lesbianism was not criminal it neither attracted nor merited support'. This invisibility has similarly haunted the history of British cinema, and apart from a few fleeting appearances – such as the sad and lonely figure of Cicely Courtneidge's middle-aged Mavis in Bryan Forbes' *The L-Shaped Room* (1962) – lesbians had never before occupied a central narrative role until the 1968 release of Robert Aldrich's 'shocking revelation of a hidden world' in *The Killing of Sister George*. Whilst on one level the film can be seen as an important contribution to British queer cinema by the very nature of its long overdue existence, the mixed critical response that the film has received since its release has revealed a very real uneasiness with the ambivalent way in which it tended to 'construct "the lesbian" as pathological, and as marking the boundary of the sinister and the bizarre'.

However, despite accusations of voyeurism, stereotype and homophobia, Thynne illustrates how the disruptive performance of 'straight' comedy actress Beryl Reid as 'Sister George' 'brings to the film a different set of pleasures' that in many ways subvert its problematic characterisation of a libidinous 'monstrous dykery' as essentially tragic and abnormal. By camply invoking innuendo, inauthenticity and a 'female disorderliness', the film presents 'queerness as something which is endemic not only to the margins or "demi-monde" of British society, but to the establishment'. Reid's rich and complex portrayal of Sister George / June Buckridge in the film may be read as conforming to the typical cultural perception of the lonely, middle-aged 'butch', but as Thynne maintains, her 'refusal to remain in the closet, disguise her sexuality or maintain a façade of respectability' – thus 'performing' her socially required role – can be seen as a very deliberate attempt at interrogating the boundaries between 'public' and 'private' that moral and legal discourses were, at the time, trying so exhaustively to preserve: 'Given the relative public invisibility of lesbianism, making "the lesbian" a sight is an important part of the film's address'.

In their divergent discussions of the relationship between homosexuality and the heritage film, however, Michael Williams (Chapter 7) and Glyn Davis (Chapter 14) agree that of all the cinematic genres, it is the one genre that 'has afforded considerable screen time to characters that would normally remain in the margins'. The heritage canon has, as Richard Dyer earlier established, proved to be 'sur-prisingly hospitable to homosexual representation' (2002: 204); a fact echoed by John Hill, who asserts that unlike any other genre 'the heritage film . . . invests many of its male relationships with a clear homo-erotic dimension' (1999: 98). So iconic celluloid moments such as the all-male nude bathing sequence in Merchant-Ivory's *A Room with a View* (1986), or the passionate, boundary-crossing love-triangle of *Maurice* (1987), present us, as Williams argues, 'with a tantalisingly queer glimpse of utopia'. By placing these texts within mythically Arcadian settings, 'of both pleasure and beauty and danger and panic', an iconographic queer frame is thus constructed for 'legitimating a homoerotic desire that is often all but spoken'. For this aesthetically lush and fluidly symbolic mise-en-scène subsequently allows these texts to invoke a world of forbidden desire that was conversely inconceivable in their Victorian or Edwardian socio-historical and generic contexts. Interestingly, Williams also finds echoes of this mythic classical utopia within more contemporary sited queer films, such as Stephen Frears' *My Beautiful Laundrette* (1985), Simon Shore's *Get Real* (1998) and Paul Oremland's *Like It Is* (1998) which, despite their gritty urban locales and social-realist preoccupations, commonly contain secluded spaces – or 'queer oases' – that diegetically infuse the films with a distinctly nostalgic impulse; consequently enabling their protagonists to 'make defiant performative gestures towards a mythically liberal classical past in order to transform and *dis-place* the cultural boundedness of the present'.

In contrast, however, to Williams' valorisation of such profoundly queer poetic escapism, Glyn Davis alternatively sets out to 'identify the limitations of the heritage genre with regard to its representations of queerness'. Focusing upon Brian Gilbert's acclaimed biopic *Wilde* (1997) as a particularly useful example, Davis suggests that the genre is actually unable to fully contain the 'untamed' disruptive potential of queerness. And even though the heritage film apparently grants significant narrative space for homosexual representation, it is a depiction that usually operates from within a quite specific representational regime, in which distinctively 'queer forms of sexuality are markedly absent'. The portrayal of lesbian and gay characters in such heritage-biopic hybrids as *Wilde* are actually, upon greater scrutiny, rather limited by their persistent sub-textual recourse to the dully historiographical political rhetoric of the 1970s gay rights movement, that mobilises – as Dyer observes – a 'narrative of realization' (2002: 208); problematically imposing contemporary lesbian and gay political ideologies onto socio-historic narratives set in a much more apolitical past. What conversely concerns Davis, however, are the fuller subversive implications of Oscar Wilde's life and writings, which contribute to the film's more radical queer agenda as it attempts to trouble the heritage genre's limitations.

In drawing upon earlier assessments of Wilde's proto-queer politics, Davis locates the more transgressively queer aspects of the film in those moments that directly call upon his writings. And it is the film's manipulative use of language that enables, as Andy Medhurst has also earlier observed (1997: 32), the destabilising affectiveness of 'the Queer wit in full flow, the man who dares to say the unsayable'. But what is also again quite common here to the film's relevance to a queer British cinema, is the strategic importance of casting, since as Davis acknowledges, 'Stephen Fry and Jude Law bring with them a host of associations and connotations that serve to problematise the positivist "gay liberation" form of the homosexual heritage film'. Fry's own personal history in particular, as a rather unpredictable and caustic wit who 'frequently attacked the credibility and status of staid, dominant institutions', quite effectively merges with his portrayal of Wilde. But, ironically, his public acclaim in the role has seen him more recently morph into the benign persona of a 'respectable homosexual', which, rather surprisingly, casts a 'heterosexual' Jude Law into a much queerer position in the film that 'extends beyond the display of his body'.

In addition to the heritage film, the biopic genre has also permitted a 'safe' – and perhaps contained – space within which to explore queer identity and desire in the mainstream (see, for example: *Another Country, Caravaggio, Carrington, Love Is The Devil*, or made-for-television films *Borstal Boy, The Naked Civil Servant* and *Portrait of a Marriage*). However, Kenneth MacKinnon finds a similarly radical queerness in Stephen Frears' exploration of the life and untimely death of Wildean enfant terrible Joe Orton in *Prick Up Your Ears* (1987). What is remarkable about this film is that unlike most 'authoritative' mainstream biopics, the film 'refuses to authenticate one vision', and alternatively constructs a clearly opaque account in which 'truth remains elusive, half glimpsed'. And in a similar vein to *Wilde*, MacKinnon discusses how Frears' film refuses to participate in the genre's 'chosen self-image of neocracy and liberation', preferring instead to present a deconstructive meditation on the hegemonic function of the 'authoritative voice' in film, in order to echo the limitations of socio-discursive models that construct and regulate the depiction of 'the outlaw homosexual' in society: 'the meanings bestowed upon them [Orton and lover Kenneth Halliwell] by their several observers are no more authenticated in the film than those that they see (and often fail to see) in their own lives'.

This more fluidly ephemeral notion of authenticity and biographical representation that is teased out in *Prick Up Your Ears*, however, takes on a much more disturbing dimension in Jim Ellis' discussion of the gothic 'home movies' of Terence Davies. For at the centre of his autobiographical texts 'stands an unrecognizable version of the self' that is symbolically analogous to those much darker 'truths' that go 'unrecorded'. Ellis describes how Davies rejects any attempt to accurately document his childhood in post-war Liverpool, in favour of a more abstract and contemplative 'memory realism'. So, contrary to some reductive perceptions of his films as merely proffering nostalgic portraits of northern working-class life in the 1940s and 1950s, they are, as Ellis demonstrates, more queerly fluid evocations 'of a subjectivity refusing to settle into an identity'. As some of the first British films to focus on a burgeoning homosexuality in childhood, *Distant Voices, Still Lives* (1988) and *The Long Day Closes* (1992) dramatise 'the split between the remembered and the pictured', and the queer potency of fantasy and cinema as a means by which to escape from the 'traumas of existence'.

As Ellis contends, Davies' filmic structures consequently attempt to mirror the fragmented, suggestive functions of memory, in order to provoke a detachment that re-positions the spectator to contemplate the 'torments' of sexuality and marginality. For Britain's alienated queers – as for Davies and his on-screen alter-egos – the oppressive conformity that they complicitly faced is seemingly transformed when viewed through the lens of fantasy and projection, which underscores how 'cinema makes a familiar observation about the ideological institutions that fabricate reality for us'. The queer characters in these films therefore see the performance of reality for what it is, 'both the fragility of the illusion and its necessity'. Their 'deviant' sexuality makes it impossible for them to truly identify with the socio-cultural fantasy of the (heteronormative) happy family, and so it is within the cinematic world that their 'fullest emotional life is lived'.

This queer revisionism in terms of authenticity, biography and the socio-historical past probably reached its apotheosis with the release of Derek Jarman's postmodern re-envisioning of *Edward II* in 1991. The only feature-length British film to be included by critic B. Ruby Rich as part of the radical 'New Queer Cinema' movement of the early 1990s,[7] Jarman's 'shocking pink triangle of passion, poetry and politics' is, as Raymond Armstrong asserts in Chapter 10, one of the 'godfathers' of queer cinema's 'most formally accessible and emotionally absorbing' works. The film uniquely projects a 'triply distilled' image of gay experience in England throughout the ages, but in contrast to usual queer rejections of generic strategies that codedly suture gay liberationist agendas to films irrespective of their contextual relevance, Jarman quite explicitly parallels the plight of England's queerest monarch 'with the insidious persecution of the gay community under the successive Conservative governments of Margaret Thatcher and John Major'. Armstrong notes how, unlike other queer filmmakers, Jarman has persistently highlighted the conflict between the 'totems of the establishment' and the taboo of homosexuality, in order to foreground how queers have always been trans-historically incompatible with the 'symbolic trappings' of the British state.

However, for all his irreverent political urgency, and the transgressive promise of a shift to more 'mainstream' work, Jarman's untimely death from an AIDS-related illness in 1994 – followed swiftly by the proclaimed death of New Queer Cinema – subsequently allowed for the emergence of a more accessible and mainstream-friendly gay cinema in the 1990s that was, as Gregory Woods puts it in Chapter 12, 'distinctly dull'. For despite a few transgressively potent cinematic anomalies, more notably Neil Jordan's 'terroristically' romantic exploration of the queerly performative spectacle of gender and racial identity in *The Crying Game* – as discussed by Andrew Moor in Chapter 11 – mainstream British queer cinema was, at the time, very much in a state of crisis.

In contrast to the short-lived radical impetus of New Queer Cinema as a response to the AIDS epidemic, British gay-themed cinema in the mid-1990s ultimately became burdened by the clinical prescriptiveness of 'gay positivity'. As Woods explains, the post-AIDS 're-branding' of queerness that occurred in this period was usually associated with a rather simplistically re-imagined notion of the 'good gay man' in relation to a more threateningly fluid bisexuality, and a hedonistic queer sub-culture that 'was still stigmatised as dangerous, immoral and diseased'. In such a cautiously 'PC' climate, the discriminating moralism that is usually ascribed to homosexuality and AIDS is thus displaced onto the much more transgressive figure of the closet bisexual – particularly as a threat to both the sanctity of marriage and the policed socio-sexual boundaries of homo- and hetero-normativity. As Woods observes, films such as Stephen Walker's *Closing Numbers* (1993) commonly present the narrative scenario of a 'picture-perfect' middle-class family (iconically represented here to perfection by Jane Asher as betrayed housewife Anna) that is invaded by this supposedly 'gay disease' via the unregulated body of 'the irresponsibly secretive and promiscuous bisexual'. A process that also simultaneously elevates a rather saintly and much more 'civilized' gay male identity to 'a position of much greater knowledge of the ways of the world', in contrast to the sexually repressed and socially ignorant heterosexual.

This fairly anodyne positivism that dominated British queer filmmaking throughout the 1990s – with only a few exceptions – is reiterated by Ros Jennings in her discussion of one of the most commercially successful – though 'unoriginal' and 'unsophisticated' – films to emerge, Hettie MacDonald's *Beautiful Thing* (1996). Jennings argues that although the film possesses none of the 'distinctive aesthetic and narrative strategies' that were so critically productive in the other new queer films of the decade, its actual efficacy as a British queer film is traceable more through the filmic world of 'the everyday'. In contrast to more abstract formulations of queer desire and identity in cinema that usually dominate the subject, Jennings constructs a much more specific and situated type of critique 'that tries to link an analysis of the film's core engagements (that of burgeoning queer identities and everyday/ordinary existences) to both its British production context and the specificities of a particular set of reading/viewing circumstances'. Utilising the broad conceptual frame of 'positive unoriginality', her close reading of the film encompasses a much wider range of politically inflected debates about ideas of the 'everyday', the affirmative drive for positive images, and the formation of queer identities and communities.

As a classic romance narrative, *Beautiful Thing* positions itself within discourses of 'ordinariness' that inscribe the text with a tension that is less about its two main characters' archetypal 'coming out' narrative, and more specifically connected to the consequences that their queer identities might provoke in relation to both family and community. The film is in many ways 'emblematic' of British cinema itself, in that it more directly, as Jennings contends, 'serves the purpose of emphasising the place of family and community in film'. However, contrary to readings of the film as a straight-forwardly positive attempt at gay-affirmation, its much queerer potential lies in its more subtle interventionism. As Jennings concludes, the film is not just a political move to validate same-sex desire, but more queerly it 'works to destabilise all available roles and desires of the community at large, making them both more plural and more contradictory', especially with regard to its allegedly 'straight' female characters. The film ultimately projects a much more complex notion of sexuality, that knowingly demonstrates 'how precarious the glue holding together heterosexual hegemony is' – and reveals, as Paul Burston and Colin

Richardson have argued, how queerness can quite readily be located 'in places that had previously been thought of as strictly for straights' (1995: 1).

The rise to power of a progressive 'cool Britannia' New Labour government in 1997 – complete with its very public embrace of queer celebrities at Number Ten – has arguably initiated a tentatively renewed phase for queer experimentation in British cinema and culture in recent years. And coupled with the controversial impact, and unexpected 'cross-over' success, of Russell T. Davies' glorious and uncompromisingly 'deviant' *Queer as Folk* television series (in a pre-millennially tense 1999), queer Britannia has witnessed a new currency for exploring 'alternative' sexualities on the screen. But despite this notable increase in queer-themed filmmaking in the UK over the past few years, the films produced have, on the whole, again been largely ignored by the mainstream film community, and have instead been forced to court a far more appreciative international market.

Films such as Duncan Roy's auto-biographical split-screen triptych *AKA* (2002) or Lab Ky Mo's outrageous queering of Guy Ritchie with the stylishly offensive *Nine Dead Gay Guys* (2002), for example, illustrate the real potential that still exists for a renaissance in contemporary British queer film. But despite winning awards and critical acclaim (or in some instances general derision) at film festivals across the globe, films such as these have struggled to secure even a modicum of attention, finance or distribution in the UK. Roy's *AKA* in particular, with its dogma-esque aesthetic and complex deconstruction of narrative identity, desire and the practices of cinematic viewing, exhibits a very real potential for finally dissipating the general malaise that has gripped British queer film production over the past decade. And whilst *Nine Dead Gay Guys* is, on many levels, one of the most controversial films to emerge, due to its relentless and politically incorrect (though exaggeratedly ironic and camply reflexive) representation of every gay and racial stereotype and sexual taboo imaginable, it also demonstrates the radical efficacy that a queer cinema (or perhaps in this case *queersploitation*) still possesses to shock and unsettle the indifferent (hetero-) mainstream cinematic establishment.[8]

This growing optimism for the future of queer filmmaking in Britain is echoed by director Lisa Gornick in her discussion with Ani Ritchie that concludes this anthology. Gornick's landmark 'thesis on love and its labels', *Do I Love You?* (2003), is as Ritchie describes, 'the first full-length film about UK lesbian life in more than a decade', and, more importantly, a critical success. For in contrast to more problematically 'labelled' lesbian films such as Fiona Cunningham Reid's rather bland *Thin Ice* (1994), or the killer lesbians featured in Nancy Meckler's *Sister My Sister* (1994) and Michael Winterbottom's *Butterfly Kiss* (1995), Gornick's very personal film attempts to more queerly articulate those socio-cultural uncertainties that surround understandings of performative lesbian identity and sexuality in the twenty-first century. But rather than conform to the reductive representational prescriptions of a positivist lesbian identity-politics, *Do I Love You?* is, more ambiguously, 'not complete, it's about allowing the uncompleted thought . . . the lack of

Figure 0.3 'The Queen is dead?' Michael Praed as 'the Queen' in Lab Ky Mo's infamous 'queersploitation' film *Nine Dead Gay Guys* (2002).

Source: Courtesy of Guerilla Films.

answers'. And even though the film's final romantic narrative resolutions are rather conventional (mainly due to commercial pressures as Gornick acknowledges), it still quite effectively reflects the 'branding crisis' that has dominated British queer culture in the aftermath of queer theory, and the ongoing and necessary position that British *sin*cema occupies for re-articulating and re-configuring popular assumptions of 'normative' identities and desires on the screen/s of the new millennium.

Notes

1   See Richards' 'Rethinking British Cinema' and Higson's 'The Instability of the National' in Ashby and Higson (eds.) (2000), pp.21–47.
2   The most significant critical study of sexuality in British cinema is undoubtedly John Hill's definitive *Sex, Class and Realism* (1986). However, it is heterosexuality that really forms the thrust of Hill's landmark thesis on the subject, and homosexuality or any preliminary form of 'queer' sexuality plays a fairly peripheral role in the proceedings.

    And in her discussion of non-heterosexual sexualities in 1990s British cinema (2000), Stella Bruzzi appears to totally misconstrue 'queer' cinema as somehow associated with essentialist lesbian and gay representational politics. As Bruzzi mistakenly contends, films such as '*Priest, Sister My Sister* and *Love and Death on Long Island* – are *less queer* and more interested in acknowledging sexual plurality, fluidity and individuality (125) . . . these three films go one step further than earlier new queer cinema in that they represent the diversity of that other, so it is not merely heterosexuality's binary opposite, but is celebrated as the site where fixed identity and definition are dispensed with' (133).

3   Cited from Howes' foreword to Stephen Bourne's *Brief Encounters* (p.ix), the only publication to begin to explore lesbian and gay representation/stardom/authorship in British cinema to date.

4   As Lisa Duggan initially cautioned (1992): 'There is a tendency among some queer theorists to engage in academic debates at a high level of intellectual sophistication, while erasing the political and activist roots of their theoretical insights and concerns. Such theorists cite, modify or dispute Foucault, Lacan, and Derrida, whilst feminist, lesbian, and gay innovations and political figures disappear from sight'. For a lively discussion of the efficacy of queer theory, see also Dennis Altman's controversial 1996 article 'On Global Queering' and the heated responses it elicits in the *Australian Humanities Review* [online: www.lib.latrobe.edu.au/AHR/archive/Issue-July-1996/altman.html].

5   Altman, ibid.

6   See Doty's 'The Queer Aesthete, the Diva, and *The Red Shoes*', in *Flaming Classics*, pp.105–30.

7   In her seminal essay 'Homo Pomo: The New Queer Cinema' for *Sight and Sound* (Vol. 2, Issue 5, September 1992), Rich described that year as a 'watershed' for independent lesbian and gay filmmaking, heralding as it did the start of a new transformative 'wave' that had potential to radically re-define 1990s cinema. However, despite a passing reference to Isaac Julien's very under-rated *Young Soul Rebels* (1991), it is only Jarman's *Edward II* that warrants inclusion in her largely North American-centric definition of the canon.

8   As Vanessa Thorpe described in her review of the film's controversial reception at Cannes for *The Observer* (26 May 2002), *Nine Dead Gay Guys* was the most shocking film to be screened at the festival that year, and 'had critics and hardened film industry executives walking out from screenings in droves'. Despite the fact that its Asian-British writer and director was a previous winner of the prestigious Carl Foreman Screenwriting Fellowship, the film was initially ignored by UK distributors. But following surprise commercial success in the US, it finally secured a limited release in the UK through British independent distribution company Guerilla Films.

Bibliography

Aaron, M. (ed.) (2004), *New Queer Cinema: A Critical Reader*, Edinburgh: Edinburgh University Press.

Ashby, J. and Higson, A. (eds.) (2000), *British Cinema: Past and Present*, London: Routledge.

Benshoff, H. and Griffin, S. (eds.) (2004), *Queer Cinema: The Film Reader*, London and New York: Routledge.

Bourne, S. (1997), *Brief Encounters: Lesbians and Gays in British Cinema, 1930–1971*, London: Cassell.

Bruzzi, S. (2000), 'Two Sisters, the Fogey, the Priest and his Lover: Sexual Plurality in 1990s British Cinema', in Murphy (ed.) (2000), pp.125–34.

Burston, P. and Richardson, C. (eds.) (1995), *A Queer Romance: Lesbians, Gay Men and Popular Culture*, London and New York: Routledge.

de Lauretis, T. (1991), 'Queer Theory: Lesbian and Gay Sexualities', *differences: A Journal of Feminist Cultural Studies*, 3, 2, pp.iii–xviii.

Doty, A. (1999), *Flaming Classics: Queering the Film Canon*, London and New York: Routledge.

Duggan, L. (1992), 'Making it perfectly queer', *Socialist Review*, 22:1, Jan–March, p.26.

Dyer, R. (ed.) (1984 [1977]), *Gays and Film*, revised edition, New York: Zoetrope.

—— (1990), *Now You See It: Studies on Lesbian and Gay Film*, London: Routledge.

—— (2002), 'Homosexuality and Heritage', *The Culture of Queers*, London and New York: Routledge, pp.204–28.

Farmer, B. (2000), *Spectacular Passions: Cinema, Fantasy, Gay Male Spectatorship*, Durham: Duke University Press.

Hanson, E. (ed.) (1999), *Out Takes: Essays on Queer Theory and Film*, Durham: Duke University Press.

Higson, A. (1995), *Waving the Flag: Constructing a National Cinema*, Oxford: Clarendon Press.

—— (ed.) (1996), *Dissolving Views: Key Writings on British Cinema*, London: Cassell.

Hill, J. (1986), *Sex, Class and Realism: British Cinema 1956–1963*, London: BFI.

—— (1999), *British Cinema in the 1990s: Issues and Themes*, Oxford: Clarendon Press.

Jagose, A. (1996), *Queer Theory: An Introduction*, New York: New York University Press.

Lovell, A. (1969), 'British Cinema: The Unknown Cinema', BFI Education Seminar Paper, March.

Medhurst, A. (1997), 'Licensed to Cheek', *Sight and Sound*, Vol. 7, No. 10, October.

Monk, C. and Sargeant, A. (eds.) (2002), *British Historical Cinema*, London and New York: Routledge.

Murphy, R. (ed.) (2000), *British Cinema of the 90s*, London: BFI.

—— (ed.) (2001), *The British Cinema Book*, second edition, London: BFI.

Russo, V. (1981), *The Celluloid Closet*, New York: Harper and Row.

Street, S. (1997), *British National Cinema*, London and New York: Routledge.

Wollen, P. (1969), *Signs and Meaning in the Cinema*, London: Secker and Warburg/BFI.

1 In search of nebulous nancies

Looking for queers in pre-gay British film

Andy Medhurst

You need to be careful when you go looking for queers. There are many questions to ponder. Where might you find them? Where are their haunts? If you do discover a likely locale, can you be sure of who you're looking at? What do queers look like? How can you tell? Is it their clothes or their faces or their gestures or the way they speak? And what if you make a mistake – what if you pin the wrong label, pin all your hopes, and consequently make the wrong move? How might they react if you assume that they're queer when in fact they are something else entirely? The answer to that last question can vary from a gently amused rebuff to a knife in the guts, or worse, but happily feature films are not parks or alleyways or public toilets (not even *Carry On At Your Convenience*). Scanning the clientele of a celluloid story in order to see if there are any queers about carries no immediate health risks, and might indeed qualify as the safest sex ever invented.

Textual analysis and looking for queers have much in common. There was a time when one occupied a sphere of social respectability while the other defined scandalous marginality, but these days you can be a professor of either – or both. Teasing a text apart in order to unearth the meanings you want to emphasise is, among other things, a matter of glances, suppositions, gambles and bluff, and looking for queers plays with much the same cards. Neither activity, I'm happy to say, is a job for a real man. Real men, or at least the academic world's limited approximation of them, busy themselves with statistical tables or immerse themselves in dusty archives. Textual analysis is for softies, weeds, those who got their mums to write them a note to get out of PE, those who preferred to stay indoors in the warm reading a book or watching television and in later life have the effrontery to earn a living by rekindling those armchair delights. There have, of course, been textual analysts keen to disown that indoor-softie heritage by garnishing their work with all manner of stern accoutrements, from Leavisite moral trumpeting to the demented algebras of Lacanian psychoanalysis, and if that soothes their consciences then who am I to carp? But the wanton speculativeness of textual analysis, its determination to remain opinionated and unverifiable, refuses to go away, and it is no surprise that it took one of us queers to spill the beans about

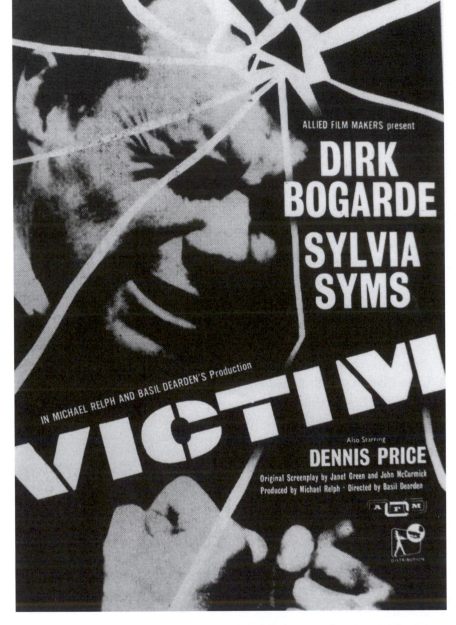

ALLIED FILM MAKERS present

DIRK BOGARDE
SYLVIA SYMS

IN MICHAEL RELPH AND BASIL DEARDEN'S Production

VICTIM

Also Starring
DENNIS PRICE
Original Screenplay by Janet Green and John McCormick
Produced by Michael Relph · Directed by Basil Dearden

Figure 1.1 The love that dares to speak its name!: Dirk Bogarde, the *Victim* (1961).

Source: Courtesy of Stephen Bourne (Allied Film Makers/Rank).

the whole business: 'imagination plays a fundamental part in the production of narrative pleasure and narrative meaning . . . it . . . reveals one of the great open secrets of textual interpretation: namely, that we make it up as we go along' (Quinn, 2000: 314).

In the light of such brazen candidness, this chapter makes no claims to a systematic, testable survey of how queers were represented in what I have decided to call pre-gay British film. Instead it zooms in on a few piquant examples and mulls over a few tendencies and trends. Pre-gay British film means films made before *Victim*, that battered old landmark wherein one queer at last got to say 'I wanted him' about another one, and as such made it possible, eventually, for homosexual lives to occupy the centre of certain films. *Victim* did not inaugurate a lavender goldrush, and many of the films that tiptoed in its wake were as beset with anxious stereotypes as the films that preceded it – and with far less excuse, but *Victim* remains a watershed moment. So what exactly were the films that 'preceded' *Victim* and what did their queers look like? Stephen Bourne's book *Brief Encounters* has already made a game stab at assembling a directory of relevant films, though some may feel he lets enthusiasm overwhelm him when the mere sight of a painted portrait of a notorious queer in a film earns that film inclusion in the inventory (Bourne, 1996: 80). Then again, if we make it up as we go along, who gets to set the boundaries?

I have set myself the boundary that the queers I'm writing about here should at least play some part, however minimal, in the films in which they appear. For reasons of political decorum, my quarry is male, though there are easily enough half-glimpsed dykes and mannish ladies in pre-gay British film to fill, at the very least, an analogous chapter, starting perhaps with the splendidly uncommented-on lesbian iconography of the head teacher of the deaf school in *Mandy* (1952). I have my sights set on the nebulous nancies who hover in the background of heterosexual narratives (until *Victim*, the only acknowledged narrative possible), the ambiguous friendships and the sidelong looks, the platoon weaklings and the sniffy shop assistants, the chorus boys and the secondary gangsters, the character actors who majored in mincing and all those queer little moments which set my antennae twitching.

There are many routes into this shady and bewitching territory, all of them inevitably drenched in guesswork and hindsight. One could follow a path pivoted on directorial sexuality (directors do not appear on screen, but they can appear in their films' meaning, even if much less often than is lazily supposed), seeking out queer reverberations that might, with a smidgeon of interpretive dexterity, be extrapolated from the sexual preference of a film's director. If any of the actors on screen had queer connotations, so much the better. A BBC biographical documentary about Alec Guinness, broadcast Christmas 2003, noted the bisexual Guinness' close working and social relationships with the queer director Peter Collinson, illustrating its inferences with loaded-by-association scenes from *The*

Prisoner (1955). For this chapter, however, I prefer to stay with on-screen queerness, though that in itself is hardly a simple category. It could mean stereotypes of effeminacy, or known-to-be-queer actors, or roles and situations which can be scrutinised for signs of that frequently overdrawn currency, the 'homosexual subtext'. As for the politics of a project like this, they remain, not inappropriately, ambiguous. These pre-gay queers are almost always ludicrous, villainous, monstrous, shadowy, pained, paranoid, edgy, guilty, doomed, or mocked. They need to be looked at, however, for three reasons.

Firstly, because without locating and investigating them, we will never grasp the pre-history of all those earnest young films analysed by earnest young things elsewhere in this book (as you will have gathered by now, I try not to be earnest and it is with much relief that I acknowledge I have not been young for some time). Secondly, at the risk of falling into that it-was-more-fun-when-we-were-still-illegal rhetoric with which vintage queens sometimes used to belabour the gay liberationists of the 1970s and 1980s, there is something memorable and evocative about the cornered secretiveness of pre-gay film queers which makes discovering them oddly satisfying. As the almost infallible gay music journalist Kris Kirk once wrote, responding to the increasing number of unapologetically gay pop songs and performers appearing in the 1980s, 'as the number of gay and gay-oriented releases increases, I find I'm less and less interested . . . partly because the thrill of the hunt has gone and . . . also because I'm becoming increasingly suspicious of . . . ghetto mentality' (Kirk, 1999: 28). In terms of film, I could echo that by expressing a preference for ten fleeting seconds of Michael Ward's outrageous wrists and elasticated eyebrows over the preachy correctness of something like *Young Soul Rebels*. And thirdly, just once in a very long while, the hunt that sent Kirk scouring through old records and me rummaging through old videotapes yields up something so cherishable, whether it's some intimation of same-sex love fenced in behind the barricades of censorship or some past-caring queer refusing to be just a stooge or a gag or a pre-*Victim* victim, that it deserves remembrance and respect.

The importance of being Michael

If you go looking for queers in British films made between the 1940s and 1960s, there is one recurring personage you cannot avoid. Michael Ward was an actor who usually played, in Keith Howes' incomparable description, 'gossamer-accented minor functionaries . . . and sundry boneless morsels' (1993: 900).

It is regrettably likely that he is most familiar to British viewers as a foil ('straight man' would be the most inapplicable phrase imaginable) for the comedian Norman Wisdom, offering a target of haughty snootiness and effete gentility to be knocked down remorselessly by Wisdom's capering proletarian man-child. In their defence, the Wisdom comedies (such as *Trouble in Store* and *Man of the Moment*) did give Ward considerable screen time, yet ironically it is in those dozens of films that utilised him

Figure 1.2 Michael Ward – A 'nebulous nancy'?

Source: BFI stills, posters and designs, courtesy of Stephen Bourne.

briefly, often in single scenes and with single lines, that Ward's real importance resides. Used so often, and so often used so briefly, he came to be not so much an actor as a sign – a sign that said queer and a sign that could guide you to interesting destinations. He was often comic relief in serious dramas. *Lost* (1955) is a thriller about an abducted child, with Ward in one scene as a temperamental dress designer, hissing 'oh do keep *still*, Fiona' at a recalcitrant model. In offering camp respite from the search for the missing child, he underscores the seriousness and implied social centrality of the heterosexual family unit by reminding the audience how frivolous and girlish and unconnected with real life those silly queers are. Yet to buy into that meaning, even though we are heavily advised to by the film, is to miss at least part of the point, since his presence, however derided, still claims a tiny foothold for queers in the London of the time. Is this being grateful for crumbs? Better that than starving to death.

The Ward one-liner also bobbed into view in comedies. A glorious example can be found in *Carry On Cabby* (1963), where Ward, as ever the elegant metropolitan pansy, exits from Kenneth Connor's taxi. Connor finds something left behind in the cab and calls out to Ward, 'Excuse me sir, is this your pearl earring?'. Ward smiles in reply, indulging such a male heterosexual ignorance of correct accessorising, 'What? With tweed?'. He has no narrative function in the film, but is needed (perhaps because this is one of the few Carry Ons where Kenneth Williams is absent) so that the requisite joke about queers can be made, but there is no malice in the joke and it is in any case debatable as to who the joke leaves looking more ridiculous.

Two of Ward's earliest appearances reward particular attention. In both films he appears only once, but his cameo camping can be seen as key points – key, at least, to those of us fixated on nebulous nancies. *Once A Jolly Swagman* (1948) is a star vehicle for the emergent Dirk Bogarde, who plays Bill Fox, a young working-class South Londoner who becomes a successful professional speedway rider in the late 1930s.

Success brings temptations, however, including a rich Mayfair hostess glorying in the name of Dottie Liz. She holds frequent parties – soirées, most likely – and one of these underlines the incompatibility between her and Bill. It is a scene saturated with post-war disapproval of pre-war luxury: cocktails are flowing, aristocratic girls drawl languidly, a lone black guest adds a touch of demi-monde daring, there is sexual gossip and arty chatter, and a young man wearing sunglasses indoors (the decadence!) throws his head and wrists around with feminised excess. Bill arrives late, and opens the door at the exact moment that Michael Ward is saying to a fellow male guest, 'My dear, surely you know there are times when Tony can be *deliciously* devastating' in a perfect Noel Coward cadence. (Connoisseurs of queer in-jokes can make what they will of the fact that Tony was the name of Bogarde's off-screen partner.) Bill and the Ward character exchange looks – looks that were over in a blink for the Odeon throngs in 1948, but which thanks to videotape and fetishistic curiosity can now be slowed, rewatched and unpacked. Bill looks Ward up and down, in a look saturated in masculine dismay and driven by the need to brand and then distance the owner of that extravagantly queer voice. Ward looks back, likewise up and down, a look that is partly nervous recognition at being so clearly caught out and so contemptuously filed under 'queer' but also partly a sly sexual appraisal of Bogarde's attractiveness, an appraisal of another man that is at once split-second surreptitious and daringly unmissable.

After this, Bill demands that Dottie Liz throws out her guests, branding them 'fakes and no-goods'. He means them all, but the only one who he has interacted with significantly is Ward, the figure who condenses all the sybaritic excess of this indulgent Mayfair set into a single despised creature. Dottie Liz refuses, they argue, and their relationship is over. The film's next scene shows a march through London by the British contingent of the International Brigade, returning from fighting Franco's Fascists in the Spanish Civil War (we previously saw Bill's brother leaving to join the Brigade) and in this juxtaposition the film proposes a stark binary comparison between the party, a chattering parrot-cage of pretentious dilettantes, and the march, a celebration of progressive, manly collectivity. The Spanish Civil War is not the film's only overt political reference – Dottie Liz had cheerfully explained to Bill earlier that a photograph of her with two uniformed Nazis had been taken at Hitler's Nuremberg rally. So in this rather reckless conflation of hints and symbols, the presence of Michael Ward, an unnamed one-line character at that self-centred and decadent gathering, gathers even more weight as the film clumsily, but fascinatingly, tries to evoke connections between sexual deviation and political perversity.

Fast forward three years, and Ward once again has his moment of singular significance in a melodrama displaying an explicit interest in politics. *High Treason* (1951) is British film history's one genuine example of McCarthyite Cold War hysteria. It follows a police investigation into a network of Communist saboteurs, several of whom meet covertly at a Music Society. A detective attends a meeting incognito, and finds himself sitting next to Michael Ward, who once again confirms the queerness suggested by his appearance and demeanour (somehow even Ward's eyelids look queer) by his manner of speech. A fellow music lover asks how keen he is to hear the evening's recital, to which Ward effulges 'Dying, absolutely *dying*'. As in *Once A Jolly Swagman*, the verbal flourish discloses the sexual deviance – Ward speaks in effeminised italics, and he uses (the grammatical giveaway) adverbs. The detective shoots Ward the same recognition/distaste glare that Bill Fox had bestowed, which this time Ward can only answer with a shrug (the detective is not as attractive as Dirk Bogarde, and this is the early 1950s not the late 1930s). At this point, some deliberately dissonant classical begins, Ward assumes a rapt-aesthete pose of concentration, and the detective is horrified to find himself trapped in a pincer movement of dandified perversity and sonic modernism. As the plot unfurls, it becomes clear that Ward is not in fact part of the Communist cell, but his positioning (along with an exceedingly mannish upper-class lady) at the Music Society yet again locates queers in the realm of threat. The demonised foreign danger with which queerness is associated may have switched here from Nazi Germany to Soviet Russia, but this simply mirrors the abrupt redirecting of British foreign policy at that time. What persists in both films is the use of Ward to act as sissified shorthand for something other, something dangerous, and something that could trouble the established patterns of British family life, which both films hold up as a microcosm of national stability. Hence a silly queen in two little scenes becomes ever more intriguing the closer you look.

I thought it was a goat

Michael Ward is not the only queer in *High Treason*.

The first saboteur shown in the film is a middle-aged bachelor civil servant, who goes home after work to feed his cat – 'Hello Tibby dear, have you missed me? Yes of course you have' – before typing out a secret list of arms shipments to pass on to his fellow subversives. Moreover, the ringleader of the Communist plot later turns out to be an upper-class MP who exudes all the silky grace of the well-heeled queer and lives alone with only a collection of Greek and Etruscan vases for company. It isn't hard to read these men as queer, especially the first ('Tibby dear', indeed), given the interweaving of anxieties about Commies and homos that fuelled many Cold War nightmares, but what gives such a reading an extra, pleasurable tweak is that both of the actors concerned (Charles Lloyd Pack and Anthony Nicholls) would later play two of the blackmailed queers in *Victim*. There is probably some interesting work to be done on how that later film drew, presumably unconsciously, on *High Treason*'s visual and narrative economies of a secretive group under police investigation. For now, I want to emphasise the importance of casting in our comprehension of queers. Actors that repeatedly played queerish roles, or are now known to have been homosexual themselves, can carry echoes of that on-screen or off-screen queerness into otherwise ostensibly straight situations. The queer look that Bill Fox attracts in *Once A Jolly Swagman* can't help but gain resonance from the fact that Fox is played by Dirk Bogarde. The role of Fox could have been plausibly played by many other actors, but Bogarde's sexuality and subsequent career profoundly deepen the queerness of his encounter with Michael Ward.

Other examples may be helpful here. There is not much in the surface story of *The Astonished Heart* (1951) to detain an audience today, it being an emotionally constipated study of infidelity among the frightfully well-bred, but it is also a rare example of an off-screen homosexual couple appearing on-screen together. Noel Coward plays the husband who errs, while his long-term companion Graham Payn plays his devoted secretary. They have only two scenes together without others present, but in at least one of these the creative queer viewer (it may be pertinent here to reiterate Vincent Quinn's insistence on the importance of imagination in criticism) might discern some shared-joke flirtatiousness in their acting that hints at levels of significance beneath the mere dialogue. (They also both wear pinkie rings – a ring on the little finger being a sartorial semiotic for signalling homosexuality to others of a subcultural inclination.) A suitably attuned queer eye might also note that Payn's character has not even the mention of a girlfriend and that throughout the film he exudes a lapdog devotion to his employer.

As actors' careers take shape over time, some casting decisions become shriekingly queer with hindsight. The presence of Kenneth Williams in *The Seekers* (1954), a laboured epic tracing British settlers' conflicts with the indigenous Maori in nineteenth-century New Zealand, may have looked uncontentious once, but after decades in which Williams' bravura queening made him one of the pre-eminent queers in British popular culture, his scenes in the film look like unintentional camp comedy – not least because the imperialist epic is just the kind of genre the 1960s radio series *Round The Horne*, featuring Williams at his finest, loved to parody. It is hard to believe that 'I thought it was a goat', his most dramatic line in the film, uttered just before a Maori warrior attacks him, was not actually part of a *Round the Horne* send-up. (The 'goat' was in fact the Maori's beloved dog, which Williams has killed, prompting the attack.) For further intertextual queer delight, consult Williams' comments on the making of *The Seekers* in his posthumously published diaries, where the miffed petulance of the effete queer required to undergo the exertions of an action picture rings loud and clear: 'work on this film *The Seekers* . . . I was in a trench waist high in cold water. It was awful. I bet I get flu. . . . To studio for shots of fight twixt me and Rangiruru. Tony (who plays Rangiruru) is big and hell to fight with. I am bruised all over and feel awful' (Davies, ed. 1993: 95–6). In other, less macho genres, it is hard to ignore the thought that some queer actors had a wonderful time by playing up the camper elements of the work in hand. Dennis Price's contribution to the 1940s cycle of Gainsborough melodramas would repay attention in such a context, most particularly when teamed with the elaborately effeminate Robert Helpmann in *Caravan* (1946). Price is the film's chief villain, Helpmann his creepy servant, and they seem employed throughout the film in a competition to out-queen each other. Helpmann's rendition of the line 'Was the paella palatable, Sir Francis?' (the film is set partly in Spain) probably wins him the trophy.

Unspoken loves

One last return to *High Treason* is needed at this point. Thanks to the ways in which queerness seeps across that film, and to the broader cultural climate around homosexuality and subversion alluded to earlier, there are times when the whole story starts to veer towards a coded tale of unspeakable desires. The film's pivotal character is Jimmy, a nervous young shopkeeper caught up in the Communist plot. Kenneth Griffith's taut, nervy performance as Jimmy, combined with certain lines of dialogue and the film's proto-*Victim* tropes of concealment and pursuit, make such an interpretation very tempting.

Jimmy keeps secrets, his (significantly fatherless) family are worried, he is meeting strange people, he is urged to confess – you get the picture. His mother is surprised at his enthusiastic membership of the Music Society – 'he was always fond of a good tune but I never thought he'd turn out so musical', she says, presumably unaware that 'musical' was a covert codeword among queers in the 1930s to denote queerness ('Oh no, my husband's not musical at all', Celia Johnson's character announces brightly in the Noel Coward-written *Brief Encounter* in 1946). She is increasingly worried about her son – 'I don't know what it is, but he's had

Figure 1.3 A 'taut' and 'nervy' Kenneth Griffith in *High Treason* (1951).

Source: BFI Stills, posters and designs.

something on his mind for a long time'. And when Jimmy 'comes out' about his political leanings, he says it all started when he was in the RAF, and 'got friendly' with 'a chap in our barracks'. What a tragedy, his mother concludes, that he didn't 'grow up straight'. Threading all of this together, underpinned as it is by Griffith's haunted, hunted look, another film emerges counterpoint to *High Treason*'s other-wise rather laughable Red Menace scaremongering. Could it be that it wasn't just like-minded left-wingers that Jimmy was hoping to meet at the Music Society? As we know from *Once A Jolly Swagman*, where there's art there's queers.

Sometimes, however, subtextual homosexuality cannot risk coming even that near to the surface. Consider, for example, an obscure middlebrow melodrama made in 1948, *Mr Perrin and Mr Traill*. At face value it is a rather quaint, fusty, dated story (the novel it is based on was published in 1911, though the setting has been updated to the 1940s) about a rivalry between two teachers at a mediocre boarding school for boys. Perrin is well into middle age, pompous and pernickety, enmeshed in a rut of petty hierarchy and protocol. Unmarried, he lives in rooms at the school, visits his mother regularly, and makes unconvincing plans to propose to Isabel, the much younger woman who works with the school's doctor. His life and plans are upset by the arrival of Traill, a war hero who played rugby for Cambridge, and who wastes little time in becoming more popular with both the pupils and Isabel. Perrin, already made somewhat unstable by the vindictive power games of the school's headmaster, begins to lose control over his emotions. At breaking point, he tries to kill Traill, but Traill falls unconscious over the cliff edge (the school is, conveniently for a melodrama, located near cliffs) and is in danger of drowning until Perrin saves him from the incoming tide. Perrin, however, dies in the rescue.

I have dwelled on the plot outline since I am aware that this is a little-seen film. It merits inclusion here, however, thanks to the feverish intensity of its unspoken homoeroticism. As many examples ranging from art cinema to pornography would testify, the English boarding school is a favoured site for the depiction of same-sex desire (Lindsay Anderson's treatment of this theme in *If . . .* is still perhaps the most movingly lyrical image of queer love in British film history), yet *Mr Perrin and Mr Traill* is hardly a tale of secret passion in the dorm. It is, for most of its ninety minutes, concerned primarily with the clash of tradition (Perrin) and innovation (Traill), tracing what happens when a suffocatingly enclosed culture is disrupted by a newcomer determined not to abide by ossified rules. At the end, though, very strange things happen. Firstly, there is a scene where Perrin, plagued by dreams about how he is a failure and an embarrassment, sleepwalks through the school to Traill's bedside, before waking up at the point where he. . . . Where he does what, exactly? Ostensibly, where he plans to attack his hated rival, but the wordlessness of the scene lends it other ambiguous possibilities, leaving faint traces of sexual undertones to this nocturnal visit. The film's register shifts towards the horror film during this sequence (though it must be noted that murderous zombies do not often wear flannelette pyjamas), and it remains tantalisingly unclear why Traill actually wakes up as Perrin sleepwalks into the room, but lies back in a pretence of sleep, almost for a moment an unusually beefy vampire's victim awaiting the deadly touch.

The curiosities of the sleepwalking scene are little more than an aperitif before the film's deranged conclusion. As Perrin climbs down the cliff to reach Traill's body on the beach below, a three-minute sequence without dialogue begins, a protracted and outlandishly suggestive watery pas-de-deux which begins with the desperate Perrin throwing the unconscious Traill over one shoulder. A running spat between them earlier in the film concerned Perrin's predilection for hogging the bathroom they shared because he liked to fill both of the available baths – one very hot, the other freezing cold. This left Traill waiting outside while Perrin, seeking to inflame and then icily quench who knows what thoughts or feelings, splashed about. They may never have got to share the bathroom, but here at their story's spumy climax they get to be wet together at last. Perrin's face is straining and distressed, but also beatifically transcendent as he carries Traill aloft through the ceaselessly crashing foam and spray, until he humps him to safety, heaving him on to a ledge out of harm's way. Traill at last rouses himself from comatose passivity, only to see Perrin's final, despairing grasp at survival swept away by the pounding tide. He cries Perrin's name, but his nemesis turned saviour is never seen again. The last image we have of him is that tortured yet transfigured face, a momentary petrification of doomed adoration and death-welcoming ecstasy so dementedly compelling it's as if some fragment of sado-masochistic Baroque religious statuary has somehow broken its way into a post-war British middlebrow melodrama.

It would not take a genius to suspect that the preceding paragraph contains some rather excitable over-interpretation. Nonetheless, when I first saw this film about fifteen years ago I recall being stunned by its unhinged climax, and watching it again for the purposes of this chapter it still strikes me as an extremely odd way to end a film of this type. After all the provincial bitching, the status-hungry bridge parties and the squabbling over where to place the common-room copy of *Punch*, the elemental ferocity of what happens in the sea, where just bodies and water and music conspire to say what the rest of the film leaves silent beneath its surface of back-biting verbosity, is memorable, unsettling and somehow compellingly queer. Of course, this is a British film, so the actors aren't as forceful or physical as one might have hoped – it isn't John Wayne carrying Montgomery Clift through the waves, more's the pity, it's Marius Goring carrying David Farrar (though John Wayne would have made for a pretty bizarre Mr Perrin). And it's a 1940s melodrama, so the film can't end where it should, there on the edge with Traill crying out for his dead deliverer, it has to retreat back indoors to a talkative wrap-up scene where Traill tells the headmaster what a beast he was to poor old Perrin. Even so, if you squint past its enforced limitations, it shows that you can find queerness in the most unexpected places.

Thoughts at breakfast

There are numerous other roads that this chapter could travel, many other questions it could ask. Why are there so many queens flitting in and out of George Formby's films? Why does that primped, reptilian queen sit at the bar in *Sapphire*

(1959), eyeing up the policemen who visit with a sly lasciviousness that even Michael Ward might have thought too risky? Did Ivor Novello's make-up in Hitchcock's *The Lodger* (1926) have to be quite so lavish? Who was laughing at who by making Frankie Howerd play a character called Willie Joy and then getting him to order a double ginger beer (in 1955's *Jumping for Joy*)? Not to mention the flamingly flamboyant set designer in *Simon and Laura* (1955) and Norman Evans' totally unexplained satin cocktail dress at the end of *Demobbed* (1944).

Sixty years after *Demobbed*, you no longer have to scent out the nancies: we're everywhere. In January and February 2004, Britain's Channel 4 restructured its breakfast-time schedule. This mostly involved the screening of American sitcoms, but it also involved a daily repeat of the previous evening's episode of *The Salon*, a reality TV series set in a hair and beauty salon. The series drew on two interlocked narratives, the short-span stories of the clients' visits and, more involvingly, the longer-term saga of the relationships and rivalries amongst the salon's staff. Thus it was that I breakfasted, for two months, watching a show in which three of the main protagonists, and many of the supporting players, were, to use a profoundly dislikeable but somehow unavoidable phrase, openly gay men. One episode even featured a gay customer receiving a proposal of 'marriage' from his partner. As I chomped through my bowl of Crunchy Nut Red, this got me thinking.

Twenty-odd years ago, when I first started writing and teaching and agitating about gay men and media representation, I could videotape every single television programme or broadcast film which I knew to contain some reference to homosexuality. There weren't very many, so this wasn't very difficult. Today, we have reached a state of queer ubiquity where declarations of same-sex love are so unremarkable that they can be shown twice a day, to audiences of (potentially) all ages, and if I wanted to tape every gay-relevant show or film on every channel I would need a small army of video recorders. I don't want this to sound naively utopian, since many of this vastly increased number of representations remain voyeuristic or gestural (some, but not me, would include *The Salon* in those categories). Yet it would be equally blinkered not to acknowledge that huge gains have been made. We no longer live in the world of nebulous nancies – indeed the nancies on *The Salon* wouldn't recognise nebulousness if it unplugged their hairdryers. Very much the grandchildren of Michael Ward, but with added fangs and attitude, and absolutely no intention of simply firing off one queeny line before retreating into the shadows, their centrality to the series can serve as a marker of how everyday queers have become. Viewed from some political vantage points, becoming everyday is not necessarily an achievement to welcome, and I have some sympathy with those views, but I wouldn't be able to write this chapter, and you wouldn't be able to read this book, if we were all still Michael Wards. He was a treasure, the grand duchess of all nebulous nancies, and I savour and relish him and his ilk, but would I rather live in his world than this one? My dear, can you *imagine*?

Bibliography

Bourne, S. (1996) *Brief Encounters: Lesbians and Gay Men in British Cinema 1930–1971*, London: Cassell.

Davies, R. (ed.) (1993) *The Kenneth Williams Diaries*, London: HarperCollins.

Howes, K. (1993) *Broadcasting It: An Encyclopaedia of Homosexuality on Film, Radio and TV in the UK 1923–1993*, London: Cassell.

Kirk, K. (1999) *A Boy Called Mary: Kris Kirk's Greatest Hits*, Brighton: Millivres.

Quinn, V. (2000) 'Loose Reading? Sedgwick, Austen and Critical Practice', *Textual Practice*, 14: 2, 303–26.

2 Behind the masks

Anthony Asquith and Brian Desmond Hurst

Stephen Bourne

Homophobia, ignorance and a preoccupation with American cinema mean that queer representation in early British films has largely escaped the attention of critics, historians and academics. Said Keith Howes in his Foreword to *Brief Encounters: Lesbians and Gays in British Cinema 1930–1971* (1996) (see Bibliography), the only exhaustive study of the formative years of queer British cinema to be published:

> For too long British cinema has been depicted as sexless, featureless and passionless: an Old Dark House. No surprise then that queer (non-100 per cent heterosexual) British cinema, with few exceptions, always used the servant's entrance. Because of prejudices and misconceptions, this vast pink and lavender arena has mostly escaped the attentions of the orthodox critic and historian.
>
> (Bourne, 1996: ix)

A recent example of this can be found in Pam Cook's *I Know Where I'm Going!* (2002), published in the British Film Institute's Film Classics series. Cook's analysis of this 1945 romantic drama, produced and directed by Michael Powell and Emeric Pressburger, failed to explore one of the film's most important subtexts: the fear of sexuality. Cook also failed to acknowledge the ambivalent sexuality of Catriona (played by Pamela Brown), one of the featured characters, who is described in the film as a 'queer girl'. Cook's heterosexual reading of the film overlooked some queer possibilities, but this is just another example of what escapes the 'orthodox critic and historian'.[1]

Anthony Asquith (1902–68) and Brian Desmond Hurst (1895–1986) are two gay directors who have been constantly overlooked or marginalised in histories of British cinema. Both enjoyed long and productive careers in the British film industry but their films have never been given proper critical attention. Asquith was once rated as highly as Alfred Hitchcock. In fact, comparing the two became a favourite hobby in the 1930s, with film critic C. A. Lejeune describing them as 'the most imaginative' and 'the most ingenious' of the makers of fiction films.[2]

Figure 2.1 The 'imaginative' and 'ingenious' Anthony Asquith.

Source: Stephen Bourne private collection.

Another omission can be found in books about gay cinema. Neither director is mentioned in the work of key gay writers on film such as Richard Dyer, who is mostly concerned with European and North American works. Vito Russo (*The Celluloid Closet: Homosexuality in the Movies*, 1987) and Richard Barrios (*Screened Out: Playing Gay in Hollywood from Edison to Stonewall*, 2003) are mainly concerned with documenting the history of queer Hollywood. Neither are there any references to Asquith or Hurst in books about gay social history in Britain.[3]

Charming, gentle, effeminate and a closeted gay, Anthony Asquith was affectionately known to his colleagues as 'Puffin'. In her autobiography, Ingrid Bergman remembered her first encounter with Asquith: 'I was on the set of *The Yellow Rolls Royce* [1964] when along came this shabby little man in frayed blue overalls and an old shirt, carrying a bunch of flowers which he handed to me'. Believing he was a stagehand, or one of the electricians, Bergman was informed that he was her director. She added, 'He was the kindest and most polite director I have ever known. He was so polite that if he stumbled over a cable he would turn back and say, "Oh, please forgive me". When he needed the extras he would say, "Ladies and gentlemen I don't want to disturb you – please finish your tea by all means – but when you have a few moments would you please come up and stand in the background, because I need a few people there. Don't rush"' (Bergman and Burgess, 1980: 440–1).

Asquith was the son of Lord Herbert Asquith, the first Earl of Oxford and Britain's Prime Minister from 1908–16. Born in 1902, he was a tiny, delicate baby with curly blond hair, and a hooked nose, hence the nickname 'Puffin'. A schoolboy 'aesthete' who described himself as 'hopelessly incompetent' at sport, he was educated as Winchester and Balliol, and later went to Oxford. A radical who was always ready to take up the cause of the underdog, for thirty-one years he was president of film technician's trade union ACCT, which upon joining in 1937, he became the first film director to become a Trade Unionist.

With a kind, considerate, sensitive nature, Asquith's films sometimes included public schoolboys of a similar disposition. These included Ronnie Winslow, who is falsely accused of stealing in *The Winslow Boy* (1948), and Taplow, whose defence of an unpopular schoolmaster could be read as a queer attraction in *The Browning Version* (1951). At Oxford, Asquith belonged to a literary group, known to attract homosexuals, who called themselves the 'Aesthetes'. A fellow student, Richard Crossman (Asquith's 'fag'), who went on to become a cabinet minister in Harold Wilson's government, once recalled:

> In college we had two groups – the Aesthetes and the Athletes – We (the Aesthetes) had readings of plays, drawing on world literature . . . we read in fact an astonishing amount of modern drama; the small boys took the female parts . . . I was tremendously influenced by Puffin – indeed all of us were. He never beat a fag nor would he allow any other Aesthete to beat us. But the Athletes not only beat their fags but beat us too. . . . Puff had at that time a shrill high-pitched voice and his Adam's apple stuck out. . . . He was sensitive, an epicure, snobbish only so far as books were concerned. . . . The Aesthetes had a special way of dressing up. They used to wear mauve shirts and flowing ties and took a delight in flaunting their get-up before the Athletes.
>
> (Minney, 1973: 34–5)

At Oxford Asquith showed an enthusiasm for cinema, and in 1925 he became a founder member of the original Film Society along with such distinguished people as George Bernard Shaw and H.G. Wells. After submitting a script to British International, he was taken on by that studio and given his first chance to direct in 1928, a light comedy called *Shooting Stars*. From the 1920s to the 1960s Asquith divided his time between directing semi-documentaries and adaptations of drama and literature. He made films in a range of genres, including thrillers, war dramas, musicals, historical dramas and comedies, and worked with a number of gay men including screenwriters Terence Rattigan (on ten occasions from 1939 to 1964), Rodney Ackland and Paul Dehn, and actors Eric Portman, Michael Redgrave, Douglass Montgomery, Dirk Bogarde and Dennis Price. In addition to *The Winslow Boy* and *The Browning Version*, his most important films include the exquisite romantic drama *The Young Lovers* (1954), a Cold War variation on *Romeo and Juliet*, and *Orders to Kill* (1958), a compelling drama about a war-time mission to assassinate a suspected double agent. There are also several polished adaptations of stage classics such as George Bernard Shaw's *Pygmalion* (1938) and Oscar Wilde's *The Importance of Being Earnest* (1952).

When it was announced that a screen version was going to be made of Shaw's 1913 stage success *Pygmalion*, directed by Asquith, Shaw disapproved of the casting of Leslie Howard as Higgins, a 'confirmed bachelor' and professor of phonetics who transforms Eliza Doolittle, a cockney flower seller, into a lady. Shaw preferred Charles Laughton, believing that Howard would provide too much tenderness, when it was not a tender part, and not a love story. When the film was being made, he wrote to Gabriel Pascal, the film's producer, and acknowledged that the public would like Howard, and probably want him to marry Eliza, which is just what he didn't want.

Apart from Mrs Pearce (Jean Cadell), the elderly housekeeper, women do not figure in the lives of bossy, overbearing Higgins and his kind, sensitive companion, another 'confirmed bachelor', Colonel Pickering. Says Higgins to Pickering, 'I'm a confirmed old bachelor and likely to remain one! . . . I've taught scores of American millionairesses to speak English . . . the best-looking women in the world . . . they might have been blocks of wood!' When Eliza enters their lives, her relationship with Higgins remains platonic, and Pickering is very protective of her. In one of the film's many enchanting and intimate scenes, Higgins and Pickering demonstrate to Eliza how to dance at the ball, and for one fleeting moment, as the two men swirl around the room in each other's arms, it becomes the most natural thing in the world. And when Eliza is preparing for her appearance at the ball, Mrs Pearce, upon seeing two effeminate hairdressers in conversation, looks towards the camera and exclaims, 'Did you ever see the like!'

The grand ball sequence is among the film's alterations of Shaw's original play. Written by Shaw himself, it allows the audience to witness Eliza's triumph, but Higgins is more concerned about the presence of the effeminate, long-haired ('if I cut my hair, nobody notices me!') but dangerous Count Aristid Karpathy, played by Esme Percy,[4] who, he fears, might expose Eliza. The Count is presented as a threat, a blackmailing queer. Wendy Hiller, whose portrayal of Eliza earned her a Best Actress Oscar nomination – the first for a British actress in a British film – had no doubts about the importance of Shaw's text. In an interview she gave to the *Radio Times* in 1973 she said, 'Shaw quite simply wrote the most brilliant anti-romantic comedy of the century. To me there was never any question of her marrying or being in love with Higgins. Those who want that sort of ending are running absolutely counter to the author. We've all been brainwashed, if you like, into wanting conventional, happy-ever-after endings. So we get them' (Hiller, 1973: 70–5).

Asquith's screen version of *The Importance of Being Earnest* captured most of the sparkle of Oscar Wilde's wit. Originally produced seven weeks before Wilde's arrest in 1895, it is regarded as a masterpiece of comic theatre, with its vocabulary, characters, subversion of the theatrical convention of the 1880s and 1890s, and its coincidences, mistaken identities and skeletons in cupboards. Asquith's casting of British theatricals, such as Joan Greenwood (Gwendolen), Michael Redgrave (Jack Worthing), Dorothy Tutin (Cecily), Margaret Rutherford (Miss Prism) and, best of all, Edith Evans as Lady Bracknell, is perfect. Michael Denison (Algernon) later recalled, 'I loved Asquith as a director. He was an interpreter and that is how I like my directors to be. I like them to know the script and subject. He obviously loved the play, loved the wit and shape of it, and loved the characters. He was completely in tune with the subject and, indeed, with the players' (McFarlane, 1997: 172). At every turn Wilde's play, as directed by Asquith, ridicules heterosexual romantic fantasies while keeping the sugar coating that allows the bitter pill to be swallowed. In the last shot, Redgrave and Greenwood appear to be kissing but they are not. Instead they are adopting an absurd pose, which is typical of the mischief the film makes. For years audiences have been conned into thinking that Wilde's sparkling, witty production is a romantic, heterosexual comedy but, says Jack Babuscio in *Gay News*, *The Importance of Being Earnest* is:

> a play whose homoerotic undertones lie closer to the surface than in any other Wilde work, excepting *The Picture of Dorian Gray*. There is little doubt why, when asked on opening night if the critics were likely to understand the play's real meaning, Wilde quickly replied, 'I hope not!' The author was alluding not to the play's surface intentions, which are plain enough to polite audiences; but, rather, to the gay insinuations lurking behind the cunningly contrived charades and chiselled chatter of the two central characters – all of which would be totally unacceptable to the conventional middle-class audiences of Wilde's day. For *The Importance of Being Earnest* is essentially the story of two men who engage in dandyish dating of females as a convenient cover-up for the pursuit of 'Bunburying', i.e. illicit and, it is strenuously suggested, *homosexual* pleasures.
>
> (Babuscio, 1976: 21)

Unlike some of his gay American contemporaries, such as George Cukor (who, in 1964, directed *My Fair Lady*, the Hollywood musical version of *Pygmalion*) and Edmund Goulding, who had reputations for directing female stars, Asquith directed male actors with great sensitivity and success. Examples of this can be found in two war dramas, *We Dive at Dawn* (1943), set on board a submarine, and *The Way to the Stars* (1945), set in and around an RAF station. In both films Asquith is preoccupied with male-bonding, the disruption of heterosexual relationships, and the emotional impact of the war on men. In these films, men from different regional and class backgrounds pull together when confronting danger, and some of them reveal ambivalent attitudes towards women. In *We Dive at Dawn*, though he is constantly trying to arrange a date, Lieutenant Taylor (John Mills) is never seen with a woman, Hobson (Eric Portman) hates women as a result of his wife's desertion, and the rugged Irishman Mike (Niall MacGinnis) is reluctant to wed, and tries everything he can to avoid his impending marriage. Needless to say, at the end of the film, Mike marries his fiancée, and Hobson is reunited with his wife. In *The Way to the Stars*, Asquith directs John Mills again, as well as Michael Redgrave, two of Britain's most sensitive, understated actors. With a script by the gay dramatist Terence Rattigan, they create a compelling study of the frailty of masculinity. For example, when Archdale (Redgrave) is killed in action, Penrose (Mills) grieves for his friend and rejects his girlfriend, fearing that he could also be killed. At least two of the actors Asquith directed in these films, Eric Portman and Michael Redgrave, were troubled, closeted gays. Off-screen, Portman was an unhappy, self-loathing gay man whose screen performances are marked by the edgy, tense manner he embodies in *We Dive at Dawn*. Similarly, Redgrave led a double-life, concealing his bisexuality, but giving queer dimensions to a number of memorable screen characters, including the killer ventriloquist Maxwell Frere in *Dead of Night* (1945) and the schoolmaster Andrew Crocker-Harris in Asquith's *The Browning Version* (1951).

In *The Browning Version*, adapted for the screen by Terence Rattigan from his own stage play, Redgrave gives an extraordinary, understated performance, drawing out the deep-felt emotions and mannerisms of a repressed, frustrated martinet. *The Browning Version* isn't *Goodbye Mr Chips*. It's cruel, unsentimental and full of unsympathetic characters, including the headmaster who tactlessly asks Crocker-Harris to make his end of term leaving speech to the boys before the popular sports master. The story resembles Edward Albee's *Who's Afraid of Virginia Woolf?* in its painful study of Crocker-Harris' loveless, torturous marriage to the selfish, callous and adulterous Millie (Jean Kent). There is only one character who shows warmth and compassion, and it is the schoolboy Taplow (Brian Smith), a soft-spoken, gentle lad who defends Crocker-Harris when some of the boys describe him as 'barely human'. This pleasant chap is keen to please the master, and he is completely unselfconscious in his outspoken defence of him. Unlike Crocker-Harris, and others in the story, Taplow shows his feelings. He is the only one to show an interest in the schoolmaster, and express affection for him. Taplow is the only boy in the school who says goodbye to the master, and applauds enthusiastically for him when he takes the stage to make his farewell speech. Clearly, Taplow is attracted to the older man. In some ways the boy 'liberates' Crocker-Harris from his repressed state. And even though the story appears to be preoccupied with Crocker-Harris' heterosexual 'impotence', it seems that Taplow's desire to be 'friends' with the master hints at something much deeper. Finally, Crocker-Harris' farewell speech at the end unexpectedly becomes a memorable, emotional 'coming-out' statement. He admits he has been a failure as a teacher, and apologises to the surprised congregation. When he asks for their forgiveness, the boys applaud wildly.

Throughout his life, Asquith concealed and repressed his sexuality, while friends and colleagues tactfully avoided it. Asquith's biographer, R.J. Minney, offers a celebratory and glowing appraisal of the man and his work, but touches only briefly, and discreetly, on the director's sexuality. Asquith's collaborator, writer Terence Rattigan, explained to Minney that the director liked the company of young men, 'but it never went further than talking or going to a concert, or playing cards'.[5]

Taking into account the time in which he lived, facing imprisonment if he was ever caught with another man, it is hardly surprising Asquith hid the fact that he was gay, and probably remained celibate till the day he died. However, he did find pleasure and enjoyment in the company of lorry drivers, as revealed in 1950 by the *Daily Mirror* when they published an article about Asquith's 'secret life',

> To the lorry drivers on the Great North Road, the dish washer in Joe's transport café is just Tony. . . . For when Mr Asquith gets bored with the beauty of film stars and cocktails at film premieres, he turns into [a] dishwasher . . . Mr Asquith's explanation is: 'I enjoy myself here. It is a complete change from the film work I do and the lorry drivers I meet are grand fellows'.
>
> (*Daily Mirror* Reporter, 1950)

Sadly, in the late 1950s, Asquith and Rattigan were unsuccessful in bringing to the screen what might have been their greatest collaboration: *Lawrence of Arabia* starring Dirk Bogarde. Asquith worked very closely with Bogarde on the development of the project, but ten days before they were due to begin filming, the Rank Organisation 'pulled the plug'. Said Bogarde, 'It destroyed Asquith and it practically destroyed me'.[6] Asquith died in 1968 after a battle with cancer.

Though Brian Desmond Hurst may not have achieved the great heights of some of his British contemporaries, such as Asquith, David Lean or Carol Reed, his film career deserves greater recognition. The son of a distinguished surgeon, Hurst was born in 1895 in South Belfast, and enjoyed an adventurous and varied career before becoming a film director. At the age of fourteen he ran away from his Belfast school and joined the Army. As a young man he was in Gallipoli with the Royal Irish Rifles, and by the end of the First World War, having survived a bayonet wound, malaria and being a prisoner of war, he had been promoted to the rank of Captain, but decided to retire from army life.

In his unpublished autobiography, Hurst is quite open about his sexuality, and recalls his first sexual experience at the age of sixteen: 'I was in an alley-way with a boy called Robert Montgomery. It was so nice and exciting that I made him do it again the very next night. We went for walks after that into the wasteland round about where we lived. I'm not sure whether I did the same to him or not, but I certainly used to feel him in those dark places' (Hurst, 1986: 14).

After the war, Hurst studied medicine but dropped that in favour of newspaper reporting. On a trip to Canada in 1922 he worked as a lumberjack, and then took up art. After studying in Paris at L'Ecole des Beaux Arts and L'Academie Julien, he migrated to America and became a painter of portraits and murals. In 1925 a lucrative commission took him to California and, while in Los Angeles, he met his cousin, film director and fellow Irishman John Ford. Hurst acted as his assistant and art director on a number of silent films and, years later, the film historian and film critic of *The Times*, David Robinson, remembered an incident involving Ford and Hurst when he was a guest at a dinner party in a London restaurant attended by Ford. He recalled, 'Ford asked someone to call Brian, and invite him to join the party. One of the guests made a remark about Hurst being gay and Ford responded, "So what if he is? Doesn't *everyone* have a gay cousin?"' (Bourne, 1996: 27). Settling in Britain in the early 1930s, Hurst decided to enter the film industry and began directing in 1934. For almost thirty years he found regular work in a variety of genres, everything from Ivor Novello's musical *Glamorous Night* (1937) to *Simba* (1955), a drama about the Mau Mau uprising. Perhaps Hurst failed to achieve the status of other British film directors because he has been difficult to pigeon-hole, but he did excel at romantic melodramas, such as *Dangerous Moonlight* (1941), one of the most popular films in Britain during the Second World War. Interestingly, a number of gay men had key roles in the production of this film: Hurst co-authored the script with Rodney Ackland; there were gowns by Cecil Beaton; its star was the attractive Anton Walbrook; and Richard Addinsell's stirring, passionate 'Warsaw Concerto' became one of the best-loved movie themes of all time.[7]

Hurst's other films included the much-admired war-time documentary *Theirs is the Glory*, a record of the landings at Arnhem in 1944 and the subsequent battle for the Rhine bridge. He later filmed Daphne du Maurier's nineteenth-century Irish family saga, *Hungry Hill* (1947), the delightful musical *Trottie True* (1949), *Scrooge* (1951), a highly praised version of Dickens' *A Christmas Carol*, *Dangerous Exile* (1957), a colourful costume drama set in 1790s France and Cornwall, and *Behind the Mask* (1958), in which Vanessa Redgrave made her screen debut.

In *The Black Tent* (1956), filmed on location in Libya, Charles Holland (Donald Sinden) searches for his older brother David (Anthony Steel), who went missing during the war, but may still be alive. Charles discovers his brother wed a Sheik's daughter, was betrayed to the Germans and then killed in action. Though *The Black*

Tent is mostly concerned with the war-time exploits of the older brother David (told in flashback) and his relationship with the Sheik's daughter, Charles is the more interesting of the two characters. He has reluctantly inherited his brother's land and vast wealth which, he discovers, rightfully belongs to a nephew he didn't know existed. He lacks his older brother's blond good looks, charisma and virility. He's presented as a somewhat lonely, troubled, unfulfilled, tense Englishman, un-married, without any female contact. At the end of the film he fails to persuade David's mixed-race son to return to England with him, and claim his inheritance. The boy prefers to stay with his own people, and culture. Hurst is a good storyteller, and *The Black Tent* is one of his best films. It's part romantic drama, and the director handles the inter-racial theme with delicacy and sensitivity, and part study of an 'outsider', a lonely, troubled Englishman.

Off-screen, Hurst had a reputation for being something of a bully on the set of his films, as recalled by the director Bryan Forbes in his autobiography. Early in his career, when Forbes was employed as an actor on Hurst's *The Black Tent*, the film's producer, William MacQuitty, asked him to rewrite Robin Maugham's first draft screenplay. Forbes remembered Hurst as:

> an amiable but wicked old queen who did not take kindly to my employment [as a writer]. Bill MacQuitty had forewarned me that I would meet with a hostile reception and urged me to answer in kind. Sure enough when I encoun-tered Brian for the first time, he immediately went on the attack. 'Why have they given me a third-rate writer like you?' he said in his thick Irish brogue. Thanks to Bill I was prepared for this. 'Probably because you're a third-rate director', I said. From that moment on we got on famously.
>
> (Forbes, 1992: 307–8)

Hurst never hid the fact that he was gay, at least within the 'safe' worlds of film and theatre. However, before the 1967 Sexual Offences Act partially decriminalised 'homosexual practices', it seems incredible that Hurst was never caught and arrested. A few years before he died, 1950s glamour queen Diana Dors gave a revealing insight into Hurst's private life:

> Brian was, and still is, one of the most colourful characters I have ever met. He lived in great splendour amidst wealth inherited from his Irish ancestors. . . . His conversation was always spiced with acid witticisms, and his imper-sonation of Queen Victoria on the lavatory . . . was unsurpassed, and famous throughout show business. He always had a penchant for beautiful boys, loving to have them around all the time. Brian always insisted that in order to gain his favour, *everybody* must be 'pretty, witty or rich'!
>
> (Dors, 1979: 99–100)

J. Arthur Rank, the powerful head of the Rank Organisation, expected everyone connected with his film productions to behave in a respectable manner, and yet he showed unexpected tolerance towards Hurst's sexuality. Hurst later recalled that Rank confronted him about his homosexuality, to which the director, a devout Catholic, responded, 'Arthur, I am as God made me'. The next morning Hurst signed a three-year contract with the Rank Organisation (Hurst, 1986: 141). In 1952, Hurst's dream of making *The Last Romantic*, a film about Ludwig II, the so-called 'mad' King of Bavaria, got underway, but was quickly abandoned. A project close to the director's heart, he later said, 'Though I made a lot preparation for the film, the (Bavarian) Royal Family didn't want any mention whatsoever of the King's homosexuality so it became pointless to continue with it. A year or so later, Count von Molo made a film about Ludwig, which was not a success. Neither was the more recent version by Visconti' (ibid.: 175). After directing his last film, a critically acclaimed version of *Playboy of the Western World* (1962), based on John Millington Synge's poetic stage drama, set in a remote part of rural Ireland, Hurst decided to retire. He died in 1986 at the age of 91.

The lives of Asquith and Hurst were worlds apart. They existed at a time when they could have been imprisoned for their sexuality, but each dealt with it in a completely different way. Gentle, effeminate Asquith concealed his sexuality, and was more than likely celibate throughout his life, while flamboyant, outrageous Hurst enjoyed an active sex life. Said film producer Michael Relph, who, with his collaborator, director Basil Dearden, was responsible for making *Victim* (1961), the first British film to deal with homosexuality:

> In those days film directors like Asquith and Hurst, as well as Noel Coward and Ivor Novello, were protected by the theatrical world. There wasn't any harassment of gay people in our profession. Asquith was a very sweet, nice person who was not open about his homosexuality. In fact, I don't think it was dominant in his life. So he was quite safe and happy working within the protected world of film and theatre. On the other hand, Hurst was quite flamboyant and did venture outside the theatrical world. He walked a very dangerous path by picking up guardsmen, but I don't think he was ever caught! However, a cat-and-mouse game existed with the police if gays stepped outside their particular world. I remember when John Gielgud was caught cottaging in the early 1950s. Sometimes the police turned a blind eye because the law was transparently ridiculous and hypocritical as far as homosexuality was concerned. From their point of view, provided you didn't overstep the mark, they were quite tolerant. But the law that existed seemed distasteful and out-of-date to me.

> (Bourne, 1996: 156)

Notes

1   *Brief Encounters* (1996) (see Bibliography), which included a section on *I Know Where I'm Going!*, was not included in Cook's comprehensive notes, bibliography and sources. It can only be assumed that Cook consulted the book and ignored it, or ignored it altogether.

2   See Lejeune, 1931: 11; Grierson, 1932: 12–13; Armes, 1978: 96–103 and 198–204. A recent attempt to address this oversight has been made by Mansel Stimpson in collaboration with the National Film and Television Archive. Their two-part retrospective at the National Film Theatre in London in February and March 2003 was the first given to Asquith since John Gillet's tribute in the 1970s. Though an entry for Asquith is included in Brian McFarlane's *An Autobiography of British Cinema* (1997), there is none for Hurst. For a rare critical assessment of Hurst see McIlroy, 1994: 25–39.

3   For example, Jivani, A., *It's Not Unusual: A History of Lesbian and Gay Britain in the Twentieth Century* (London: Michael O'Mara, 1997) and Aldrich, R. and Wotherspoon, G. (eds.), *Who's Who in Contemporary Gay and Lesbian History* (London: Routledge, 2001). Biographies of Asquith and Hurst, as well as references to a number of their films, are included in *Brief Encounters* (1996) (see Bibliography).

4   Esme Percy (1887–1957) was a distinguished stage actor, noted for his performances in the plays of George Bernard Shaw. In addition to Asquith's version of *Pygmalion*, his other queer screen roles of the 1930s included the effeminate transvestite killer in Hitchcock's *Murder* (1930) and the flamboyant impresario in *Song of Freedom* (1936) starring Paul Robeson.

5   See Minney, 1973: 34–5.

6   See McFarlane, 1997: 68.

7   Ackland (1908–91), playwright and screenwriter; Beaton (1902–80), photographer, stage and film designer; Walbrook (1900–68), a major star in British films of the 1930s and 1940s, played the gay ballet impresario in Powell and Pressburger's *The Red Shoes* (1948); Addinsell (1904–77) composed the music for a number of British classics including *Fire Over England, Goodbye Mr Chips, Love on the Dole, Blithe Spirit* and Hurst's *Scrooge*.

Bibliography

Armes, R. (1978) 'Style in the Interwar Years – Hitchcock and Asquith' and 'Literary Cinema – Asquith, Reed and Lean', *A Critical History of British Cinema*, London: Secker and Warburg.

Babuscio, J. (1976) 'Screen Gays No 19 – Shooting Wilde: Oscar on the Screen', *Gay News Number 89*, 1976: 21.

Barrios, R. (2003) *Screened Out: Playing Gay in Hollywood from Edison to Stonewall*, New York and London: Routledge.

Bergman, I. and Burgess, A. (1980) *Ingrid Bergman: My Story*, London: Michael Joseph.

Bourne, S. (1996) *Brief Encounters – Lesbians and Gays in British Cinema 1930–1971*, London: Cassell.

Cook, P. (2002) *I Know Where I'm Going!*, London: BFI.

Daily Mirror Reporter (1950) 'The Hon. Anthony Washes Dirty Dishes at Joe's', *Daily Mirror*, 30 May 1950.

Dors, D. (1979) *Behind Closed Dors*, London: A Star Book.

Forbes, B. (1992) *A Divided Life: Memoirs*, London: Heinemann.

Grierson, J. (1932) 'Asquith-Hitchcock Trials', *The Clarion*, January.

Hiller, W. (1973) 'Lynn, Julie, Anne, Yvonne, Margaret, Mrs Pat and Wendy – All Doing a Lot for Miss Doolittle', *Radio Times*, 15–21 December: 70–5.

Hurst, B.D. (1986) 'Hurst [Travelling the Road]'. Unpublished manuscript. British Film Institute.

Lejeune, C.A. (1931) *Cinema*, London: Alexander Maclehose.

McFarlane, B. (1997) *An Autobiography of British Cinema*, London: Methuen.

McIlroy, B. (1994) 'British Filmmaking in the 1930s and 1940s: The Example of Brian Desmond Hurst' in Wheeler Winston Dixon (ed.), *Re-viewing British Cinema, 1900–1992 – Essays and Interviews*, New York: State University of New York Press.

Minney, R.J. (1973) *Puffin Asquith*, London: Leslie Frewin.

Russo, V. (1987) *The Celluloid Closet: Homosexuality in the Movies*, New York: Harper and Row.

Thomas, N.D. (1988) 'The Contribution of Anthony Asquith to British Film Culture'. Unpublished MA dissertation. School of English and American Studies, University of East Anglia.

3 An instrument with a flaming sword

Conservative queerness in *A Canterbury Tale*

Alexander Doty

In his autobiography *A Life in Movies*, director Michael Powell says that his – and collaborator Emeric Pressburger's – 1944 film *A Canterbury Tale* 'looks on the surface conventional, but it was filled with subversive material' (438). What is conventional about the film is easy for Powell to articulate: '[W]e were explaining to the Americans, and to our own people, the spiritual values and traditions we were fighting for' in World War II (437). What he thinks is subversive about the film Powell never directly states, but he does note that '[t]here was a loony squire, who was so anxious to preserve British traditional values that he poured glue on girls' hair when they went out at night with soldiers' (437). Called 'The Glueman' by the locals, Thomas Colpeper, the middle-aged, 'loony squire' is also queered as he lives with his mother even as he carries out his sticky scheme to break up heterosexual couples so that soldiers will come to his romantic lectures on the English countryside and English history.

But, while Colpeper may be queerly coded, and while his modus operandi may be bizarre, his role as mouthpiece for Ye Olde England virtues and values makes his subversive potential nil for progressive viewers. Paradoxically, for these viewers, the only way that Colpeper could be a subversive agent would be for the character's queerness to trigger viewer homophobia, which would encourage them to reject Colpeper's conventional ideas. But when he called the film 'subversive', maybe Powell was thinking of more conservative viewers who supposedly make up most of the mass audience for mainstream films. I guess it is subversive in a certain way to have these viewers be forced to admit that a queer, 'loony squire' has the same ideological beliefs they do.

Most likely, Powell and Pressburger wouldn't have called Colpeper 'queer', except in the sense that he does some strange things. But I am going to talk about Colpeper as queer in the sense that he is not strongly or definitively represented as homosexual or heterosexual. Similarly, a character who is not clearly coded as either conventionally masculine or feminine could be considered queer. Since he is a conservative, it is no surprise that Colpeper is a masculine-coded queer man.

Figure 3.1 'Land Girl' Alison Smith (Sheila Sim) and Thomas Colpeper (Eric Portman) explore what's lurking in the closet in *A Canterbury Tale* (1944).

Source: BFI stills, posters and designs (Archers Film Productions).

Though masculine, the 'loony squire' of Chillingbourne inhabits a liminal sexuality position that represents a narrative challenge for most mainstream films – namely, how can this queerness be contained so that it does not pose a threat to dominant ideology? Often this queer challenge – and its potential for suggesting positive alternatives – is dealt with by treating queer characters to undercutting humour or violence. But these strategies still leave room for 'reading against the grain' or 'oppositional' readings wherein readers, themselves in the position of queer challengers, understand queer characters as being unfairly treated by heterosexist, heterocentrist, or homophobic cultural and narrative machinations. Less open to such politically progressive reader reclamation are those films that contrive to have their queer characters buy into dominant culture's institutions and values. By constructing assimilationist 'place at the table' queers, these films are relatively unconcerned about using laughter, force, or some other narrative ploy, as a containment device.

It's strange that these gay, lesbian, bisexual, transgender, and less clearly defined queer characters, with their middle- or upper-class 'we're the same as everyone else' looks and attitude are generally considered positive and politically liberal representations when their purpose is to support hegemony. Some of the more prominent film characters that fall into this category are FBI agent Clarice Starling in *Silence of the Lambs* (1991), military and company women Ellen Ripley and Pvt. Vasquez in *Aliens* (1986), and those ever-popular figures whose raison d'être is to assist straight folks in various ways, usually in relation to romantic or family matters: Frank, the Greg Kinnear character in *As Good as it Gets* (1998); Simon, the Harvey Fierstein character, and his partner in *Mrs Doubtfire* (1993), Nancy Blake in *The Women* (1939), and many others. These are good queers who are generally given a supporting role within mainstream narratives and the dominant culture that produces them.

Thomas Colpeper is perhaps the most spectacular and complex example of this type. If, as Graham Fuller notes, *A Canterbury Tale* 'is a High Tory lesson in cultural conservatism', then Thomas Colpeper is the self-proclaimed 'missionary' who will employ extreme methods, if needs be, to teach traditional lessons (Fuller, 1995: 34). If he has an ideological failing, it is that his attitude about certain things – especially about the role of women – is a bit too conservatively old-fashioned for war-time England:

> He rejects the services of Alison as a land girl on his farm, preferring a male farm worker. At almost his first appearance he demonstrates with approval the use of the ducking stool, for dealing with gossiping women, to Sergeant Johnson.
>
> (Richards and Aldgate, 1983: 49)

To this can be added his activities as The Glueman, which he does, in part, to control the (hetero)sexuality of local women. As The Glueman, conservative Colpeper mimes the action of a fetishistic straight man as he pours glue (read: semen) into women's hair. While most of the older local men approve of the results of The Glueman's attacks, the film sides initially with women like Alison who declares that far from being frightened into staying at home, she will be out every night trying to catch The Glueman. It is not surprising that more than one critic calls Colpeper a misogynist (Wicking, 1984: 356; Richards and Aldgate, 1983: 49), but, more often than not, this misogyny is linked to the queer coding surrounding the squire. 'Colpeper's Freudian attacks on the girls may have a cultural rationale,' says Graham Fuller, 'but it is also the work of a troubled man' who the film treats with 'homosexual implication[s]' (Fuller, 1984: 36). In this manner, Colpeper's one ideological problem area is connected to his queerness: 'There is a distinct element of misogyny in Colpeper's stance . . . [h]e is a bachelor, living with his mother' (Richards and Aldgate, 1983: 49). Ironically enough, then, a conventional and conservative understanding of queer men (that is, they hate women) is deployed by the film to explain the one weak spot in Colpeper's otherwise exemplary traditionalism.

Complicating this cultural and narrative move, however, is Colpeper's relationship with Alison Smith, a London shop girl-turned-Woman's Land Army volunteer. Alison's love of the English countryside and English heritage is almost as strong as Colpeper's, although her connections with the land and its history are a result of caravan trips with her fiancé, who is now missing in action. Over the course of the narrative, Colpeper's queerly motivated misogynistic attitudes will be challenged by his encounters with Alison. Attending one of Colpeper's men-only lectures, Alison is the first one to take him up on an offer to drop by his house in order to learn more about local history. Her remarks on the Kent countryside and her offer to give Colpeper some old coins for his museum cause him to look at her with real interest for the first time. The source of this interest is made intriguingly ambiguous in their next scene together. Walking in the countryside, Alison, now in a feminine floral dress, is surprised by Colpeper, who is lying in some tall grass. Telling him she heard medieval Canterbury pilgrims on the road just then, Colpeper remarks that those sounds come from inside, implying that he hears them too. 'I was very mistaken about you. I'm sorry', Colpeper says as he invites Alison to sit with him.

Then things become queerly interesting – or frustrating, depending on your point of view. Alison tells Colpeper that she spent 'thirteen perfect days' around where they are sitting with her fiancé, and that she feels his soul there. 'He loved it so much', Alison says finally. 'I love it, too', Colpeper responds, as the pair are posed and photographed like lovers, with Alison leaning on Colpeper's shoulder as the sun and breezes play upon them. While the 'it' Colpeper speaks of is most obviously the countryside, given the romantic mise-en-scène, the 'it' could also refer to Colpeper's role here as a replacement for Alison's fiancé. Although the moment indicates certain longings in Colpeper, it is not at all clear whether these longings are fundamentally heterosexual, or whether Alison's status as English heritage 'soul sister' causes Colpeper (and the film's mise-en-scène) to temporarily indulge in a fantasy of heterosexual romance (Wicking, 1984: 356). Or, perhaps, the film is suggesting that a queer man and a straight woman can romantically bond over something non-sexual — once that queer man has got over his narrow view of women. However you read the scene, though, Colpeper's misogyny is being tempered here in a context that connects a romantic love of English land and history with heterosexuality. In order to make up for his one ideological blind spot, and become 'the film's heart', Colpeper must affirm his empathy with heterosexuality, if not clearly be represented as straight himself (356).

This narrative and cultural demand of the good queer is reaffirmed when Colpeper explains The Glueman's motives toward the end of the film as the four principals (Colpeper, Alison, American Sergeant Bob Johnson and British Sergeant Peter Gibbs) are on the train to Canterbury.

What is amazing about this sequence is how the misogynistic glue attacks that Colpeper / The Glueman has been criticised for earlier in the film are now justified as a patriotic means of preserving normative heterosexuality, since they keep the women of the town faithful to their soldier husbands and boyfriends while the latter are away:

> *Colpeper*: [to Johnson] You have a girl at home?
> Would you like her to go out with soldiers while you are away? Most of our girls here have men in the services. The older people didn't like them going out with every soldier who came along.
>
> [Shot of Alison silent and staring.]
>
> *Colpeper*: No one wanted to stop the soldiers from having a good time.
> *Gibbs*: So you stopped the girls from having one.
>
> [Shot of Sergeant Johnson with pipe and Alison.]
>
> *Colpeper* (voice over): Exactly.

While one could say that preventing the women of the town from going out also 'stop[s] the soldiers from having a good time', the emphasis in this scene is on how Colpeper has contributed to the war effort by looking out for the interests of straight men. Even the older men who were taken to task by Alison earlier in the film for their repressive attitudes toward women are excused. Besides, as Colpeper has said earlier, if the soldiers couldn't get women, they 'went to the movies to see glamour girls on the screen' to get their erotic jollies. So it is, finally, only women's desires that are being policed by the conservative queer man, whose Glueman misogyny is repackaged as being in the patriotic service of patriarchy. It is important here to recall that Colpeper conducts his attacks in a Home Guard uniform and that we are told that 'every second man' in the area has a Home Guard uniform: The Glueman, as it turns out, could be almost any man. One might recall here an earlier scene in the film in a new light. After Alison is attacked by The Glueman, a number of men help wash her hair. One shot reveals many men's hands lathering and washing her hair simultaneously. In retrospect, the shot seems disturbingly fetishistic and the men's action less benevolent than controlling, as their hands push her head down toward the water in a large bowl.

During much of Colpeper's confessional scene on the train, usually outspoken Alison has remained silent, but she finally speaks up to challenge Colpeper one last time, though with a smile on her face:

> *Alison*: Mr. Colpeper, didn't it ever occur to you to ask the girls to your lectures?
> *Colpeper* (unsmiling): No.
> *Alison*: Pity.

Not missing a trick, the film allows Alison to point out Colpeper's queerly connected failing one last time. His negative response to her question reveals that he has not yet moved beyond his appreciation of Alison as an exceptional woman to see all women in a new light. But while Alison's 'pity' suggests that Colpeper still has some work to do in changing his misguided queer ideas about women, the narrative also has her defend and, implicitly, forgive Colpeper/The Glueman a minute or so later, thereby bestowing the exceptional woman's seal of approval on the idea that men (queer or straight) can monitor women's sex lives for the good of the nation, especially during war-time, when these women have more social latitude. Having gone from being The Glueman's victim to become an active narrative agent (she leads the search for The Glueman), Alison is finally placed firmly within conservative patriarchy, just like Colpeper, her English heritage 'soul sister'. It makes sense that Colpeper's last major scene is when he surprises Alison during her inspection of the caravan she and her fiancé lived in when they travelled through Kent. Colpeper comforts Alison after she breaks down. But when Alison receives word that her fiancé is alive and that her prospective father-in-law (who had initially opposed the marriage on class grounds) wants to meet her in Canterbury Cathedral, Colpeper mysteriously vanishes from the scene, his work as good, dominant culture-supporting, queer being done.

Before he vanishes from the film entirely, however, Colpeper passes the conservative queer baton on to another character, Peter Gibbs. Peter is the only one to question Colpeper's explanation of his Glueman activities, and he plans to turn Colpeper over to the authorities once they reach Canterbury. But, then, Peter is caught up in an attraction–repulsion relationship with Colpeper throughout the film, telling Bob at one point: 'He's a bit cracked, but I like him too'. In standing up for the women The Glueman attacks, Peter is, from a progressive ideological position, actually on stronger ground than anyone else in the train compartment. Indeed, he appears to take on Alison's function here as the defender of women's rights just at the point that the narrative has her conservative nationalistic and romantic sentiments swamp her feminist impulses. Peter has stood up for, and in

Figure 3.2 On the road to Canterbury: before playing his 'big organ', Peter Gibbs
(Dennis Price) denounces conservative 'queer' Colpeper's dark little secret.

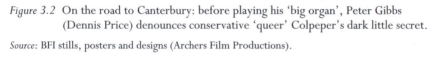

Source: BFI stills, posters and designs (Archers Film Productions).

for, Alison on other occasions: he convinces her to attend Colpeper's lecture, and
he, rather than Alison, is the first person we see visit Colpeper at home after the
lecture. While looking for clues that would indicate Colpeper is The Glueman,
Peter critiques Colpeper and men like him for their misguided 'missionary' zeal
about the land and its history – that is, he critiques what he sees as 'every second'
British man's sentimental relationship to church and state. It soon becomes
apparent, however, that the 'lady doth protest too much', as Peter starts talking
about his former life as an organist. He reveals that although he has wanted to be a
church organist since he was a kid, he plays the organ in a cinema. When Colpeper
asks if he's ever played a church organ, Peter replies, with longing in his voice, 'Not
a big one'. Before the end of the film, he will get his chance to play 'a big one'
– and for an audience of fellow soldiers, no less.

After this double-entendre exchange, suggestively connecting male queerness
with Christian spirituality, it is apparent that cynical urbanite Peter is a progressive
queer man ripe for the converting by Colpeper. As indicated above, Peter's last
stand as a rebellious – and, by the logic of the film, unhappy – queer man is on the
train to Canterbury, where he has his final show-down with Colpeper:

Colpeper: If I've done harm, I must pay.
Peter: In order for that to happen, someone must denounce you.
 I want to make that quite clear.

[Colpeper looks out of the train window.]

Colpeper: There are higher courts than the local bench of magistrates.

[Shots of Canterbury Cathedral. A choir is singing. Alison and Bob Johnson look at Colpeper with wonder in their eyes. Peter seems troubled, yet engaged, by Colpeper.]

Peter: Rum sort of pilgrimage for you.
Colpeper: A pilgrimage can be either to receive a blessing or to do penance.
Peter: I don't need either.
Colpeper: Perhaps you're an instrument.
Peter: Do I get a flaming sword?
Colpeper: Nothing would surprise me.

[An abrupt cut to the train entering the station.]
[Back in the train compartment.]

Peter: I'll believe that when I see a halo 'round my head.

[Noise and steam from the train fill the background of a closeup of Peter, who is then shot with backlighting which creates a glowing silhouette.]

Moving beyond his earlier patriotic, nationalistic justification for his Glueman activities, Colpeper, with the filmmaker's approval (shots of the cathedral, heavenly choir), suggests that his actions would be favourably judged by God himself. Finally, queer Colpeper works for the interests of both state and church, as Peter will when he plays the organ in Canterbury Cathedral at a service to see the soldiers off. At this point, however, Peter is still an unconverted queer man, and Douglas McVay notes that Colpeper's 'Christlike function is most plainly denoted by the fact that [Peter] Gibbs, Judas-like, plans to denounce him as the Glueman to the police' (19). While there may be some frisson for many viewers once they realise the film is comparing a queer man not only to Judas (which they might expect) but also to Christ, Colpeper's commitment to, and containment within, dominant culture's institutions and ideology more than makes up for the audacity. Besides, he is also the 'missionary' for traditional values who converts the 'Judas' who dares to question the sexual policing of women and who dares to say, 'The beauty of the countryside – who cares about these things during wartime?'

While Peter says he doesn't need a blessing or to do penance during his visit to Canterbury, he does become Colpeper's 'instrument' when he is forced to seek out the police superintendent in the cathedral and is diverted from his mission by the organist, whom he follows into the loft, guided by a dropped piece of sheet music

– treated here like the dropped handkerchief in a heterosexual scenario. 'That's some organ!' Peter exclaims upon reaching the top of the stairs. The Canterbury Cathedral organist, who is another queerly coded man (he wears a pinky ring, first played the organ in a circus, and snaps out 'Do I look like a charwoman?' when Peter asks if he is the organist), allows Peter to fulfil his dream of playing a 'big' church organ. Playing 'Onward Christian Soldiers' for the troops and towns-people assembled in England's most tradition-soaked cathedral, Peter has finally become the 'instrument' with 'a flaming sword' Colpeper spoke of earlier: the good, assimilationist, conservative queer man who uncritically serves the interests of dominant culture.

But that 'flaming sword' cuts two ways, and, for a queer progressive reader at least, it is difficult not to see that part of the process of becoming an English Christian soldier with a flaming sword requires that Peter douse and suppress his other 'flaming sword' and forgo any queer personal and sexual life. Colpeper is an excellent example: a 'bachelor' who lives with mother, has no romantic inter-ests, and who devotes all his time and energy to tending the land, running the town, policing the morals of its women, and lecturing soldiers on England's glorious history. As Fuller puts it, Colpeper becomes 'the archetypally repressed [Powell and Pressburger] hero' (36). It might briefly be noted here that many of Powell and Pressburger's 'repressed' heroes (Lermontov in *The Red Shoes* being the prime example) are queerly coded. This repressive psychosexual sacrifice is not required of any of the straight characters in *A Canterbury Tale*. It is telling that while Colpeper's 'miracle' or 'blessing' is having the soldiers come to Chillingbourne so he has the opportunity to lecture them, and Peter's 'miracle' is playing the organ for the soldiers in Canterbury Cathedral, the final 'miracles' the film contrives for both Alison and Bob have to do with their heterosexual relationships. Land Girl Alison Smith will be reunited with her fiancé and is taken into the bosom of his family, while Sergeant Bob Johnson receives word that the reason he has not heard from his fiancée is because she has joined the WACS and is in Australia – but that she loves him. Colpeper even talks to Bob about bringing his future son to England; and, as noted earlier, the squire has commiserated with Alison over her apparently lost lover.

So, while heterosexuality and serving a conservative church and state agenda do mix, *A Canterbury Tale* tells us through its representation of Colpeper and Peter that the only good queer is one willing to sublimate his/her sexual desires and translate them into a desire to serve dominant culture. If Alison and Bob receive unqualified miracles or blessings in Canterbury, the miracles or blessings Colpeper and Peter receive are simultaneously forms of penance. But the film does hint at what these two queer men are sacrificing by having Colpeper compare the psychosexually charged act of pouring the glue on to women's heads to pouring knowledge into the soldiers' heads, while Peter ecstatically plays an organ he calls a 'big one' for his fellow soldiers as the film's finale. Clearly, the film encourages viewers to understand these queer men's penetential sacrifices of a personal and sexual life as appropriate and noble. Indeed, it is part of how they are able to be blessed by church and state. But while Colpeper and Peter appear content with their lot, most queerly positioned viewers – even conservative ones – cannot help but feel some frustration and anger at the clever narrative and cultural programme laid out for these men, which ties war-time patriotism to the denial of their personal and sexual desires. The queer men in *A Canterbury Tale* are like the women The Glueman attacks in relation to the narrative and cultural pressures they are under to police their non-normative desires, so it is both ironic and fitting that Colpeper should be an instrument of dominant culture as The Glueman.

It is also both ironic and fitting that Prudence Honeywood, the most queerly coded woman in the film, should want to meet The Glueman: 'I wish he'd go for me,' she tells Alison, 'I'd "Glueman" him!' Prudence's remarks betray a desire to fight The Glueman in reprisal of the women he has attacked, to have The Glueman 'go for her' romantically, and to become The Glueman. As it turns out, Prudence, like Colpeper, doesn't need glue poured on her hair to convince her to regulate her queerness, because, also like Colpeper, she has channelled these energies into the war effort by running a farm. In this, she is assisted by Land Girls, who are to her what the soldiers are to Colpeper, younger vessels that she can pour knowledge into – here, about working the land rather than about establishing a metaphysical connection with the land.

At one point, Alison tells Prudence about living in a room in one of the 'tall, sad [row] houses [that] were all the same'. 'The only man who ever asked me to marry him wanted me to move into a house like that,' Prudence confides, 'I'm still a maid – an old 'un, but a free one.' Taking its cue from this vague statement, the film isn't fully clear about whether tie-wearing Prudence prefers men to women. However, she is represented as strongly gender non-conformist. Even granting that the film is set in a period where women were allowed greater gender mobility, women of the period were expected to be conventionally feminine at the end of the day (and the war). But Prudence is coded as thoroughly masculine in her looks, attitudes and speech, whereas the other women in *A Canterbury Tale* actively pursue men, are engaged or widowed, talk about 'girly' things, dress in traditionally feminine clothes, or display feminine touches while dressed in more masculine work garb. At one point, Prudence contrasts her attitude to The Glueman's attacks to that of her sister's, saying that Susanna likes to 'dramatize things': 'It's happened to other girls. None of them died.' Prudence's cool remarks about The Glueman's victims become even more interesting after Land Girl (and Glueman victim) Fee Baker tells Alison that The Glueman 'might be a woman'. One of the marks of Prudence's good, conservative queerness is this nonchalant, 'masculine' attitude about women being attacked to keep them in line – just as one of the marks against Peter is his dramatic feminist outrage at these attacks. Reinforcing Prudence's conservative queer position, the film also implicitly contrasts Susanna's work running an inn with

Prudence's work running a farm. Whereas the widowed sister's entrepreneurship – and whatever 'masculine' qualities she displays – can be excused because of the domestic context, within the conservative ideology of the film, 'old maid' Prudence's thoroughly masculine endeavours and attitude can only be presented as positive because she puts her gender (and, perhaps, sexuality) queerness at the service of a nation at war.

In spite of – or because of – the persuasive and pervasive narrative and cultural forces at work in *A Canterbury Tale* to de-sexualise queerness as part of a conservative ideological programme, the film is full of queer sexual joking and innuendo, some of which has been mentioned already. Graham Fuller finds that 'coursing through the film is a weird sexual energy' (36). Among the examples he cites is Prudence telling Alison she turned down her one chance at marriage and is still 'a maid' (and 'a free one') within an hour or two of their meeting – just after, it should be added, she confesses to Alison that leading a 'straight harrow' is not one of her farming skills. Fuller also mentions, but does not elaborate upon, the scene where Susanna tells Bob Johnson 'a ribald joke about the bed he just slept in at the inn' (36). The joke – and many of the other jokes and innuendoes in the film – refers to male homosexuality. After Bob tells Susanna that he slept well, but was 'lonely', she informs him that 'They say two six foot men couldn't shake hands across that bed'. When Bob asks 'Why would they want to do that, m'am?', Susanna replies, 'Depends upon who's in it, young man'. Bob actually initiates the film's series of homosexual jokes and innuendoes, when, during the film's opening, he jumps off a train and into the arms of the station master: 'I'll sit the next dance out', he tells the flustered man. More than once during the film Bob, or some other character, will talk about his having a 'date' with a fellow soldier. The one 'date' we do see him on takes place at the end of the film. It is telling that this male date brings Bob word of his fiancée and, by this, effects one of the film's two heterosexual 'happy ending' reunions, which closes off the jokey queer energy the film has been generating.

That straight Bob Johnson should be the source of so many of the film's male–male jokes and innuendoes seems odd until you recall that an important political mission of *A Canterbury Tale* was to firm up war-time Anglo–American relations. British male critics were certainly taken with American amateur actor Sergeant John Sweet, who plays Bob Johnson. 'What a man this Sergeant John Sweet is . . . he has toughness and charm', rhapsodised Ernest Betts in the *Sunday Express* (14 May 1944). Winifred Horrabin of the *Tribune* found Sweet 'charming and endearing' (20 May 1944). Indeed, most of the men reviewing the film found Sweet and his characterisation 'charming'. Above a picture of Sweet/Johnson surrounded by English boys, the headline of one of the 'exploitation' schemes offered in the film's publicity materials suggests that theatre owners 'Run a "Get-Together Go-As-You-Please" Party on Stage each night with US and British Soldiers'. In an obvious afterthought, this headline adds ' – and don't forget the Ladies!' before going on to suggest how to best promote 'good fellowship amongst "the boys"' during screenings of the film (*A Canterbury Tale*, promotional brochure: 12).

Before Colpeper's lecture, Bob and a British solider, both smoking pipes, get to know each other in a dialogue rife with queer innuendo. The British soldier mentions he has a brother in 'Butt City', Montana [obviously meaning Butte], to which Bob replies 'I come from Three Sisters, Oregon'. 'I come from Seven Sisters Road, London', the soldier remarks warmly as he offers his hand to Bob. American and British 'sister' soldiers bond here over pipes and talk of 'Butt City' – the American city where the British soldier's brother lives. Fittingly, one of American Bob's 'date' scenes involves British Peter, who tells Bob and Alison at the end of the film that he's off on a secret mission. When Bob presses him about where he's going, Peter tells him: 'Don't worry. I'll be seeing you'. 'It's a date', Bob replies, to which Peter adds, 'And the more of us – the merrier'.

In earlier drafts of the film's script, the queer humour was even more pronounced – but also more centred around Peter. Returning to the sergeants' quarters at camp one night, one of his mates, Len, decides Peter has been out with nurses (he's actually been out with Bob and Alison looking for The Glueman):

> *Len*: Pretty nurses? Cool hands in the night? Lovely white forms ministering to your every want? [He demonstrates. Peter resists. There is a free fight, Len yelling.] Come on, nurses! Let's remind him of hospital! Let's wash him with tender hands! Are you friend or enema?

When Peter tells some of the sergeants that he thinks he has helped catch The Glueman, '[m]ore sergeants in scanty night clothes come rushing in asking questions'. Len then casts Peter in the role of Dorothy from *The Wizard of Oz*, singing 'Heigh-Ho! The Glueman's dead!' and exclaiming 'All the boys will want to kiss you!' 'I haven't shaved!' is Peter's retort. Later, anticipating the sentiments of British male film critics, Peter tells Bob that he is the person to get men in the village to talk about The Glueman case because 'They fall for you'. 'Maybe it's the uniform', Bob replies. 'And maybe it's your fatal charm', Peter suggests.

Perhaps this final remark is too much for Bob – or the narrative – to bear, because, soon after, the draft script offers this exchange:

> *Bob*: Get lots of girls on your trail, I'll bet.
> *Peter*: I'm hard to catch.
> *Bob*: But you had a girl – I hope?
> *Peter*: Yes. I had a girl.
> *Bob*: Where is she now?
> *Peter*: She married a Finn.

Bob is intrigued by Peter's apparent calm, remarking, 'I don't get you at all . . . you're not mad if somebody steals your girl. What makes you tick?' 'I may be new to you, old-timer, but I know a lot of other fellows like me', Peter replies. Adding, 'We do all right'. As if sensing what Peter is suggesting about his sexuality here, Bob toasts Peter with a 'The skin of your nose!' while Alison offers, 'Glue in your hair!' – the former toast alluding to the male member (castrated or merely circumcised?) and the latter toast placing Peter in the role of someone with semen in his hair.

But, as the narrative requires Peter to become a model conservative queer and take up where Colpeper leaves off, all these striking queer – and more specifically male homosexual – references surrounding Peter were purged from the final script for *A Canterbury Tale*. The script drafting appears to have gone through the same process the film demands of Peter and other good queers – the suppression of any indication of desire (not that, as noted earlier, the film or Peter are fully successful at this). In any case, shifting the burden of queer humour to Bob in the final script makes it more acceptable. Because he is more insistently represented as straight (he talks about his 'girl' back home at regular intervals; the American version of the film has Bob take 'girl', June, to the places he had seen during the war, triggering flashbacks to the central narrative), the queer jokes Bob initiates or that are connected to him will be attributed to war-time male homosociality by most viewers. As long as Peter was the focus of the joking and innuendo, the ideological project of the film to contain queerness and put it to conservative uses was threatened, as Peter turns out to be queer. Displaced on to charming, straight Bob, the film's queer humour actually helps promote male Anglo–American relations. Score another one for the film's clever exploitation of queerness for dominant culture uses.

One way to understand *A Canterbury Tale* is to think of it as enforcing a 'don't ask – don't tell' policy. It's war-time Britain and the country needs every man and woman. Every man and woman is exhorted to serve king and country or risk being called unpatriotic, a slacker, or worse. Because of the demand for man- and woman-power, even queers are expected to do their duty. However, in order to carry out this necessary and required service, queer men and woman, unlike their straight counterparts, must set aside all personal and sexual desires, as any direct expression of these desires would be disruptive and, therefore, subversive to the war effort. Certainly there can be a bit more leeway for women to express non-normative gender characteristics – after all, war is a masculine business – just as long as they clearly indicate somehow that they are fundamentally feminine, heterosexual women. And as for the men, what better method than humour to let off some of the suppressed queer steam and to defuse any of the male–male intensities encouraged by wartime circumstances? In this way, no one need take any of it seriously. All the better if this queer humour is largely associated with a straight foreigner – it's that much more distanced from the queer British characters. These discreet characters can then conservatively go about serving church and state by running a farm, playing a cathedral organ, being a soldier, governing a town, and lecturing about England's glorious history. Shots under the end credits of *A Canterbury Tale* return us to Colpeper and his talks. Strolling into a lecture at the Colpeper Institute are men and women in couples or in two men-with-a-woman-between-them trios. Colpeper doesn't appear. Reinforcing the central message about queerness in the narrative proper, the film's epilogue has the queer man represented not as a bodily presence, but as a poster reminding us that his value is as someone who serves the dominant culture – and as someone who can only do this by the denial of his body. Even if we consider the male-female-male trios in the epilogue as echoing Bob, Alison and Peter, the queer member of that trio ends the film as an 'instrument' with 'a flaming sword' – a newly 'converted', conservatively queer, soldier-church organist playing for other soldiers, their 'girls' and their families. To any queers in the audience, especially in 1944, the message of *A Canterbury Tale* is clear: Close your eyes and think of England!

Bibliography

Betts, E. (1944) 'You'll like this U.S. sergeant in a truly British film', *Sunday Express* [London] 14 May: n.p.

A Canterbury Tale. Dir. Michael Powell and Emeric Pressburger. With Eric Portman, John Sweet, Sheila Sims and Dennis Price. The Archers-Eagle Lion, 1944. All quotes from the film are transcribed from a videotape distributed in the United States by Home Vision Cinema of Janus Films' copy of the original British release Print.

A Canterbury Tale, promotional brochure, 1944. Information Department, British Film Institute, London.

Fuller, G. (1995) '*A Canterbury Tale*', *Film Comment* March–April: 30–6.

Horrabin, W. (1944) 'Shows', *Tribune* [London] 20 May: n.p.

McVay, D. (1982) 'Michael Powell: Three Neglected Films', *Films and Filming* January: 18–25.

Powell, M. (1987) *A Life in Movies: An Autobiography*, New York: Alfred A. Knopf.

Powell, M. and Pressburger, E. *A Canterbury Tale*, Script #S13976, n.d. Information Department, British Film Institute, London. All quotes are taken from this copy of the script, which has no pagination.

Richards, J. and Aldgate, A. (1983) *The Best of British: Cinema and Society, 1930–1970*. London: Basil Blackwell.

Wicking, C. (1984) 'Retrospective: *A Canterbury Tale*', *Monthly Film Bulletin* November: 355–6.

4   Are there stars out tonight?

Keith Howes

Let's begin with those six degrees of separation. Michael Redgrave appeared in *The Importance of Being Earnest* (1951), which would be remade fifty years on with Rupert Everett playing the Redgrave role's 'Bunburyist', Algy. Rupert Everett shot to stardom on stage and screen as the future Cambridge spy Guy Burgess (but named Bennett) in the public school set *Another Country* (1984). Michael Redgrave's most prestigious and best remembered full-length screen role was that of a public schoolmaster facing the abyss in the screen version of Terence Rattigan's *The Browning Version* (1950). Rattigan it was who scripted the ill-fated *Lawrence of Arabia* in 1958, which was all set to start filming when the Rank Organisation pulled the plug. Its star was to be Dirk Bogarde who, four years later, would become the first box office male star to play the role of a homosexual in a contemporary screen subject. Michael Redgrave was, according to the film's producer, Michael Relph, the number two choice should Bogarde – as was thought fairly likely – decline the role of the blackmailed lawyer in *Victim* (1961). Playing a supporting role in the film was Dennis Price, briefly a star of British films of the late 1940s such as *The Bad Lord Byron* and *Kind Hearts and Coronets*, two roles for which Rupert Everett would be eminently suitable. Everett would also be uncommonly convincing in a number of Dirk Bogarde's roles such as *The Spanish Gardener*, Sydney Carton in *A Tale of Two Cities*, *The Servant*, *Accident* and *HMS Defiant*.

The one outsider is Ian McKellen who, though a star of sorts on the London and Broadway stage, had no pulling power on screen until he was nominated for an Oscar in 1998 for *Gods and Monsters* before accepting the coveted role of Gandalf in *The Lord of the Rings*, parts 1 to 3. In *Gods and Monsters*, McKellen played gay director James Whale, an Englishman in Hollywood. Whale once directed Charles Laughton in *The Old Dark House* (1932). And as for *Six Degrees of Separation*, the movie, McKellen played a leading supporting role in Fred Schepsi's film which was the starting point for the theory that most people are linked by a few short leaps.

And it is an unbroken chain from Michael Redgrave and Dennis Price in the 1940s, Price and Dirk Bogarde in the 1950s, 1960s and 1970s to Everett and McKellen in the 1980s and onwards today. Out they may be, but in actual terms,

Figure 4.1 Standing out from the crowd: Guy Bennett (Rupert Everett) in *Another Country* (1984).

Source: BFI stills, posters and designs (Goldcrest).

McKellen and Everett's contribution to queer British cinema, in its narrowest sense, is but a few hours of screentime – McKellen's brief supporting role in *Bent* (1997) and Rupert Everett's wordless man dying of AIDS in *Remembrance of Things Fast* (1994), and his contribution to something called *South Kensington* (2001). Other out non-movie star gay actors like Antony Sher and Simon Callow have played no more than a couple of roles in UK films made on low budgets, which are redolent of the kind of insolence and 'in your faceness' of what we regard as queer cinema. On closer inspection, it is the now deceased actors Michael Redgrave, Dennis Price, Dirk Bogarde – and let's not forget Alec Guinness – who laid the foundations.

Starting with Redgrave, who appeared in what is arguably one of Britain's very first post-war queer films, Ealing's *Dead of Night* (1945). The film tweaks the devil's tail more than somewhat, moving confidently through tales morbid and jaunty, saving the best for last in the gradual corruption, manipulation and emotional destruction of a ventriloquist by his dummy. As Maxwell Frere, Redgrave, with his tremulous voice and not quite at home in his body jerkiness, adroitly indicates the dependency and love he feels for this plaster nemesis whose identity is part and parcel his. The film, and especially this episode, captured public imagination at the time and Redgrave's ghastly end, in a prison accused of murder and taunted by his former stage partner, still garners respect because of its sharply etched portrait of aesthetic concentration and frenzied theatricality. It was during this period in films such as *The Way to the Stars* and *The Captive Heart* that Redgrave became recognised by the British public, though never with the same warmth or longevity bestowed upon his co-star in *The Way to the Stars*, John Mills. Redgrave's own angst over his heterosexual and family obligations, and his affairs with men, were eventually made public in his autobiography in the 1980s. It could be said that his inner turmoil finds an appropriate temporary resting place in the guise of poor, trapped Maxwell Frere. But he's equally good in the full-length roles he plays, such as Andrew Crocker-Harris in *The Browning Version* or as John Worthing in *The Importance of Being Earnest*. Crisp and dry, shot through with icy disdain, Worthing is every inch a Wildean dandy and pillar of society, and markedly livelier than Colin Firth's limning of him in the recent remake. Despite a few Hollywood forays – notably *The Secret Beyond the Door* (1948) for Fritz Lang, and *The Quiet American* a decade later – Redgrave never became the second-tier star that Stewart Granger and James Mason did. Too cerebral is the general verdict. Lots of music, little fire. Look carefully at *Secret Beyond the Door*. Too queer, more likely.

The 'too nervous' persona also spelt doom for Dennis Price; first a Gainsborough employee, he reached his apogee with his serially killing Louis Mazzini in Ealing's *Kind Hearts and Coronets* in 1949, deliciously camp and fluted, offing all the d'Ascoyne family members who stand in his way to the earldom. Although heterosexual, the character, especially in his frisky scenes with lover-girlfriend Joan Greenwood, displays a kittenish relish which is fascinatingly queer. Despite appearing as a female d'Ascoyne, Alec Guinness is relatively restrained in his various guises, and it is Price who scores the most bullseyes with both dialogue and visual interest. However, as one Gainsborough stalwart told me recently, 'He was queer and it showed'. A suicide attempt – at that time illegal in Britain – and a seeming move towards more or less open homosexuality, at least in private life, put paid to his career as a leading man. Far from disappearing, though, he thrived in scores of supporting roles with names such as Bertram and Cecil, and he became the walking, breathing emblem of British shiftiness and hooded cynicism, whether as the blackmailer in *The Naked Truth* (1957) or Robbie Ross in *The Trials of Oscar Wilde* (1960).

He was certainly the first name actor to play a more or less overtly gay role on television (*Crime On Their Hands*, 1954) and to consistently tinge his screen roles with lavender, pink and purple, culminating in a brace of overt queers in 1961 with his West End matinee idol in *Victim*, and an unapologetically foulard flying scream-ing queen photographer in *No Love for Johnnie* (1961). He never stopped working, playing leads on TV (notably as the imperturbable butler, Jeeves), second, third or fourth string parts in British films, until he went to Spain in the early 1970s to do vampire movies. I saw him at Pinewood a few months before his death, grinding out a wretched quickie set in a film studio. He was a gracious, deracinated man by this time, apparently with gambling problems which necessitated ceaseless work even in the most inauspicious circumstances. It was a long way from the man who danced with Margaret Lockwood in *Hungry Hill*, ravished – offscreen – the cream of English society as *The Bad Lord Byron*, and did in four or five Alec Guinnesses in *Kind Hearts*.

There were of course scores of Guinnesses – he was noted, celebrated even – for having no star persona as such, though after his Oscar-winning role in *The Bridge on the River Kwai* (1957) he was a big name around the world. The singular queerness of most of his performances, whether disguised with whiskers, moustache, pebble glasses, false nose or skin dye, shone through. The schoolgirlishness of his Herbert Pocket in *Great Expectations* (1946), the spinsterishness of *Father Brown* (1954) or his Col. Nicholson in *Kwai*. He can also release a seductive feline quality, as with his Feisal in *Lawrence of Arabia* (1962). This corresponds with the asexuality of his Wormold in *Our Man in Havana* (1959), where he is seemingly propositioned by two men, one of whom is played by Noel Coward, whose other major contribution to British queer cinema is his prison 'queenpin' in *The Italian Job* (1967). It must be noted that Coward was the first choice for Harry Lime in *The Third Man* and for Col. Nicholson.

With Guinness the quintessential chameleon, Price relegated to supporting parts, Redgrave increasingly middle-aged and in gruff authority roles, Coward earning stacks of dollars in Las Vegas and only doing the occasional guest role, screen queerdom on the grand if covert scale was virtually the sole domain of one man, a star who, like Rupert Everett would do three decades later had a second 'star' career, and then a third, as a writer. Unlike Everett, Dirk Bogarde was a genuine star, at least in Britain, for over a decade. 'The Dirk Bogarde Homepage' calls him in one section the Idol of the Odeons, a reference to the cinemas owned by the Rank Organisation who placed Bogarde under contract from the beginning of the 1950s to the mid-1960s. The devotion to building up Bogarde's star status through a series of lightweight adventures and comedies, coupled with appearances at premieres and on radio, was rewarded with financial if not critical success, especially with the long-running Doctor series. In 1955 and again in 1957, Bogarde was voted the top star by British film exhibitors, placing him above the likes of Rock Hudson, John Wayne and Doris Day. However, this exaltation did not last. There were Hollywood offers, refused *Gigi*, and unwisely accepted Franz Liszt's story. And sufficient funds were not forthcoming to make the *Lawrence of Arabia* project a reality. There were intimations of a waning of interest even in Britain. Then came *Victim*, which tackled homosexuality in a fashion at once corny and compelling. I've seen the film at various queer festivals. Certain factions in the audience initially laugh at Bogarde's overwrought barrister, then become more engrossed in his predicament and that of his wife played by Sylvia Syms. They were supposed to appear together again in *The Servant* (1963), but in the event she became pregnant, so he destroyed Wendy Craig's upper-crust boyfriend instead. Much queerer than *Victim*, it apparently lost at least one semi-explicit scene between the master and servant. The dialogue by Harold Pinter, the direction of Joseph Losey and the sustained contempt of Bogarde's trissy Hugo Barrett, made this a telling piece of *grand guignol*, well in the tradition of *Dead of Night*'s ventriloquist tale, though this time with a flesh-and-blood servant as the dummy.

Bogarde forged ahead as an actor of note in films such as *Accident* for Losey, *Darling* (1965) for John Schlesinger, and then in the 1970s in *Death in Venice* under Luchino Visconti's direction and *The Night Porter* for Liliana Cavani. Despite the acclaim, his services were not massively in demand in Hollywood where he was apparently known as 'that fag actor', and he and his longtime partner Tony Forwood relocated to France where he wrote seven successful volumes of autobiography, and several novels. He became Dirk Bogarde, former star, now writer, on the talk show circuit.

Now the game was on in earnest. Being ironic and arching an eyebrow was one thing. Being gay was quite another. Bogarde side-stepped every ambush, whether it was Russell Harty's in the 1970s or Sue Lawley's on BBC Radio's *Desert Island Discs* a decade later, when he returned to London after his companion Tony Forwood's worsening illness and subsequent death. He himself suffered a stroke in 1996. Now he was no longer the teenage girls' idol who became a serious actor. He was now the popular author, still in need of money, approval, acceptance, recognition.

Figure 4.2 'The Idol of the Odeons': Dirk Bogarde in *Once a Jolly Swagman* (1948).

Source: BFI stills, posters and designs.

Unmarried he may be, devoted to his manager he might be, but part of a gay relationship, no, definitely not. It is scary to open up a package that has been signed, sealed and delivered and not to be opened for one hundred years. While he had a breath left in his body he would be a man who was not in a fifty-year relationship with the man he'd lived with for fifty years.

In matters sexual political there was and always would be *Victim*. He was brave. It could have capsized his career. But by standing up for 'Them' he had been rewarded with greater respect and prestige. But he would profess to not being in a homosexual relationship with the man he had lived with for close on half a century. He seemed to want to portray himself as the slightly tarnished hero who had fought the good fight, taken the big step, stood up for them and theirs, never us and ours. And the chatterboxes, the fingerpointers and the militant gays or queers or whatever they called their dreary selves, could leap up and down and their newspapers could make requests in vain for interviews when he rode out on his annual book-selling trail.

At least that is how it appeared. In truth, though, Bogarde had been laying luscious clues throughout his career. Take a look at most of his films, and there is a gay man at the heart of everything he says and does. In his private life he, commendably some might say, remained a bachelor boy until his dying day. At least in the conventional sense. Then there is the television documentary 'Dirk Bogarde By Myself'. This is essentially somebody pretending not to be pretending, and it's fascinating, as all star behaviour is. And the man was a star. Just how much was revealed in Arena's 'The Private Dirk Bogarde' on BBC television in 2001? The truth was out. Thanks to Tony Forwood's home movies, we saw Dirk at play, at home, on holiday. But where were the diaries, the letters, the unguarded moments? Up in smoke these had gone. On a bonfire lit by Dirk himself. And very likely Michael Redgrave had his bonfire, too. And possibly even Dennis Price. During a large part of their lives, homosexuality was a criminal offence, indictable and punishable. It could mean disgrace, ruin, imprisonment. Maybe in the case of one or more of them, their form of sexual enjoyment may still have been taboo.

Bogarde exemplifies the gay fine art of being the keeper of his own flame. He managed to preserve the niceties of the Idol of the Odeons while being one of the screen's most finessed decadents. As his screen father John Gielgud confides to the audience in *Providence* (1977): 'When in doubt, attempt a little style – surprise them, keep them off balance. Establish your unpredictability.' There is so much still to unravel about this man who is described by the Dirk Bogarde Homepage as 'Decadent, handsome, brooding, alluring, sadistic, charming, vulnerable, explosive, intelligent, beautiful, subtle, distinctive'. He was all these things the one and only time I saw him in 1984 at a special screening of *The Killing Fields*. David Puttnam, who produced the film, was at that time trying to woo Dirk to play the role of the older priest in *The Mission*. Bogarde wasn't interested. He would not appear in any film where his name was not above the title. However, he did come

to see Puttnam's new film about Cambodia. I remember coming out of the audi-
torium after nearly everybody else had poured out. I saw, on the opposite side, a
still handsome man prepare to make his exit down a small flight of steps. He paused,
looked around at the small group of people leaving the cinema, then descended,
Zorro-like down the steps. It was one of the most thrilling feats of theatricality I'd
ever seen. Suddenly, a man in late middle age was a handsome screen idol again.
Except he was far more handsome at that moment than I had ever found him on
the screen. And his composure, his intense sexuality were those of someone thirty
years younger. This wasn't Norma Desmond or Norman Maine. It was a small
chamber performance for the benefit of a few stragglers like myself. Thinking back
on that moment now, I do believe what he wrote in his book *A Perfect Relationship*:
'I simply hated being a Film Star. For about 10 years, I was never able to be free
. . . I had my flies ripped so often that eventually, in public, I had to have a side
zip . . . can you imagine anything more humiliating than that? I have an absolute
horror of being "looked at". An eye phobia or something. So I'm quite in the wrong
profession, obviously.'

That same year, I was in Glasgow working on a project to promote the British
film industry, and persuade the British public to return to cinemagoing, a habit they
had rejected in their millions from more or less the same time that Dirk Bogarde
was Britain's top male star. We had brought some actors to Glasgow for that grisly
exercise known as a 'personal appearance'. One of those subjected to the stares and
finger pointing of the assembled crowds was Rupert Everett who was publicising
his new film, *Dance with a Stranger*. That Rupert 'simply hated being a film star' was
obvious from his massive sulk. He didn't carry this beyond the hotel room, and
was stallion charm himself during his brief speech and audience interaction. It was
obvious, of course, that he was a man of extraordinary sensuality, and a shyness
which came across as arrogance and ill grace. At least that was what my assistant
told me later. She had been told to figuratively hold his hand during what for him
was an ordeal every bit as great as Dirk Bogarde found in his much more intense
brushes with fandom. But in Rupert's case he told my young assistant that he hated
having to live a sexual lie, promoted as he was as Britain's latest male heterosexual
sex symbol.

With his sculpted face and body, coupled with his air of knowing provocation, it
was obvious that Rupert Everett could be every bit the star Bogarde was. He could
certainly play many of Dirk Bogarde's roles. Barrett in *The Servant*, for example:
'Get out of the way. I'll show you what I am. I'm a gentleman's gentleman, and
you're no bloody gentleman.' The vicious first lieutenant in *HMS Defiant*: 'Take
your hands off me, you mutinous filth!' And the mother-fixated archvillain Gabriel
in *Modesty Blaise*: 'One of these days I shall have to tell mama who I am.' And he'd
be a knockout as the Mexican bandit in the dark glasses and tight leather trousers
in which, at least in still photos, Dirk displayed his cock, astride a white horse. He
could also do Michael Redgrave's *Dead of Night* turn, and something along the lines

of Dennis Price's Louis Mazzini. Certainly he'd be an interesting *Bad Lord Byron*. There was just one problem. There was at that moment in time, no British film industry to nurture a new Dirk Bogarde, nor a mass audience to go and see his films.

Like Dirk Bogarde, Rupert Everett was – and is – a glamour boy. He has the thrust and recoil that hits the spot and stirs the loins. His decision to come out as gay – initially bisexual – in the late 1980s, means that there need be no fold-up façade marriage or customised bachelorhood for him. No secondhand imitation of life. Gone were the days when the stars had to check every impulse. Ian McKellen, who could have been the Dirk Bogarde of his day, came across as sexy as chillblains on the screen. It was only, heavily camouflaged as Gandalf the Wizard, that he broke through and was brought finally to the altar of star, albeit aged and sexless.

Maybe McKellen will be the exception that proves the rule – a star of mature years who gets to have the boy/girl. Meanwhile Everett, flagrantly disobeying the twentieth-century code, marches on through his forties playing heterosexual and homosexual lovers, and being paid quite handsomely for it. And along with the *acting as* Rupert Everett is the *being* Rupert Everett on talk shows and in magazine articles and modelling spreads. His every appearance challenges the humdrumness of the Either/Or: 'It's time for people to be honest about what they do.'

But is he a real star? It is some years since he announced he was writing a 'gay James Bond movie' in which he would star. And the screen adaptation of his novel *Hello Darling, Are You Working?* seems stalled indefinitely. No sign either of the project with Julia Roberts. She and Rupert were going to play a movie star couple in a lavender marriage. Instead he has played decadent creatures and looked beautiful doing it. His contribution to queer cinema has been less through playing gay roles, but playing heterosexual roles as an openly gay man, something Dirk Bogarde could not do for a long time, and then when he could, decided not to.

This has led to some interesting questions for an audience to consider. He was Wilde's Lord Goring in *An Ideal Husband* in 1999. Wrote the *Sydney Morning Herald*'s critic Paul Byrnes: 'Wilde's obscured gay puppet and dandy is made straight, but only in the writing. Everett's performance remains mischievously bent, bringing to the role ambiguity which is presumably what the director, Oliver Parker, wanted. The ironies here are a tangle. Wilde wrote a character who was secretly gay, Parker makes him straight but hires an actor to play him gay' (21.10.99).

Maybe this was also partly behind the decision to cast Ian McKellen, who is not only openly gay but, unlike Rupert Everett, a gay political activist, in the pivotal role of Gandalf, messenger from the immortals. McKellen had been seeking screen stardom for years and found it playing a character who is a whole galaxy in himself. Like real stars his light is boundless, his existence beyond right or wrong. He is there. He is.

In the 1986 biography *Ian McKellen* by Joy Leslie Gibson, much is made of McKellen's star appeal, and whether he has true star potential. A TV special on the actor shown on ITV's *The South Bank Show* the previous year found that McKellen would like to be Robert Redford. But at that time the chances of Ian McKellen joining the ranks of instantly recognisable faces and voices seemed highly unlikely. As Joy Leslie Gibson wrote,

> Stars form part of our fantasy life, we like them to be more glamorous, more fantastic, almost untouchable, so that we can dream about touching them. We can even dream about making love to them. Noel Coward said that when he appeared on stage he had to make every member of the audience, men and women, want to go to bed with him.

Certainly, as a result of his participation in both *Lord of the Rings* and *X Men*, I would suspect that a great number of people, mainly young children, do go to bed with Ian McKellen, at least as some kind of wise/dangerous iconic presence. Maybe now that Rupert Everett has moved into the children's film area (*Inspector Gadget*, *Shrek 2*) he will also be an under-the-pillows companion to many a child around the world.

Bibliography

Bogarde, D. (1988) *Dirk Bogarde: The Complete Autobiography*. London: Methuen.

The Dirk Bogarde Homepage. *Elegance and Eloquence. The Idol of the Odeons*. http.// members.aol.com/Alpheratz9/dirkbogarde.html (listed since 1998).

Bourne, S. (1996) *Brief Encounters. Lesbians and Gays in British Cinema, 1930–1971*. London: Cassell (appendix: The 'Victim' Letters, pp. 238–54).

Everett, R. (1995) *Hello Darling, Are You Working?*, London: Arrow Books.

Gibson, J.L. (1986) *Ian McKellen*, London: Weidenfeld & Nicolson.

Hawthorne, N. (2003) *Straight Face*, London: Hodder & Stoughton.

Katz, E. (ed.) (2001) *The Film Encyclopaedia. 4th edition*, New York: HarperResource.

McFarlane, B. (ed.) (1992) *Sixty Voices. Celebrities Recall the Golden Age of British Cinema*, London: BFI Publishing (Dirk Bogarde interview pp. 23–30).

Sir Ian McKellen Official Homepage, http.//www.mckellen.com (listed since 1997).

Murray, R. (1996) *Images in the Dark: An Encyclopaedia of Gay and Lesbian Films and Videos*, New York: Plume.

Redgrave, C. (1996), *Michael Redgrave: My Father*, London: Trafalgar Square Press.

Redgrave, M. (1983) *In My Mind's Eye*, London: Hodder & Stoughton.

5 Sad and angry

Queers in 1960s British cinema

Robin Griffiths

the way it questioned sexuality, male sexuality in particular – I think people found all of that very uncomfortable, very disturbing. We can look at it now and say, what was all the fuss about? But in 1969 people weren't as steeped in these sort of subjects through the movies as they are now. Now it all seems commonplace. But people said it was *dirty* – not pornographic, but *dirty*.[1]

The nature of the game

In the notes that append his fairly definitive analysis of one of British cinema's most complex and under-rated 'classics' – Nicolas Roeg and Donald Cammell's surreal meditation on the 'nature' of identity: *Performance* (1970) – Colin MacCabe (1998) casually proposes that 'It cannot be too long before somebody recognises *Performance* as the first "queer" film'.[2] And though MacCabe neglects to elaborate further on such a provocative assertion, it's not very difficult to see his reasoning, nor query why this is only an afterthought to his already characteristically *queer* textual negotiations (whether intentionally so or not):

> [T]he film delivered an anatomy of masculinity which promised a genuine liberation from the cage of gender.
>
> (1998: 8)

> There is a simple symbolic journey at the heart of *Performance* [. . .] from the narcissistic repressed homosexuality of the opening sequence to the open liberated sexuality of the final minutes of the film.
>
> (1998: 74)

Anticipating queer theory 'guru' Judith Butler's groundbreaking work by over two decades,[3] *Performance* is seemingly – on a number of intricate levels – one of the queerest films to emerge in post-war British Cinema. It's impossible in any analysis of the film to ignore the fact that its underlying premise is to limn social and moral binarisms and the constructed, performative 'nature' of gender and sexuality from within a decadent, 'hermetically sealed alternative social and psychic space' (MacCabe, 1998: 32); a space detached from an extra-textual outside world that was also, ironically, beginning to exhibit a similar fascination with more fluid and transgressive re-configurations of identity.[4] The film is in many ways the proto-typical Butlerian text, wherein the boundaries of prescriptive gender and sexual identity are gradually 'erased' as the film unravels: each character methodically dissolves into one another irrespective of their assigned gender, class or narrative function, to reinforce, as Adrian Danks proposes, 'its ideas of dissolution, archetype and the chimerical nature of identity'.[5]

Filmed in the summer of 1968 – a time of great political and social upheaval in the UK, Europe and beyond, and only a year after homosexuality was finally decriminalised between consenting adults over the age of 21 – *Performance* remained in limbo for a couple of years due to the nervousness of Warner Bros executives, who were all too aware of the controversial nature of their 'dirty movie'.[6] And though most initial (and rather limited) critical responses to the film tended to

Figure 5.1 'Polymorphously perverse'? Lucy (Michéle Breton), Pherber (Anita Pallenberg) and Turner (Mick Jagger) engage in a spot of gender-bending in *Performance* (1970).

Source: BFI stills, posters and designs (Goodtimes/Warner Bros).

assess its importance in heralding a 'new wave' in the British gangster film, it was, more significantly, the first to truly address a growing social impetus to question conventional 'hetero-normative' notions of gender and sexuality that had captured the cultural imagination – both positively and negatively – of late 1960s Britain: 'The 60s were, in general, the decade in which representation came under attack' (MacCabe, 1998: 53).

As a rather queer re-working of Billy Wilder's *Sunset Boulevard* (if it's possible to be any 'queerer' than the original!), the film charts the final days in the life of a narcissistic, violent, East End thug – Chas Devlin (James Fox) – who, whilst on the run from his criminal past, seeks refuge in the isolated bohemian abode of a reclusive former rockstar – Turner (Mick Jagger) – a man whose final, very extreme, 'close up' (far removed from Gloria Swanson's) involves us following the trajectory of a bullet through his head.

The apparent queerness of *Performance*, however, is evident from the start. In the opening sequence in which we first encounter Devlin – one of the film's two central 'performers' – it is clear that he's hardly the 'straight' man we would expect of the gangster genre's typical anti-hero. For despite being caught in the final throes of (narratively obligatory) heterosexual lovemaking (a scene described by MacCabe as 'a soulless display of sexual pyrotechnics' [74–5]), 'confirmed bachelor' Devlin exhibits very little actual erotic interest in the marginalised female member of this rather awkwardly staged coupling (a woman called Dana [Ann Sidney]). But rather through a fairly abstract mise-en-scène, he is 'constructed' via an ambivalent process of fetishised hyper-masculinity (that emphasises his potent virility and physique) and conversely coded effeminisation (through his narcissistic fascination with his own erotic image in the mirror, and obsession with order, style and appearance). He is literally making love to himself (his own face trans-sexually superimposed upon Dana's as she fellates him), and is all too eager to expel her presence from his 'swishy' ultra-modern London 'bachelor-pad' post coitus.[7]

This ambiguity in the way that Chas Devlin is coded is even further 'queered' as the film develops, when it is not only revealed that his 'role' is to provide the 'muscle' for openly gay East End crime boss Harry Flowers (Johnny Shannon), a man whose 'entire language is made up of a series of metaphors [. . .] with a constant undertone of perverted, specifically homosexual, sex' (ibid.: 28), but that he also has a mysterious 'double personal' relationship with rival bad boy Joey Maddox (Antony Valentine). Ironically, it is the break-up of his repressed relationship with Maddox, which violently climaxes in a pseudo gay rape 'gangbang' and murder in which Devlin is held down, stripped and forced to admit that he is a 'poof' before shooting Maddox dead (in a fit of homosexual panic perhaps), that leads him to seek sanctuary in the purportedly queerer world of Jagger's 'degenerate' Turner:

> Jagger posited an altogether more flagrant challenge to the values of the day. His unapologetic narcissism – the pouting, voluptuous lips, the animal grace

of his gestures – lay somewhere beyond received ideas of sexuality, at a point
which was neither masculine nor feminine. Quite simply, he *was* sex.

(Brown, 1999: 93)[8]

In stark contrast to the violent, homoerotic landscape of the East End ganglands
(that regulate Chas' identity through the threat of exposure of his repressed homosexuality and its associated feminised weakness), the hallucinogenic, 'arty' interiors
of Turner's secluded Powis Square 'hippy' pad seemingly enable a space for a much
more cerebral, psycho-sexual deconstruction of Devlin's 'performance': especially
in terms of his gender and sexual identity.

However, whilst it would be logical to presume that the queerness of the film
could be seen to be mobilised around Jagger/Turner's androgynous iconicity and
its comparative dissection of Fox/Devlin's hetero-masculine identity, it is a process
that, in the end, merely re-inscribes the more 'trendy' and illusory notion of 'new
man' heterosexuality that was so central to the 1960s 'hippie' milieu. For all his
pouting, pseudo-effeminate posturing and playful bisexual flirtatiousness, Turner
remains decidedly 'straight' in terms of the actual spectacle of his sexuality that
the film presents. And despite his gender-bending ménage à trois with the volup-
tuously feminine Pherber (Anita Pallenberg) and androgynously 'boyish' Lucy
(Michéle Breton), his voyeuristic obsession with Devlin's unpredictably volatile and
butch persona remains safely unrequited, and never really transgresses any sexual
boundary beyond the heteronormative. In fact, the effects of Devlin's subsequent
half-hearted attempt at trans-gender experimentation, throughout which he
relentlessly maintains that he's 'normal', actually result in the re-affirmation of his
heterosexuality since it re-aligns (and normalises) his sexual attraction towards
the opposite sex (when he finally makes love to Lucy) – which is clearly antithetical
to the queerly narcissistic self-obsession we witnessed at the film's beginning. His
new curiosity towards exploring his feminine side – and femininity/the female
body more generally – thus, it is arguable, 'cures' him of his queerness, rather than
enabling any tangible space for a potentially erotic development in his 'relationship'
with Turner. A fact which McCabe also seemingly echoes:

> It is this acceptance of the trauma of difference; the recognition of the body's
> interchangeability that enables Chas both to embrace Turner and to make love
> to the 'boyish' Lucy [Michele Breton]. This passage of sexual initiation is clearly
> meant to transform Chas completely . . . [t]he repressed homosexuality which
> underpins the hatred of all difference of gender and race is opened out on to a
> genuine curiosity about the other: both carnal and spiritual.
>
> (1998: 75)

The 'real' queerness of the film is, therefore, more readily traceable in the
'straight' exterior world from which Devlin is so desperate to escape. The terrain

of the camply named Flowers gang, and the ambiguously coded men that populate both the 1960s criminal underworld and the corrupt London upper class. It is this world that conversely queers Jagger's pseudo-feminised Turner, whose fascination with its deviant macho 'performances' later climaxes with the iconic 'Memo from Turner' musical interlude, in which a seductive, gyrating Jagger hypnotically coerces Flowers' men to strip naked for him in hallucinatory, Dionysiac frenzy, 'tauntingly exposing the latent homosexuality within the gangster's strutting machismo' (Brown, 1999: 123). And it is with them that a seemingly immortal Turner transcendentally finds sanctuary at the film's overtly abstract climax, rather than remaining in the more feminine, heterocentrically inclined interiors of Powis Square. As Andrew Spicer describes:

> In the final scenes the identities of Chas and Turner have become inter-changeable. Both have entered a surreal, unrestrained, Nietzschean space where 'all is permitted'. The film's baroque, allusive style allows this fantasy to play itself out in an ambiguous allegory.
>
> (Spicer, 2001: 143)

It is within those marginalised homosocial sub-cultures of the late 1960s, therefore, with their deviant criminals, anti-establishment rebels and damaged men, all at odds with both accepted social ideology and hetero-masculine norm, that the film's most subversive potential can really be located. *Performance* is, as McCabe rightly surmises, a 'queer' film, but whether or not it was 'the first 'queer' film' to emerge in British cinema is open to debate, as this very anthology attests. But as a film 'on the edge' of polymorphous perversity, however, *Performance* was, more importantly, the apotheosis of a whole decade of potentially queer flirtation in British cinema that had been slowly simmering away since the 1950s.

Films 'on the edge'

The ideological and socio-cultural shift that occurred from the volatile years of the late 1950s to the late 1960s enabled the most progressive and 'exciting period for British cinema' (Street, 1997: 81) in terms of its exploration of gender and sexuality. In fact, the critical and commercial success – both at home and abroad – of the landmark films of the 'New Wave' and 'Swinging London' cycles marked a quite distinctive break with more established cinematic themes and traditions, and, significantly for this study, introduced a renewed and reflexive period of 'sociological enquiry'.[9] In stark contrast to the more repressed, literary and war-obsessed narratives of the 1940s and 1950s, an aggressive and socially conscious new British cinema emerged that sought to reflect the disillusionment of an angry and alienated post-war working-class youth culture.

And yet despite this initial success, fuelled in part by media concern over the 'immoral' liberated hedonism associated with the 'swinging sixties', critics such as John Hill (1986) have argued that the New Wave films of the period rarely projected the liberally 'progressive' image of society that is usually associated with them. But rather they contained, on reflection, a more traditionalist and socially conservative bias:

> the films, and the views of the world which they promoted, may well have obscured as much as they enlightened, and obstructed as much as they initiated the potential for social change and reconstruction.
>
> (Hill, 1986: 3)

In narrative (and ideological) terms, the burning desire to initiate 'social change and reconstruction' that was at the heart of these apparently radical contemporary dramas usually came at a devastating price, which commonly involved the loss of any 'stable' social (and gender) identity for all concerned. And whereas Peter Hutchings proposes that the characteristic films of this 'angry' New Wave may be perceived, at face value, to embody 'Zeitgeist-like expressions of change in the social fabric' (Hutchings, 1997: 147), they were also quite problematic in that they were consistently angled from exclusively white, heterosexual and misogynist perspectives: 'which often centre on an alienated working-class male attempting to find a role for himself in a turbulent, materialistic world'. A performative 'role' which involves a transgression that, in the end, brings nothing but misery, an even greater sense of alienation, and a final resigned submission to social conformity.

For all its apparent liberalism then, many recent critics of British New Wave cinema have viewed the 'movement' as decidedly conservative in terms of its actual gender and sexual politics; despite all its sexually transgressive promise, the films produced tended to adhere to conventionally heterosexist narrative resolutions which were, as Samantha Lay puts it:

> remarkably consistent with the ideological values and assumptions of the period . . . sexual experimentation is ultimately empty and meaningless, and heterosexuality – and the gender divides that usually come with the whole package – is the norm, the ideal: there are no viable alternatives offered.
>
> (Lay, 2002: 66)

However, critical readings such as these, that accentuate the New Wave's ambivalence in its anti-establishment limning of 'unconventional lifestyles' and taboo themes (namely promiscuity, abortion and inter-racial sex), tend to ignore the potential 'queerness' of its underpinnings. The implications of the sexuality of the three leading filmmakers involved in this innovative cinematic trend have generally been overlooked in studies of the period, when it reveals much about the underlying critical and social stance of their work, and the unspoken tensions and desires that permeate it.[10]

Though by no means working under the banner of a specifically gay or queer cinema, New Wave auteurs Tony Richardson, Lindsay Anderson and John Schlesinger were revolutionary in re-defining the boundaries for thematic representation and exploration in British film, and made a very real attempt at releasing it from the 'straight-jacket' of decades of middle-class conservatism. Collectively, their films exhibit liminal conflicts between transgressive desire and social conformity that are not easily resolved in 'heteronormative' narrative or ideological terms; and they not only established a vital cultural forum for debate concerning issues of social identity and marginality, but laid the explorative groundwork for the more visible representation of queer sexuality on the British screen that has emerged since:

> The principal mood of the 'New Wave' was one of discontent and dissatisfaction, a rejection of things as they were, a powerful sense that Britain was hopelessly mired in a hierarchical Victorian world of outdated values, disciplines and restrictions.
>
> (Richards, 1997: 148)[11]

Whereas most retrospective queer critical attention to date has understandably centred upon the historical impact of Basil Dearden's 'social problem' film *Victim* (1961), as a landmark in the representation of homosexuality on the British screen,[12] it was, more appropriately, part of a wider socio-reflexive shift that owes as much to the preceding works of director Tony Richardson; and a growing curiosity in British cinema to explore, albeit cautiously, the emerging 'problem' of homosexuality as informed by debates surrounding the Wolfenden Report of 1957.[13] *Victim* was, as Andy Medhurst argues (1996: 127–8), 'made primarily for extra-textual reasons, consciously to effect social change, it is in many ways propaganda', and is therefore antithetical to the New Wave texts, whose implicit 'queerness', I propose, is more a 'reading-against-the-grain' process of 'teas[ing] out strands of meaning other than those signalled by textual mechanisms . . . to locate contradictory elements of narrative and/or *mise-en-scéne*' (ibid.).

Though his bisexuality wasn't publicly revealed until his death of an AIDS-related illness in 1991,[14] Richardson was a driving force in re-configuring 'cultural positions of resistance in regard to representations of class, gender and national identity' (Hutchings, 1997: 149), and just as importantly, sexuality. The success of his debut film adaptation of John Osborne's seminal theatrical assault on the English establishment, *Look Back in Anger* (1958), introduced an increased openness towards limning the margins of 'alienated' British social identities. But whilst most critics have been rather dismissive of both the play and film as exclusive and overly indulgent valorisations of 'masculinity-in-crisis' (with its concomitant misogyny and homophobia), the fact that Osborne was also bisexual significantly skews any reading of both the intimate 'homosocial' playfulness of Jimmy Porter's relationship with live-in lodger Cliff in the film/play, and the internalised anger, misogyny and fear of effeminacy that underlies his crisis of identity.[15] It is quite significant that the only time that Richard Burton's Porter exhibits any real affection or heartbreak in the film is when 'best friend' Cliff, frustrated with the fact that Porter 'wants something from [girlfriend Helena] that she is incapable of giving', decides to leave him to start a new life; as an emotional Porter makes it very clear, Cliff is 'worth half a dozen' of the women he's involved with.

Burton's Porter was the prototypical 'Angry Young Man', a dominant emblem of the films of the period from Richardson's later delinquent teen allegory *The Loneliness of the Long Distance Runner* (1962), to Schlesinger's loveless *A Kind of Loving* (1962) and Anderson's unsportingly homoerotic *This Sporting Life* (1963). Their angst-ridden rebellion against, and rejection of, the social systems and values within which they find themselves trapped symbolically reflected both the experiences of their respective directors, and the general dilemma of being queer in British society at the time.

In the New Wave cycle, the key institutions of 'heteronormativity' (i.e. marriage and family) are hardly the attractive or idealised prospect that one would come to expect from such seemingly 'straight' social narratives. And in comparative terms, there is a marked difference between the representation of heterosexual relationships in those New Wave films by less queerly identifiable filmmakers of the movement, such as Jack Clayton's *Room at the Top* (1959) or Karel Reisz's *Saturday Night and Sunday Morning* (1960), which despite conforming to the thematic trend of the 'wave' in their depiction of masculine social alienation and sexual promiscuity, their central female characters are far from the cold, nagging hags that tended to populate the other films. Rachel Roberts' sexually vivacious and alluring Brenda in *Saturday Night*, for example, is far removed from the frigid, emasculating Mrs Hammond that she later portrayed in Lindsay Anderson's *This Sporting Life*.

Similarly, in Schlesinger's *A Kind of Loving*, an innocent date between young draughtsman Vic Brown (Alan Bates) and virginal typist Ingrid Rothwell (June Ritchie) soon escalates into the relationship from hell as 'Jack-the-lad' Vic is trapped into a loveless marriage with a frigid wife and her battleaxe of a mother (Thora Hird). Interestingly, their first date involves a trip to the local cinema to see Dearden's *Victim*, not exactly the type of film one would expect the randy northern lad to take 'his bird' to on a steamy first date. However, this by no means implies that their queer sexuality necessarily contributed to the misogyny inherent in these narratives per se, but rather that the strategically marginalised asexuality of the women in these films thus enabled the foregrounding of their more homosocial/erotic dimensions, and a necessary disruptive space for the textual activation of queer pleasures.

In the same year that Dearden's *Victim* was unleashed upon an unsuspecting British public, the subject of homosexuality also emerged more ambiguously in Richardson's adaptation of another pivotal social realist play, Shelagh Delaney's *A Taste of Honey* (1961). This film was a unique departure from the male-centred films of the movement – in that it was more a case study of the stormy relationship between a pregnant working-class teenager and her irresponsibly self-centred mother – but more crucially, it also featured one of the first fairly sympathetic portrayals of a working-class homosexual in British film: an effeminate outcast named Geoffrey (Murray Melvin).[16] And whereas the fate of Dirk Bogarde's repentant, middle-class and 'straight-acting' Melville Farr in *Victim* envisaged some optimism for the future of a more acceptable, 'un-closeted' gay presence in British post-war society, *A Taste of Honey*'s Geoffrey is left with a much more uncertain fate. Confined to the cinematic gay stereotype that Richard Dyer iconically defined as the 'sad young man',[17] Geoffrey's emergent and groundbreaking cinematic visibility is conversely quite regulated in terms of the unthreatening asexuality that the film actually presents.

Beginning the film as a stereotypically homeless loner, art student Geoffrey finds a very 'boyish' soul mate in the form of pregnant teenager Jo (Rita Tushingham), who has also been abandoned by both her uncaring mother Helen (Dora Bryan)

Figure 5.2 A Taste of Honey's unthreatening 'sad young man', Geoffrey (Murray Melvin).

Source: National Film Archive, courtesy of Stephen Bourne (Woodfall/BFI).

and black lover Jimmy (Paul Danquah). And in a rather 'queer' reversal, faux butch Jo is immediately attracted to femme 'big sister' Geoffrey's fashionable unconventionality: 'I want to know what you do. I want to know why you do it?' But despite his refusal to comply with her need for a 'sensational confession', thus ensuring that 'the love that dare not speak its name' remains unspoken, these two social outcasts decide to performatively 'play house' together.

Gentle and passive Geoffrey is, of course, the direct antithesis of the genre's hyper-masculine 'Angry Young Man'; but, more importantly, his coding is also indicative of the general ambivalence surrounding socio-cultural perceptions of 'the homosexual' that were emerging in the lead up to the partial de-criminalisation of homosexuality in 1967. Though a common performative shorthand for homosexuality, the 'stigma' of effeminacy was, however, very suspiciously viewed by more assimilationist factions of the fledgling gay movement of the time as a stereotype that should remain confined to the closet; preferring instead to assert that homosexuals were just as 'normal' and masculine as heterosexuals (such as Bogarde in *Victim*), and not just the 'screaming queens' that they had for so long been portrayed as. For as Andy Medhurst has argued:

> A major feature of the liberal tolerance of homosexuality centred around Wolfenden is its hostility to camp, which, given camp's inherent snubbing of codes of dignity and restraint, is hardly surprising. What is perhaps odd, and not a little unnerving, is the eagerness with which those few homosexuals who found a public voice as part of those debates sought to join the condemnation of their more flamboyant comrades.
>
> (1996: 129)

The fetishised machismo and homoeroticism that was so central to the films of this purportedly 'queer' New Wave, therefore, had no place for any lavender taint of homosexuality that may reveal the subversive pleasures that they were synonymously flirting with. Geoffrey's plight can be read then as more a product of his effeminacy than his homosexuality. By visibly 'performing' the stereotypical traits of heteronormative perceptions of the child-like homosexual invert, he is consequently excluded from the erotically mobilised 'adult' homosocial spaces of his seemingly 'straight-acting' and closeted counterparts.[18] The feminine working-class interiors of *A Taste of Honey* do allow a temporary space for exploring a maternal, effeminised homosexuality, but in the end this liminal identity is no match for the 'authentic' matriarch Helen, who returns to reclaim her place from such a 'pretender'. Ultimately, however, it is Geoffrey's choice to leave and re-unite mother and daughter, and despite finding himself alone again by the end of the film, he exhibits an agency and independence in the face of social rejection that was unique in terms of the representations that had preceded him – which usually ended in suicide, murder or incarceration.

The rejection of effeminacy (and women) that seemingly dominated the New Wave, and its quite relentless fetishisation of its virulently sexual (yet unobtainable) male protagonists, says as much about these filmmakers' own complex relationship to their sexuality as it does the new social values of Britain in the 1960s. And the queerly masochistic and potentially violent undercurrent that permeates many of the New Wave narratives probably reached its most symbolic climax in Lindsay Anderson's first feature-length film, *This Sporting Life* (1963). A former leading figure in the short-lived 'Free Cinema' movement of the late 1950s, Anderson's earlier works served as a radical 'call to arms' against what he perceived to be an oppressive mainstream British film industry. But, ironically, *This Sporting Life* also signalled the end of the radical 'kitchen sink' poetic realism that had characterised much of the period. Anderson's passion for a distinctively independent social realist cinema that focused on the alienated and marginalized in society was, however, very much imbued with his own repressed homosexuality – which was only able to find some sublimating outlet in the queer sub-texts of his films (though quite often manifest in a rather disturbing and self-destructive manner).

Set in the hyper-masculine world of a northern Rugby League club – complete with requisite male nude horseplay – all is not necessarily as 'straight'-forward as it first appears. As Anderson himself stated shortly before the film's release:

> *This Sporting Life* is not a film about sport. Nor is it to be categorised as a 'North Country working class story'. . . . It is a film about a man. A man of extra-ordinary power and aggressiveness, both temperamental and physical, but at the same time with a great innate sensitiveness and a need for love of which he is hardly aware.[19]

And given Anderson's well-documented proclivity for masochistically 'falling-in-unrequited-love' with the heterosexual leading men of his films,[20] Richard Harris' brooding Frank Machin is quite clearly the focus for a whole host of queer gazes in the film, both on-screen and off.

Masquerading as a doomed heterosexual love affair between an up-and-coming rugby star and his widowed landlady, *This Sporting Life* is more an allegorical exploration of the fetishised commodification of working-class masculinity by a rather 'queer' middle class – symbolised here by the lascivious machinations of the Rugby Club committee – the sinister embodiment of which is subtly effeminate club Chairman, Gerald Weaver (Alan Badel). A man renowned for 'keep[ing] all his protégés to himself', Weaver is introduced to Machin through his 'talent scout', 'Dad' Johnson (William Hartnell), a 'sad old man' with an almost obsessive fixation for the young player. As Machin's landlady (and token heterosexual love interest) Mrs Hammond (Rachel Roberts) ominously forewarns him, Johnson 'looks at [him] like a girl', and, even more suspiciously, has 'soft hands'! It is the marginalised female perspective that is hence positioned to insinuate the covert queerness of

Figure 5.3 Frank Machin (Richard Harris) is paid for his 'services' after joining 'the Club'
        in *This Sporting Life* (1963).

Source: Rank Film Distributors (Independent Artists).

Weaver and the Club. Insinuations that are given possible legitimacy in the
unresolved mystery surrounding the death of Mrs Hammond's husband, a former
employee of Weaver, who, it is said, 'didn't feel as if he belonged'. And it is later
revealed, in a rather tragically queer turn of events, had committed suicide: unable
to live with his guilt perhaps, or find any fulfilment in the 'frigid' sham of a
relationship with his wife?

The queer temptation of Frank Machin, however, begins when, after 'joining the
Club', Weaver suggestively grasps his knee and proclaims that he is now its (and
his) 'property'. For Machin, the attainment of success and material affluence
comes to represent a transgressive loss of a 'natural' and stable working-class
hetero-masculine identity, and consequently signals his descent into hedonistic
self-destruction. His newly feminised interest in designer clothes and the 'men
only' decadent homosocial spaces of 'the Club', are a distinct departure from the
'shabby back-to-backs and industrial squalor' that Mrs Hammond and 'heteronormative' domesticity represents; spaces that are 'still ruled by values and class
relations which are essentially Victorian' (Murphy, 1992: 27). And, ironically, it is
the literal loss of these feminised good looks in a violent assault during a rugby game
(in which he loses his front teeth) that symbolises the beginning of the end. As
a stereotypically superficial queer, Weaver inevitably loses his unreciprocated
interest in Machin, whom he later cattily reveals is hardly the skilled 'performer'
he narcissistically believes himself to be. And in a final bitter twist, Machin's world

is destroyed as he pays the price for transgressing the prescriptive boundaries of both his social status and gender identity. *This Sporting Life* is thus a distinctly cautionary tale that forewarns of the dangers of transgressing one's prescribed socio-performative role in society, since as John Hill argues,

> [the film reveals] an anxiety about the demise of the 'traditional' working class, associated with work, community and an attachment to place, in the face of consumerism, mass culture and suburbanisation. In so far as these changes are also associated with a certain 'feminisation' of the working class, so these films also extend a degree of sympathy towards the virile, working-class male who seeks to resist the pressures towards embourgeoisement and social conformity (including domesticity).
>
> (2000: 250–1)

Ironically, however, the queerness that haunts this threat of 'embourgeoisement' also symbolises Lindsay Anderson's rather contradictory double status as both a leading champion of the working-class male, and as an active member of the very bourgeoisie that seeks to erotically commodify and consume him.

Walking on the wild side

The most uncompromising of the three filmmakers in terms of depicting a queer sexuality, however, is unquestionably John Schlesinger.[21] Though more widely acclaimed by gay critics for his landmark film *Sunday, Bloody Sunday* (1971) – with its first passionate on-screen gay kiss – Schlesinger's earlier New Wave works, such as *A Kind of Loving* (1962) and *Billy Liar* (1963), followed the same socio-critical themes set up by Richardson and Anderson. Both films feature alienated young men either trapped in loveless heterosexual relationships, or desperate to escape – or at least re-negotiate – the erotic mundanity of social 'normality'. But it wasn't until his 1965 film *Darling* that Schlesinger really began to explore more fully the new sexual dynamics of 1960s Britain.

In a departure from the overtly masculine northern working-class terrain of the New Wave, *Darling* heralded a new shift of focus in 1960s British cinema to the seemingly more fluid, feminine sexual realms of 'Swinging London'. And contrary to the New Wave films, in which queerness can be seen to be mobilised around an eroticised Northern working-class homosociality – framed through an infatuated middle-class gaze – the queerness of the 1960s Swinging London cycle can at first be seen to be more associated with the new sexual utopia of a mythically 'permissive' London, 'a city that comes to represent a site of pleasure and autonomy'. As Moya Luckett argues:

> [t]he narratives of these films heralded a new feminine perspective marked by the importance of sexual expression to self-identity . . . [but they] do not

simply celebrate freedom, superficiality, popular culture and affluence, but instead fuse optimism with a keen and often self-reflexive social criticism.

(2000: 233)

The burning desire to escape the prescriptive restrictions of a normative small town social identity that underpinned the New Wave is thus here seemingly enabled by the 'polymorphously perverse' metonymic context of the city: 'the capital is associated with mobility and cultural diversity in contrast to the landscape of the New Wave, which testifies to (masculine) stasis and confinement' (234).

In Schlesinger's *Darling*, ambitious model Diana Scott (Julie Christie) eagerly arrives in this 'new' London in search of the liberation that such a culturally bohemian metropolis supposedly promises. And though the capital does enable Scott a modicum of sexual agency in terms of her shifting ménage à trois relationship with stuffy BBC reporter Robert and middle-class hedonist Miles (ironically played by closeted gay actors Dirk Bogarde and Laurence Harvey), the liminal queerness of the film can be seen to be associated more affectively with a metonymic fascination towards a far more promisingly exotic and 'perverse' perception of post-war Western Europe. The 1960s cultural 'myth of Europe' was, as Jack Stevenson puts it:

> [a] myth of far away lands where a natural, open sexuality was part of everyday life [;] where innocent, free-minded teens explored sex with impish impetuosity . . . lived lives full of temptation, passion, pleasure and pain . . . engaged in sex and adventure and found themselves lured to opulent, jet-setting poolside parties in places like Rome or Paris. Exotic accents all.
>
> (2000: 17–18)

In comparison, a mythically 'Swinging' London does permit some sexual agency for women (and homosexuals) in *Darling*, but agency that is, in the end, curtailed and 'ultimately erased by [heterosexual] men, who reassert their authority over [t]he[i]r movements' (Luckett, 2000: 240). Despite its still illegal status in 1965, homosexuality is visible in Schlesinger's London, but only as both a social problem (illustrated by Robert's vox pop street interviews with members of the public about what they feel 'ashamed of in Britain today'), or again seen as synonymous with a pre-supposedly decadent (i.e. queer) upper-class bohemian fringe: stereotypically manifest within the effeminate, asexual worlds of fashion and art ('embodied' through flamboyant photographer Malcolm [Roland Curram] and camp art gallery impresario Alec [Basil Henson]). It is only during a series of 'border crossings' to Paris and Capri that any real form of queer sexuality is permitted some degree of erotic expression, albeit on a rather cursory and transient level.

Whilst on a modelling assignment to Paris, narcissist Miles introduces Diana to a local group of über-modern and 'emotionally inquisitive' bohemians, who attempt to initiate her into their more sexually fluid circle. And following an initial erotically unsettling moment, in which both of them are subjected to rather aggressively lascivious same-sex scrutiny from the group, they are quickly seduced into taking part in a gender-bending 'truth game' in which participants performatively 'exchange' gendered identities whilst 'framed' by the scrutinising gaze of a film projector. This transgressively exhibitionistic act thus allows them to mock the 'role-play'of socio-sexual identity (and narrative cinema) while deconstructively 'exposing' each other's hidden secrets to the delight of the like-minded hedonists in the room. Sadly however, despite the growing sexual intensity of the group, and its flirtatious queer advances, the rather sexually conservative duo make a swift exit from the party and return to the safety of the more heterocentrically inclined swinging rituals of London.

And later on in the film, following the disintegration of her 'unconventional' relationship with both Miles and Robert, Diana forges a much more successful (though platonic) relationship with gay photographer Malcolm, and a trip that they take to the exotically accented island of Capri finally enables a liberated space for the direct expression of queer desire. In contrast to the policed environment of London, Capri represents a much more diverse and tolerant place, where Malcolm is able to express his desire for the macho Italian men that surround him and, more importantly, have this desire reciprocated and fulfilled. Malcolm's homosexuality is thus affirmed and normalised in Capri, free of the stigma, 'shame' and social regulation that it was still subject to in pre-1967 London. And unlike the lonely, self-loathing, 'sad young men' that had populated cinema previously, Malcolm is charming, witty and totally shameless in his queer desire and visibility. Although still only a support character in the film, he is nonetheless one of the first truly 'positive' new gay characters to emerge in post-war British cinema. Free of the deception, angst and ambivalence of such films as *Victim* or *A Taste of Honey*, his presence in *Darling* is emblematic of both the shift in social perceptions of homosexuality that occurred in the mid-1960s, and the queer experimentalism that permeated Schlesinger's work throughout his career (in both Britain and Hollywood). Christie's Diana may be the narrative focus of *Darling*, but extra-textual parallels can easily be drawn between the film's underlying anti-Swinging London rhetoric on the ramifications of such casual, loveless activity, and the emergent cultural perception of a promiscuous gay subculture. However, for all *Darling*'s progressive queer potential, the narrative consequences of Diana's liberated sexuality and non-conformity are, in the end, loneliness and regret; which also reveals a rather conservative cautiousness towards these new sexual attitudes that were emerging, and the possible price that feminist and homosexual liberation may have to pay in its move towards social mobility and the rejection of 'heteronormative' values and lifestyles. As Schlesinger himself ambivalently observed: 'What this film is about is the loneliness that Diana's kind of life must lead to. The emotional coldness that descends upon her in the end is the real danger.'[22]

This uneasy, more sceptical view of (a queer) 'Swinging London' became a prominent feature in British cinema of the late 1960s,[23] as is particularly evidenced through its excessive preoccupation with socio-ideological distortion and a pervasive sense of cultural dystopia. The illusory 'permissiveness' (in terms of *what* was being permitted and *who* was doing the permitting) and sexual liberation that were so essential to the 1960s social milieu were, more generally, part of a much wider and 'volatile melting-pot of issues' which were, as Sarah Street argues, symptomatic of Britain's 'more fundamental malaise' (1997: 92). And so the constant re-negotiation of social reality in British cinema that obsessively characterised the mood of the times, in actuality reflected an underlying fear of the negative consequences of non-conformity – especially in terms of class, gender and sexuality – that was emerging during the final transitional years into the 1970s. This suspicion and social conflict that emerged between a disaffected, anarchic, and sexually irresponsible hetero-masculinity and the newly radicalised and poly-morphously perverse gender and sexual politics of the late 1960s, therefore, dovetailed quite effectively in Nic Roeg and Donald Cammell's prototypical queer odyssey *Performance*. As discussed at the start of this chapter, the film epitomised quite effectively this greater willingness to explore the implications of more liminal and 'deviant' configurations of gender and sexuality – but configurations that, in

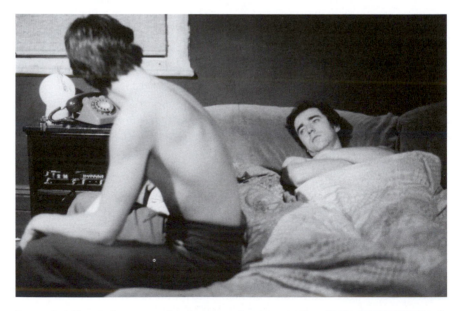

Figure 5.4 Ken Robertson as 'out' gay teacher Jim, in Ron Peck and Paul Hallam's *Nighthawks* (1978): exploring the nightly rituals of cruising the new 'scene' of the 1970s.

Source: Courtesy of Ron Peck and Paul Hallam (Cinegate).

the end, are also quite stereotypically sutured to themes of criminality, violence and socio-pathology.

Queer audiences would therefore have to wait until the final years of the 1970s for the emergence of a more 'official' – and 'positive' (or at least visible) – gay or gay-themed cinema, such as in the work of queer cinema's founding father Derek Jarman, or in films such as Ron Peck and Paul Hallam's uncompromising study of the late 1970s London gay scene in *Nighthawks* (1978). However, in spite of all its angst and ambivalence, British cinema in the 1960s subsequently played a crucial and visionary role in laying the representational and narrative groundwork for the articulation of lesbian, gay and queer desire that has evolved on the screen since.

Notes

1 Film producer Sanford Lieberson discusses the initial reception of *Performance*, cited in Brown (1999), pp.154–5.
2 Colin MacCabe (1998), p.83.
3 In particular her landmark works *Gender Trouble* (1990) and *Bodies That Matter* (1993). Butler proposes that gender and (compulsory) heterosexuality are merely categories that regulate and synonymously construct individual subjects according to how they 'perform' their sexuality and/or gender identity. They are not naturalised categories of *being*, but ones in which their *performativity* is clearly revealed: sex and gender are not therefore inherent, biological features, but socially and culturally constructed.
4 For a decidedly queer take on the Zeitgeist that writes 'against the grain of 1960s studies', see Patricia Juliana Smith's *The Queer Sixties* (1999).
5 See Adrian Danks (2001), '"What's Been Puzzling You is the Nature of My Game": *Performance*', in *Senses of Cinema* [online:www.sensesofcinema.com/contents/cteq/01/14/performance.html]. In a rather unique move for Warner Bros, the gender and sexual ambiguity that is so central (and commercially problematic) to the film was actually played upon in the advertising campaign that headed the film's British release in January 1971: the poster featured four 'gender-bending' images of its headlining stars Mick Jagger and James Fox juxtaposed in both their masculine and feminine 'drag' personas in the film, along with the provocative slogan 'Vice. And Versa'.
6 As Colin MacCabe recounts, 'At a test screening in Santa Monica in March 1970 one executive's wife vomited with shock. So vocal was the audience in its displeasure that the film had to be stopped and the paying customers offered their money back' (p.60). But after a number of imposed re-edits (much to the frustration of its makers), a studio-approved cut of the film received a rather tentative US release in the summer of 1970.
7 A scene that is later reversed when Pherber (Anita Pallenberg) also uses a mirror to 'project a female face and body on to the surface of Chas's masculinised body' (McCabe: 75).
8 As Mick Brown further elaborates, Cammell and Roeg were very much aware that in their casting of Jagger they were 'calling upon the services of not only the most famous, and most charismatic, rock singer in the world, but also the most notorious. To the British media, and huge swathes of the public, Jagger was the face of degeneracy, the personification of rock music as a threat to moral probity and order' (p.93).
9 A period that evolved from the socio-reflexive works of the 'Free Cinema' movement and the 'Social Problem' films of the 1950s.

10   'Queer' was, of course, commonly deployed as a pejorative term of abuse in the 1950s and 1960s, whereas 'homosexual' – a term rejected more recently due to its pathologising associations – was conversely regarded as the 'proper' mode of address to those individuals (mainly male) erotically attracted to the same sex. My usage of the term is thus in relation to its contemporary semantic re-deployment, which describes desires and identities that either defy or, at least, problematise the 'heteronormative'.

11   For an exhaustive overview of the key critical debates involved, and the socio-historical impact of the 'New Wave' on British 1960s cinema and culture, see Geraghty (2001), Higson (1996), Hill (1983) (1986) (2000), Hutchings (2001) and Murphy (1992).

12   Socio-historical and critical discussions of the film can be found in Bourne (1996), Dyer (1993), Medhurst (1996) and Russo (1981).

13   The 1957 Wolfenden Report recommended the decriminalisation of homosexuality in Britain, but it was not until ten years later that the legislation was finally passed. During this period, a few films did emerge that alluded to homosexuality in a fairly sympathetic way; however, in addition to *Victim*, both Gregory Ratoff's *Oscar Wilde* (1959) and Ken Hughes' *The Trials of Oscar Wilde* (1960) evaded any direct reference to homosexuality, and were set in a rather socially distant and therefore safe historical past; similarly, Terence Young's *Serious Charge* (1959), though a landmark exploration of bigotry and intolerance, once again stereotypically associates homosexuality with paedophilia and blackmail.

14   Though publicly presumed to be heterosexual, following his death in November 1991, Richardson's bisexuality was revealed upon the publication of his memoirs in *The Long-Distance Runner*, by daughter Natasha in 1993.

15   See Nicholas de Jongh, 'The Secret Gay Love of John Osborne', *Evening Standard*, 24 January 1995, pp.12–13, and *Gay Times*, Issue 198, March 1995, p.107.

16   Despite most critical readings of Geoffrey as a rather problematic stereotype of the period, in the commentary that supports the recent DVD release of the film by the BFI, Melvin sees his performance as somewhat different. He recounts that throughout the production process of both his theatrical portrayal of the role at the Royal Court and Richardson's film a year later, no discussion ever took place of Geoffrey as homosexual. In fact, Melvin sees his performance of the role as decidedly 'straight', but does not elaborate on whether this 'straightness' is more in terms of a deliberate downplaying of the exaggerated camp traits that an audience would expect from a homosexual on the screen, or that he saw the character as heterosexual. It is arguable then that readings of Geoffrey as 'gay' could potentially be more a product of perceptions of and/or presumptions about Murray Melvin himself, rather than what is traceable in Delaney's more ambiguous play or screenplay.

17   See 'Coming Out as Going In: The Image of the Homosexual as the Sad Young Man' in Dyer (1993) pp.73–92.

18   This tension between effeminacy and homosocial fetishisation that was so endemic to the queer dynamic of the British New Wave is more explicitly explored in Sidney J. Furie's *The Leather Boys* (1963). Based on Gillian Freeman's novel of the same name, the film charts the rather 'unconventional' friendship that evolves between two young bikers, Reg and Pete. Despite initial accusations of queerness from his estranged, jealous wife Dot (Rita Tushingham), young mechanic Reg (Colin Campbell) finds great solace in his newly formed friendship with fellow motorcycle enthusiast and 'funny bloke' Pete (Dudley Sutton) – a friendship that even involves the pair of them moving in together and sharing a bed. However, it is only when Pete's homosexuality is finally revealed in the film's closing moments – by two mincing queens in a gay bar – that the

productively homoerotic relationship that has been simmering between them throughout the film must finally come to an end. Reg must reject his now visibly 'queer' friendship with Pete in favour of a return to the recuperative heteronormative safety of his wife.

19 Lindsay Anderson, 'Sport, Life and Art', *Films and Filming*, February 1963, p.16.
20 The publication of his letters and autobiography by lifelong friend and fellow homosexual Gavin Lambert, *Mainly About Lindsay Anderson: A Memoir*, revealed a man tortured by his repressed homosexuality and unrequited love for married leading men Richard Harris, Albert Finney and Malcolm McDowell.
21 Schlesinger didn't publicly 'out' himself until 1991, following Derek Jarman's public letter of attack towards Ian McKellen's decision to accept his Knighthood. Schlesinger was one of a number of British lesbian and gay artists to come to McKellen's defence.
22 *Daily Mail* interview, 14 September 1965. Cited in Murphy (1992) p.125.
23 See e.g. Michelangelo Antonioni's *Blow Up* (1967), David Green's *Sebastian* and *The Strange Affair* (both 1968), Anthony Page's *Inadmissible Evidence* (1968), Roman Polanski's *Repulsion* (1965) or Michael Winner's *I'll Never Forget What's 'Is Name* (1967).

Bibliography

Ashby, J. and Higson, A. (eds.) (2000) *British Cinema, Past and Present*, London and New York: Routledge.

Bourne, S. (1996) *Brief Encounters: Lesbians and Gays in British Cinema 1930–1971*, London: Cassell.

Brown, M. (1999) *Mick Brown on Performance*, London: Bloomsbury Publishing.

Butler, J. (1990) *Gender Trouble: Feminism and the Subversion of Identity*, London and New York: Routledge.

—— (1993) *Bodies That Matter: On the Discursive Limits of 'Sex'*, London and New York: Routledge.

Chibnall, S. and Murphy, R. (eds.) (1999) *British Crime Cinema*, London: Routledge.

Curran, J. and Porter, V. (eds.) (1983) *British Cinema History*, London: Weidenfeld & Nicolson.

Dyer, R. (1993) *The Matter of Images: Essays on Representations*, London: Routledge.

Geraghty, C. (2000) *British Cinema in the Fifties: Gender, Genre and the 'New Look'*, London and New York: Routledge.

—— (2001) 'Women and 60s British Cinema: The Development of the "Darling' Girl", in Murphy (ed.), pp.101–8.

Higson, A. (1995) *Waving the Flag: Constructing a National Cinema*, Oxford: Clarendon Press.

—— (ed.) (1996) *Dissolving Views: Key Writings on British Cinema*, London: Cassell.

—— (1996) 'Space, Pleasure, Spectacle: Landscape and Townscape in the "Kitchen Sink" Film', in Higson (ed.), pp.133–56.

Hill, J. (1983) 'Working Class Realism and Sexual Reaction: Some Theses on the British "New Wave"', in Curran and Porter (eds.), pp.303–11.

—— (1986) *Sex, Class and Realism: British Cinema 1956–1963*, London: BFI.

—— (2000) 'From the New Wave to "Brit-grit": Continuity and Difference in Working-class Realism', in Ashby and Higson (eds.), pp.249–60.

Hutchings, P. (2001 [1997]) 'Beyond the New Wave: Realism in British Cinema, 1959–63', in Murphy (ed.), pp.146–52.

Jeffrey-Boulter, S. (1991) *Peers, Queers and Commons: The Struggle for Gay Law Reform from 1950 to the Present*, London: Routledge.

Jivani, A. (1997) *It's Not Unusual: A History of Lesbian and Gay Britain in the Twentieth Century*, London: Michael O'Mara Books.

Lay, S. (2002) *British Social Realism: From Documentary to Brit Grit*, London: Wallflower Press.

Luckett, M. (2000) 'Travel and Mobility: Femininity and National Identity in Swinging London Films', in Ashby and Higson (eds.), pp.233–45.

MacCabe, C. (1998) *Performance*, London: BFI.

Medhurst, A. (1996) '*Victim*: Text as Context', in Higson (ed.), pp.117–32.

Murphy, R. (1992) *Sixties British Cinema*, London: BFI.

—— (ed.) (2001) *The British Cinema Book*, 2nd Edition, London: BFI.

Richards, J. (1997) *Films and British National Identity: From Dickens to Dad's Army*, Manchester: Manchester University Press.

Russo, V. (1981) *The Celluloid Closet*, London and New York: Harper & Row.

Smith, P.J. (1999) *The Queer Sixties*, London and New York: Routledge.

Spicer, A. (2001) *Typical Men: The Representation of Masculinity in Popular British Cinema*, London: I.B. Tauris.

Stevenson, J. (2000) 'And God Created Europe: How the European Sexual Myth was Created and Sold to Post-war American Movie Audiences', in Jack Stevenson (ed.), *Fleshpot: Cinema's Sexual Myth Makers & Taboo Breakers*, Manchester: Headpress, pp.17–48.

Street, S. (1997) *British National Cinema*, London: Routledge.

Weeks, J. (1989) *Sex, Politics and Society*, London: Routledge.

Wilson, E. (1980) *Only Halfway to Paradise*, London: Tavistock.

Wollen, P. (1995) 'Possession', *Sight and Sound*, vol. 5, no. 9, September, pp.20–3.

6 'A comic monster of revue'

Beryl Reid, *Sister George* and the performance of dykery

Lizzie Thynne

In rough cut the film is quite garish, but, partly because of this quality, it gives us a good sense of the demimonde its lesbian characters share with fags, prostitutes, and even lower echelon show folk. It is tacky, tawdry, repellent – and true. A world of gay bars, vulgar talk and desperate expedients, in which Beryl Reid as the 'butch' tries with noisy desperation to hold on both to her job as a soap opera heroine and to her cruelly childish lover.

(Schickel, 1968)

Thus *Life* magazine greeted the release of *The Killing of Sister George* in 1968. Director Robert Aldrich had deliberately chosen to adapt Frank Marcus' stage hit of the same name as the first film to be made at his new studio because of its exploitation potential, and much of the press both in Britain and the US duly echoed the producers' claim that it was a shocking revelation of a hidden world. Although funded from Hollywood sources, the entire cast and the original play were British and the use of real punters from a London lesbian club was very significant in the film's bid for authenticity.

It was the first explicit representation of lesbianism in a Hollywood film and has since provoked both approval and disapproval from queer audiences and critics. As many critics have noted and as the review above echoes, the film's (and the director's) drive to reveal perversity is deliberately sensationalised and in many ways in keeping with contemporary discourses which continued to construct 'the lesbian' as pathological, and as marking the boundary of the sinister and the bizarre. Yet the performance of Beryl Reid as 'Sister George' brings to the film a different set of pleasures, derived from her long history as one of the first British women stand-up comedians and variety artists in a tradition which in many ways resists the characterisation of queer as essentially tragic, marginal and abnormal and in which female disorderliness, camp innuendo, inauthenticity and homoeroticism are indeed the norm.

The film came out at a transitional moment in film censorship and production (Russo, 1987). It capitalises on changes in the political economy of Hollywood and

Figure 6.1 Lock up your daughters! Beryl Reid as the irreverent 'dyke' June Buckridge in
       The Killing of Sister George (1968).

Source: Cinerama Releasing/Associates and Aldrich/Palomar Pictures.

its moral regulation to explicitly foreground previously taboo subject matter. These
industrial changes also intersect with wider redefinitions of public and private
behaviour occurring during the 1960s. The diverse responses to the film both at
the time of its release and since reflect its complex location within existing and
emergent discourses on sexuality. In this essay, I explore the tension between the
framing of 'the lesbian' as pathological, which is bound up with the film's claims
to seriousness of purpose, and the comedic celebration of disorderliness which
is particularly focused around Reid. These diverse elements within the film
are traced both through its assembly and reception, and some of the history of its
translation from stage to screen.

'Nobody would know what the hell you were talking about'

Robert Aldrich's decision to adapt British dramatist Frank Marcus' play, *The Killing
of Sister George*, as the first production to be made by his new company, Associates
and Aldrich, seemed to be a strange departure for a director who had just established his success with *The Dirty Dozen*, 'one of the biggest hits in the history of
motion pictures' (Production notes, press pack). The sale of his percentage on that

film enabled him to set up Aldrich Studios in January 1968 where all of the interiors of *Sister George* were shot (see Silver and Ursini, 1995). In the late 1960s, Hollywood was beset by a series of big budget flops and successful imports (Schatz, 1993). In this unfavourable market climate a space opened up for more innovative and quasi independent production. As part of a bid to establish himself as an independent, the choice of Marcus' play provided Aldrich with a number of potential marketing hooks, particularly its subject matter which could be exploited as 'controversial' and contemporary, and as offering an alternative to the safer fare offered by the majors. The play had also recently been a hit on Broadway and in London so that the film could benefit from some prior audience awareness in both the United States and Britain, and the connotations of artistic integrity associated with the more high-brow medium of theatre. However, Aldrich felt that the story situation as presented in the play offered some challenges in terms of its intelligibility to all sections of the audience (Arnold, 1986, p. 146). In the play, there is no explicit sexual action, which would in any case have flaunted current obscenity rules, and the word 'lesbian' is not mentioned – the reason Marcus claimed it escaped the censorship of the Lord Chamberlain (Fanshawe, 1995). The film, by contrast, clearly identifies and names a type whose status in Hollywood film had hitherto been veiled or ambiguous. *The Children's Hour*, directed six years earlier by William Wyler in 1961, features the close relationship of two schoolmistresses, Karen (Audrey Hepburn) and Martha (Shirley Maclaine) but despite the accusations of a pupil that the two are having an affair the L-word is never mentioned in the dialogue, nor, Maclaine reveals, in an interview in *The Celluloid Closet*, was it used on the set (Epstein, R., and Friedman, J., 1995). Martha's long disguised desire for Karen can only be articulated through the mise-en-scène and through her own eventual declaration of her 'dirty nastiness'. In the film, *Sister George*, the use of the word 'lesbian' is completely overt: When George jealously interrogates Childie about a meeting with Mrs Croft, Childie protests with 'Not all girls are raving bloody lesbians you know!' to which George quips 'Well that's their misfortune!'. Towards the end of the film, prior to taking Childie off with her, Mrs Croft calls George 'a drunken dyke'.

The film promised to show not only 'a love triangle between three women' but a 'unique sequence filmed at the Gateways club, the private club for women that for the first time, permitted extensive camera coverage within its doors' (Production notes, 1968). In particular, Aldrich's introduction of an explicit seduction scene between Mrs Croft and Childie – Reid refused to perform such a scene – is his attempt to make the nature of the relationships in the film unambiguously lesbian. The film was released in the same year as *Therese and Isabelle* and *Les Biches*, two French films with lesbian storylines (Schickel, 1968). Aldrich felt that it was 'essential to have an explicit seduction scene – or the film could be so well done that no one would know what the hell you were talking about'[1] (Arnold, 1986: 146). He himself didn't understand the nature of the relationship when he saw the play (unidentified cutting, British Film Institute, 18/8/68). In this way, he was both appropriating and competing with European art cinema which has 'the tendency to assign the cinematic convention, the love scene, a particular symbolic function: the ability to represent "lesbian experience"' (Merck, 1993: 167). The director asserted to his backers the 'honesty' of his portrayal of lesbianism 'in a manner neither approving nor disapproving' (cited in Arnold, 1986: 144) – in other words a departure from the condemnatory stance required in relation to homosexuality under the production code.

The film began shooting under the production code in the US and was completed under the ratings system which for the first time introduced a distinction between what could be shown to an adult as opposed to a young or family audience. The former was a system based on a discourse of morality to which studios were supposed to adhere and the latter assumed that people over a certain age did not need to be protected from previously taboo subjects or given moral direction, but instead shielded from overly explicit or dangerous material through a direct censorship system. On completion, the film immediately ran into censorship difficulties in the US. Aldrich finally consented to cut the seduction scene only to have the film awarded an X certificate on the basis of theme alone (Russo, 1987). In the UK, where local authorities issued their own certificates, different cuts were required in different parts of the country. This censorship environment undoubtedly influenced the way the film was received, providing useful publicity but also by highlighting the scenes cut by the censor at the expense of the film's other elements and inflecting the emphasis of reviews and audience preconceptions of its points of interest. Ann Pacey noted the film contained 'the most explicit love scene between two women seen by me at any rate' (Ann Pacey, no ref, BFI cutting). Dick Richards wrote in the *Daily Mirror*:

> John Trevelyan, the censor, demanded a 3 minute cut but the GLC only cut 40 seconds of the sex scene between Browne and York: ' Now everyone will want to see the film for the wrong reasons. . . . The scene still shows Coral Browne making love to Susannah York. She kisses and caresses Miss York's naked breasts while Susannah York pants and gurgles with mixed loathing and ecstasy. I saw nothing lascivious, disgusting, erotic or even exciting.
>
> (23/3/69)

Felix Barber, in the *Evening News* (27/3/69), compares the film to *The Fox*, saying it has a considerably more explicit 'lesbian love scene' and calls it 'a rough shod travesty of Frank Marcus' delicate and poignant play', objecting to the inclusion of a sex scene not in the original as 'outrageous'.

Despite Aldrich's assertion of his non-judgemental stance, the seduction scene is constructed, as many critics have noted,[2] as a rather sinister encounter through the music, noirish lighting and camera angles and uncomfortable performances of York

and Browne. In order to overcome the actresses' revulsion the director substituted
body doubles for York and Browne so that they could have minimal physical contact.
Reid had herself said no to the film when she saw the script:

> They had me in bed making love to the girl . . . close like baked beans. I
> thought of the fortune with the world-wide recognition, the gold-plated
> loo. But I said, 'No, not on your nelly – or maybe her nelly'. I just couldn't do
> it. The thought made me sick. It may be silly, but that sort of physical contact,
> starkers, with another woman frightened me to death.
>
> (quoted in Gardiner, 2003: 148)

These reactions underline the fact that lesbianism was still a relatively hidden
sexuality in the late 1960s. In the UK, it had been relatively absent from public
discourse. It was invisible or virtually so within the law and therefore not the
subject of open debate that male homosexuality had been in the decade preceding
the film's release. In 1957, the Wolfenden report had examined the boundary
between 'private moral conduct' and 'public order and decency' in its investigation
of homosexuality and prostitution. The concern prompting the report was mainly
to reduce the incidence of sexual behaviour in public – essentially clearing the
pros and faggots off the streets. The intention was not to end prostitution but
to drive it indoors and the result, as Weeks notes, was a vast expansion of commercial prostitution agencies and call-girl rackets. It may not be coincidental that
George's best friend in the film is Betty, a successful prostitute, not a medium as
she is in the play. Wolfenden had also recommended the decriminalisation of
homosexuality between consenting adults over 21 in private, and this finally came
into effect in the Sexual Offences Act in 1967. Male homosexuality was seen
as needing regulatory intervention not only because of its visibility through public
sex, but because of the danger that buggery was seen to represent as most nearly
approximating heterosexual coitus and therefore a potential temptation away from
it (Weeks, 1981: 240).

In this context, lesbianism does not figure as public nuisance and remains invisible
within the law. Elizabeth Wilson argues that 'while liberal progressive opinion
championed the cause of the male homosexual in the late fifties and early sixties,
there was tendency to assume that because lesbianism was not criminal it neither
attracted disapproval nor merited support'. She cites as an example *A Quaker View
of Sex* (Heron (ed.) 1963) – 'the most advanced expression of "permissive" views
in its time' which 'sternly accused lesbian relationships of being thwarted and
neurotic and expressive only of frustrated maternal feelings' (Wilson, 1980: 104).
This view of lesbianism clearly underpins the representation of both Childie, who
is obsessed with dolls, and George in *The Killing of Sister George*. George reveals
vindictively to Mrs Croft, as she takes Childie away, that Childie has herself had
a child as a teenager. Childie's bizarre habit of wearing baby doll pyjamas at all

Figure 6.2 The performance of 'dykery': June and girlfriend Childie (Susannah York) celebrate at the Gateways Club.

Source: Cinerama Releasing/Associates and Aldrich/Palomar Pictures.

times of the day also serves to infantilise her in relation to George – as her name explicitly implies. It gives the lesbian femme connotations of an immature sexuality – regressive in Childie's case because she is in fact 32. Although apparently interested in men, she prefers older dominating women who can be seen as 'mother' figures. In the play, George actually reprimands Childie for not being dressed and wearing the pyjamas with visitors present (Marcus, 1965: 54). In the film, the pyjama-wearing narratively codifies Childie as somehow both child-like and inappropriately sexual and contrasts her with the butch tweediness of George. At the same time it offers the young Susannah York as spectacle.

Given the relative public invisibility of lesbianism, making 'the lesbian' a sight is an important part of the film's address to its putative adult audience. A decision was made to include actual customers rather than extras by filming the club sequence at the Gateways – the long-standing London club with a mainly lesbian clientele. In documentary style, real Gateways punters perform themselves bravely and uncomfortably in front of the camera and the press highlighted this sequence as one of the selling points of the film. For the first time on screen a glimpse is given of a hidden subculture:

The prolonged view of women dancing which in turn has New York audiences gasping has obviously been talked about as box office bait. Frank Marcus' original play simply talked about the bent triangle conflict.

(*Daily Mail*, 25/3/69)

Reid recounts her own shock at being introduced to the Gateways: 'If I had been here before I did the play I'd never have done it. I didn't realize they held each other and went to the gent's loo' (Reid, 1984).

The film introduces scenes not only from the Gateways, but the soap opera *Applehurst* in which June stars as George, and its production at the BBC, none of which are in the original play, and which feature a number of queer characters. In this way, it presents queerness as something which is endemic not only to the margins or 'demi-monde' of British society but to the establishment – in this case the BBC, a tendency which it shares with another example of 1960s British cinema, *Victim* (Dir. Basil Dearden, UK, 1961). In *Victim*:

It is homosexuality which would appear to be normal if only by sheer prevalence . . . you can never be sure who is gay and who is not. Indeed much of the play of the film revolves around the uncertainty of sexual identity and by implication what's normal. . . . Gays are identified as existing in all walks of life (from Lord to lawyers' clerk) and one of the components of the film's strategy of surprise is the revelation of homosexuality in otherwise normal and socially well adjusted characters. Despite verbal addresses to the contrary, the gay community is to this extent 'normalized'. Far from being socially isolated, they conform exactly to the 'normal' parameters of British society.

(Hill, 1986: 92)

In the film of *Sister George*, many of the BBC personnel also appear decidedly butch, camp and/or queer, from the towering, vindictive PA Mildred, to George's *Applehurst* rival, Leo Lockhart, to the director of the show, Freddie. Mrs Croft, a BBC executive and apparently respectable widow, quickly turns out to harbour lust for 'Childie'. Scenes from June Buckridge's private life including her entangled and manipulative interactions with Childie are juxtaposed with her performance as Sister George, in the cliché-ridden soap, *Applehurst*, set in a mythical English village (intended as a parody of the genre – June being based on the actress who played Mrs Dale in *Mrs Dale's Diary* who was sacked after many years for alcoholism). After storming off the set, George gets drunk and gropes two nuns in a taxi. This episode is followed by a scene from the soap, where as Sister George, she comforts a little girl whose grandmother is seriously ill. These juxtapositions suggest disjunctions between character and role, comedian and actress, highlighting the gap between public and private. Whilst they can be read as implying George's tragedy is her sexuality they can also be read in the opposite way. June's fictional character in the soap is a sweet asexual spinster nurse and represents an English type which is anachronistic and which, as she puts it, 'makes you want to vomit'. The underlining of June's energetic refusal to remain in the closet, disguise her sexuality or maintain a façade of respectability to perform her required role can be seen as interrogating the distinction between public and private which contemporary moral and legal discourses, were, as I have indicated, trying to enshrine.

Contemporary reviews in the lesbian press nonetheless responded negatively and claimed that the film 'dealt with lesbians entirely through the eyes of heterosexual males' (*The Ladder*, xiii, v, vi, Feb–March 1969, cited in Gardiner, 2003: 151). Other lesbian viewers at the time and since have found points of identification and pleasure in the film. These include the much criticised seduction scene between Mrs Croft and Childie and the film's representation of power relationships. I held a discussion session about the film with a group of seven lesbians whose ages ranged from late 40s to early 60s, a couple of whom had seen the film near to when it came out. They were mainly professional or retired professionals, largely in counselling and social work jobs and were all white. They largely ignored the generic coding of the sex scene, which attempts to denote it as noirishly sinister, and reacted appreciatively to its openness and detail. Alice, one of the group, commented that 'the sex scene was amazingly powerful . . . I needed a glass of water or rather a bucket of water', although another group member thought Mrs Croft's attraction to Childie to be 'implausible'. Alice saw the film at the Odeon in Brighton when it was first released and said she came away 'walking along the sea front feeling really miserable' but she also said that 'back then it was a kind of revelation that there were other people – that there was a club'. I also had six questionnaires about responses to the film returned by lesbians to whom I distributed them at various events in Brighton (the launch of 'From the Closet to the Screen', Brighton Gay Pride and a women's night). These responses reflected the identities available to the women at the time of viewing and the way in which they connected the film to their current perceptions of lesbianism, their own sense of sexuality as well as the textual codification of lesbian types and lifestyles. Catherine (48) remembered seeing the film on TV aged about 21 in circa 1975, and recalled thinking that the 'lesbian club appeared sad and unusual . . . that it created conflict and uncomfortable feelings for me, – [I] did not want to be part of that world, but knew that I would'. Jan (52) 'recalls fascination and a sense of otherness' and particularly remembers the seduction scene between Coral Browne and Susannah York. Maria (50) recollects what she heard about the film:

> The film came out around the time I was a teenager and first falling in love with other girls. We just knew about it even though we didn't get to go and see it. The image I had was of a very masculine older woman dressed in tweeds and the film being about her. This was jumbled up in my mind with the general image I had of 'lesbians' which at the time was daunting and off-putting to me! I was a longhaired purple flare-wearing hippyish young person and I

couldn't relate to Sister George at all! My other impression was that it all ends in tears and the character is miserable! By contrast I did go and see 'Les Biches', a French film with some lesbian story in it where the women were all very beautiful and feminine. I identified with that more although it also ends in tears and was a pretty negative portrayal.

Interestingly, she contrasts her later thoughts on the film: 'Years later when I was "out" I felt a bit more affection for it and by then I was identifying positively as a butch so my take on it became different.'

While anger, sadness or alienation characterised some of the feelings these respondents had about the film there were other more positive ones and these were largely associated with the performance of Beryl Reid. According to Jen (57): 'she said all the things you'd love to say and got away with it' and 'she gave an amazing performance which was a mixture of tragedy and comedy'. Alice observed wittily that Beryl (George) was 'a female Falstaff with a bit of Oscar Wilde thrown in'.

As I have noted, Reid had reservations about playing a butch dyke because of the overtness of the role, but her background was nonetheless in variety and revue – genres where female disorderliness, camp innuendo and homoeroticism are the norm. While not claiming that these factors are inherently subversive, they

Figure 6.3 The 'sinister' Mrs Croft (Coral Browne) makes her move on Childie.

Source: Cinerama Releasing/Associates and Aldrich/Palomar Pictures.

certainly form an important counterpoint to the exploitative emphasis of the film's script and direction and were recognised as such (although not always with approval by reviewers and audiences). The characters who exemplify camp innuendo in British comedy are predominantly male and are associated with the *Carry On* series, such as Kenneth Williams, Frankie Howerd and Charles Hawtrey. Reid was one of the few women who over a long period was able to mine this particular vein of British humour. Some British critics criticised Reid's performance in Aldrich's film for its coarseness, which they associated with an inappropriate revue style:

> In essence the cigar-smoking gin-swilling remains as acutely observed and as pitiful as on the stage. But in treatment she has broadened out into a comic monster of revue who defies our sympathy by clowning, rampaging and boozing her way out of the programme. She comes right out with a four letter word of dismissal and clearly mouths another. She plagues her TV director (Hugh Paddick), guys Sister George's death scene and pours gin and tonic over the head of her smug co-star (Ronald Fraser). All this is very funny in a typically Reidian way but it turns the character into a caricature. Of the three women Coral Browne remains most consistently in character but the life and soul of the picture is unquestionably Beryl Reid.
>
> (Cecil Wilson, *Daily Mail*, 25/3/69)

Likewise, Patrick Gibbs commented that 'this actress's style is on the large side for the cinema' (*Telegraph* 28/3/69). I would argue, though, that this performance style and the comedy with which it is associated helps to resist the tragic narrative of abjection, which the film contains despite Aldrich's claim to be non-judgemental. Reid had had twenty-two years as a stand-up in revue and music hall before breaking into 'serious acting' by winning the part of Sister George in the stage play. One of the characters who she invented in music hall, and subsequently performed on radio in *Educating Archie*, 1952–56, was Monica, who Reid described as 'a frightfully grand schoolgirl, having her teeth put right, who spat all over everybody' (Interview with Roy Plomley, *Desert Island Discs*, 5/2/83). As Monica she engages in homoerotic banter typical of British comedy. *Educating Archie* is a series where the humour is based on quick fire innuendo, double entendre and mistaken identity. In an episode entitled *Archie's the Boy* (broadcast 8/11/54) there is a scene in a tobacconist's shop where the tobacconist sits on a burning cigar, an incident which Monica uses as the occasion for a series of double entendres, beginning with 'little does he know he's going to get a red hot tip'. When the tobacconist opines: 'if a customer comes in I won't be able to serve him', Monica quips 'Never mind, you can always bend over and give him a light'. This kind of sexual, often homoerotic, repartee is carried over into the role of George. When Mrs Croft remarks to George that she always looks so cheerful on her motorbike in the soap opera, George responds, 'You'd look happy with 50 cc throbbing between your legs'. The humour of Reid's later starring role in the 1970s ITV sitcom, *Alcock and Gander*, also continues in this vein.

Reid's revue performances depended on her ability to create her own characters, to improvise and to hold an audience. Maureen Lipman comments of Reid that 'if you can control the Hartlepool crowd in 1947, you can act' (interview, ITV News, 2000). It is this ability to hold an audience and keep their attention on you even at the expense of the narrative and the audience which Reid brought to her roles in serious scripted drama. Jenkins in his wonderfully titled book, *What Made Pistachio Nuts*, describes how 'in early sound comedy a vaudeville aesthetic based on heterogeneity, affective immediacy and performance is confronted by one that had long placed primary emphasis on one causality, consistency, closure and cohesiveness' (Jenkins, 1992: 278). During the stage performance of *The Killing of Sister George*, co-star Eileen Atkins recalls the ways in which Reid would draw attention to her own performance at the expense of the script and the story line. Much to Atkinson's consternation, Reid would begin improvising and do a whole turn by herself. When challenged by Atkins, Reid apologised profusely but said she thought that the audience were bored and that they weren't enjoying themselves as much as usual and so she thought she'd give them a laugh (interview with Eileen Atkins, ITV News, 2000). Likewise Alexie Sayle, with whom she appeared in *The Comic Strip*, recollects her power and ruthlessness and determination to dominate a scene – 'she didn't stick to her lines and would add something to the end of a scene so the director would have to finish on her' (interview, ITV News, 2000). Sayle surmises that this ruthlessness was the product of what Reid had been through personally and professionally, and her journey to becoming a 'serious' actress had been a long one, as she describes in her autobiography (Reid, 1984). In the film of *Sister George*, this vaudevillian tendency to hold the audience at all costs is exploited by George to parody her own demise. Having apparently been killed by a truck, realising she is off camera, she uses her knowledge of the recording process to make faces at the actor playing the truck driver, both disrupting his performance and making the crew laugh. As June Buckridge, Reid resists the narrative closure that the Applehurst producers have devised for her character Sister George, and it is this image of George refusing to be put down which also serves to counterbalance the closure of the film itself where she sits alone in the darkened studio, pathetically mooing in anticipation of her demotion to doing the voice-over for a cartoon cow in a children's series.

The tendency to improvise and play for laughs was turned to advantage by both Reid and Atkins when during rehearsals for the play they invented a Laurel and Hardy sequence where George and Childie engage in a bawdy slap-stick routine (Reid, 1984: 129). This sequence, which is retained and built on in the film, seems out of keeping with the narrative. It appropriates the playful homoeroticism of the male comedy duo and contrasts strongly with the couple's engagement else-where in the film in pathologised sado-masochism. It is also perhaps through this playful improvisation that Reid resisted the negative connotations of the part of a butch lesbian that some of her peers had refused to take. She was running a great risk in accepting it even though it was the means by which she could make her bid to be a serious actress rather than only a comedian.

Kenneth Allsop lamented of the film in the *Observer* (1986): 'This version is far more theatrical than in the theatre. The lines are addressed not within the situation but sententiously across the footlights.' However, in playing to the footlights in what is ostensibly a naturalistic drama, Reid underlines the bawdy humour of her character. She harnesses the female disorderliness for which she was already celebrated in her stand-up career, to making the kind of sexual innuendo normally reserved for male artists. When challenged by Mrs Croft about her very public assault on young nuns in a taxi she retorts 'How was I to know they were noviati-ates?' The delivery of the lines appears to demand off-stage laughter, arresting forward movement of the narrative. Comedian Sendman argues, comedy involves 'a dialectic between eccentric behaviour (anti-cultural drives) and social conformity (cultural values). The comedian's disruptiveness is constructed as a problem blocking his full assimilation into the social and narrative order' (cited in Jenkins, 1992: 11). In the case of *The Killing of Sister George* it is not only the verbal comedy inherited from Frank Marcus's play which undermines the film's attempt to construct 'the lesbian' through a voyeuristic gaze, but Beryl Reid's performance which has the same effect by disrupting the demands of narrative verisimilitude.

Notes

1   As Tom Dewes Matthews notes when critic Pauline Kael reviewed *The Children's Hour* she commented that lesbians didn't really *do* much at all, but that her response to *The Killing of Sister George*, by contrast, is titled 'Frightening the Horses' (cited in Russo, 1987, p. 173).
2   See e.g. Sheldon (1977: 13): 'The voyeuristically necessary seduction scene is as nasty as the women, though it is hard to work out what is happening, the dark setting and strange musical score, indicate that it is certainly perverted.'

Bibliography

Arnold, E and Miller, E. Jr (1986) *The Films and Career of Robert Aldrich*, Knoxville: University of Tennessee.

Epstein, R. and Friedman, J. (1995) directors, *The Celluloid Closet II*, USA.

Fanshawe, S. (1995) 'Moving Out of Character', *Sunday Times*, 23 April.

Gardiner, J. (2003) *From the Closet to the Screen: Women at the Gateways Club, 1945–85*, London: Pandora.

Hill, J. (1986) *Sex, Class and Realism: British Cinema 1956–1963*, London: BFI.

ITV News (2000) *The Unforgettable Beryl Reid*, 31 December.

Jenkins, H. (1992) *What Made Pistachio Nuts?: Early Sound Comedy and the Vaudeville Aesthetic*, New York: Columbia UP.

Marcus, F. (1965) *The Killing of Sister George: A Comedy*, London: Samuel French.

Merck, M. (1993) *Perversions: Deviant Readings*, London: Virago.

Reid, B. (1984) *So Much Love: an Autobiography*, London: Hutchinson.

Russo, V. (1987) *The Celluloid Closet*, New York: Harper & Row.

Schatz, T. (1993) 'The New Hollywood' in Collins, J., Radner, H., and Preacher Collins, A. (eds.), *Film Theory Goes to the Movies*, London: Routledge.

Schickel, R. (1968) 'Shock of Seeing a Hidden World', *Life*, November.

Sheldon, C. (1977) 'Lesbians and Film: Some Thoughts' in Dyer, R., *Gays and Film*, London: BFI.

Weeks, J. (1981) *Sex, Politics and Society: The Regulation of Sexuality since 1800*, London: Longman.

Wilson, E. (1980) *Only Halfway to Paradise: Women in Postwar Britain: 1945–1968*, London and New York: Tavistock.

7 'Come and have a bathe!'

Landscaping the queer utopia

Michael Williams

It is in moments such as the all-male nude bathing sequence in *A Room with a View* (James Ivory, 1986, henceforth *RWAV*), that British film presents us with a tantalisingly queer glimpse of utopia. Here, the floppy-haired Freddy, statuesque George and arch Mr Beebe romp freely in the waters of an English Arcadia. Such moments are obsolescent by design. Often the emblems of heterosexual culture are all too quick to intrude, here as visions of starched linen, parasols and Helena Bonham Carter. However, the queer moment has been too vivid to easily forget, and recent writing has challenged the film's reception as a rather starchy and con- servative artefact of the heritage canon, which as Richard Dyer has highlighted, has actually been 'surprisingly hospitable to homosexual representation' (Dyer, 2002: 204).[1] This chapter will examine the way a classical framework, that is a mythical and iconographic vernacular drawing from ancient Greece and Rome, can be seen to implicitly structure such instances of sexual encounter and experi- mentation. While my focus remains with the ostensibly more glamorous facades of E.M. Forster adaptations *RWAV* and *Maurice* (Ivory, 1987), I shall move on to briefly explore the suburban pools and wooded enclosures of 'beautiful downtown Basingstoke' frequented by the young protagonists of *Get Real* (Simon Shore, 1999).

Et in Arcadia Ego?: 'I cannot see that you should object in such a landscape'

Greece, unsurprisingly enough, forms the mythic touchstone for innumerable cinematic representations of homosexuality. The main reason for this lies not only in the almost universal familiarity of classical aesthetics but, more significantly, in their deployment since the nineteenth century as a 'mode of defence' by artists, Chris White argues, seeking to 'find discreet ways and discreet discourses of speak- ing about themselves', not least within the kind of Arcadian spaces here discussed (White, 1999: 116). By Arcadian I refer to the mythical construct of distant green landscape of both pleasure and beauty and danger and panic, the latter term deriving from Pan, the priapic Greek god and lover to both sexes that presided over the land (Schama, 1985: 526–7). The more primitive concepts of the space were moderated through the Greek and later Roman era, becoming the idyll popularised across Western Europe from the eighteenth century. Drawing from the notion that same-sex relationships were unproblematic in the classical period (see Dover, 2002: 25), a loose classical framework can be seen to frame the kind of Arcadian spaces here discussed, to some extent legitimating a homoerotic desire that is often all but spoken.

Even in films entirely disconnected with the ancient world, we find a certain recourse to the classical in the iconography of gay love, particularly in its early fumbles amid the undergrowth. These spaces are often iconographically displaced from the contemporary and often present a challenge to the demands for social realism with which British cinema is still so often burdened. Thus, Andrew Higson's discussion of the 'Kitchen Sink' film has relevance for many of the texts discussed here, albeit from a different historical context, as he explores how numerous contradictory demands compete to document the social problem or offer pleasurable, romantic atmosphere, including the poetic rural cameos glimpsed in almost all the films (see Higson, 1996). Such narrative places have a long tradition in cinema, not least in the Woman's Film and its contemporary British incarnations where, in the liminal spaces of Greece in *Shirley Valentine* (Lewis Gilbert, 1989) or the woods of *She'll Be Wearing Pink Pajamas* (John Goldschmidt, 1985), Justine King has argued, lies a 'realm of possibility' for the women involved (King, 1996: 220).[2] However, given the cultural tradition it draws from, the queerer resonances of the Arcadian space are what interests me here.

In both *RWAV* and *Maurice*, the classical vocabulary is established from the outset, whether through the dazzling display of Florence's Piazza Signoria or in a Greek interpretation class at Cambridge. What is important in both texts is the relationship of the classical to the personal lives of the characters and not the heritage pageant alone, a tension elucidated within the mise-en-scène of the Florence sequence. The camera enters the square with Lucy (Helena Bonham Carter), zooming out and craning up to embrace the magnificence of the scene, it amounts to a rather histrionic display of history: Elizabethans pretending to be Edwardian, pretending to the classical, or at least the Renaissance version of it. What matters is not just period authenticity as has often been suggested of these films, but its very artifice. We might look to David Lowenthal's deconstruction of historical memory in *The Past is a Foreign Country* at this point, as he argues that contemporary conceptions of the classical and architecture like that in the square are an 'amalgam of Hellenistic, Renaissance, Enlightenment, Romantic, and Victorian works in which extant Greek and Roman remains play only a minor role. It is not the original that seems "authentic" but current views of what the past ought to have looked like' (Lowenthal, 1985: xxiii). We are left with 'views' as if on a picture postcard, or indeed a whole series of classical visions flickering away into the past, and indeed

Lucy appears more concerned with the postcards she buys at the start of the sequence than with her 'actual' surroundings.

A striking play is made upon the statue of Perseus, brandishing the head of Medusa, whom he has slain as a sequence of three shots in quick succession scrutinise the sculpture as a Cubist pastiche, snatched out of time. The music sounds a note of discord as the third, closer shot frames the warrior's sword against his genitals, the juxtaposition implying that the classical aesthetic possesses an ambiguous double-edge. It is as if a romantic attachment to the past can also, viewed from a certain position, connote an ambiguous yet powerful sexuality. This image, I suggest, connects to the later scene of male nudity at the 'Sacred Lake' through the concept of 'the warrior ideal' which, Linda Dowling argues, saw such images of classical heroism transformed into the 'battleground of ideas' central to Forster's Oxbridge (Dowling, 1994: 31). Thus gay apologists of this period found the original Greek aesthetic of men fighting 'toe to toe and shield against shield hard driven, crest against crest and helmet on helmet, chest against chest', highly conducive to homo-erotic appropriation (Dover, 1978: 48).[3]

The shock and horror of the Piazza, with its blood and combat, links via the fountain and statues, to the lake scene. Forster himself connects the two episodes in the novel with their titles 'Fourth Chapter' and 'Twelfth Chapter', whereas all other titles assume the witty commentary quoted by the film's inter-titles. The sulking, slightly effeminate George (Julian Sands) admits that he 'nearly fainted' at the sight of the blood shed by two fighting Italians at the end of this sequence. This contrasts sharply with the passionate athletic figure that kisses Lucy and later romps naked in the lake. George's 'effeminacy' is symptomatic of his self-emburdenment with the 'question-mark' of life (the mark he scrawls on the back of a picture in Lucy's room), much like that of the doubtful Clive in *Maurice*. When George gets over his doubts and recognises the 'beauty' he has been looking for, he is then able to embrace Lucy and then his fellow men in the pool, acknowledging 'universal' and perhaps just a little queer 'yes'. When he strides boldly, nakedly, through the water of the pool, spurting water from his mouth, he is truly statuesque.[4] He possesses the 'Hellenic temperament' and 'blondness and delicacy that did not mean frailty', an implicitly queer aesthetic with which Forster constructs *Maurice* (Forster, 1972: 218).[5] The final shot of the Piazza Signoria sequence finds he and Lucy gazing at the surging torrents of the Arno. Empowered by discarding the blood-stained postcards, George has shaken off the repressive shackles of the past and will later enact a classical vision of his own in the Sacred Lake.

Maurice: Classical ruins and Bermondsey boxers

Maurice was E.M. Forster's most personal work, the eponymous story of a young man's sexual awakenings while studying the classics, among other things, in

Figure 7.1 'The unspeakable vice of the Greeks': Maurice (James Wilby) and Clive (Hugh
Grant) in *Maurice* (1987).

Source: BFI Stills, Posters and Designs (Merchant Ivory).

Edwardian Cambridge. The manuscript, which Forster ensured remained unpublished during his lifetime, was, Forster wrote in 1960: 'the direct result of a
visit to Edward Carpenter' (Forster, 1972: 217). The influence of Carpenter,
a Whitmanesque sexologist who conceived the pseudo-classical notion of the
homosexual as 'Uranian', can be seen in the passage where Maurice fantasises about
his first, imaginary, object of desire, anticipating his first 'actual' lover, Clive, a
fellow scholar. The ethereal vision of Forster's narrator arises from a heavy,
Dionysal dream. Amid a vocabulary of 'fogs' and 'shadow' (perhaps extending
into the mistiness of the classical imagery seen in the film) the young Maurice
attempts to discern a 'friend' from a haunting dream. 'Was he a Greek god,
such as illustrates the classical dictionary?', Maurice wonders, but 'most probably
he was just a man' (Forster, 1972: 26). For Forster, it seems, only the 'classical
dictionary' can make the queer visible, as the figure, first imagined to be 'Christ',
is then mediated as a 'Greek god' to become 'a man', the very process of conceptualisation in the early twentieth century when Forster and Carpenter were
writing.

In *Maurice*, neo-Arcadian spaces are also contrasted with more overtly classical
but considerably less vibrant locales. George's rejection of historical artefacts in
Florence echoes the complex relationship of Maurice (James Wilby) and Clive

(Hugh Grant) to the classical past. A relationship not only in terms of the physical landscape but also the social environment of Edwardian Cambridge where, as a don warns early on in the film, one must omit 'reference to the unspeakable vice of the Greeks' at all costs (Harvey, 1987: 72). In a key sequence, shots of Clive sitting utterly alone amid desolate classical ruins are intercut with shots of Maurice tutoring East End docker's lads in boxing in the 'darkest reaches of Bermondsey'. The brief scene in Greece stands out as a rather solitary oasis in the film, yet iconographically connects to four other scenes across the film where setting is key in facilitating character development. As a prologue to the Greek scene, we witness an awkward restaurant dinner in London where, in the presence of their families, Clive and Maurice's relationship appears quietly strained. When asked 'you sound as if you have no use whatsoever for Greece, Mr Hall?', Maurice dismissively replies 'sounds out of repair – a heap of old stones'. Indeed, the Greek trip is of *use* only to Clive as the ultimate test of his sexuality, and whose pointed toast 'to the ladies!' motivates the cut to the aforementioned 'heap of old stones'. The trip to Greece ('of all placcs' as June Perry Levine exclaims) is taken by Clive not as a Grand Tour but as a tonic for his recent illness, namely the neurotic fainting spells he has been experiencing and the associated need to 'work things out' about his feelings for Maurice, as he later confesses (Levine, 1996: 316).

The first shot of Greece is an extreme wide-shot of a sun-drenched temple on top of a hill blanketed with golden grasses against mist-enshrouded hills behind. Firstly, the image is reminiscent of both the little patch of Arcadia he and Maurice found in the breezy sunshine of the Cambridgeshire countryside where the men 'woke up each other' as if from a dream as they lay in the long grass. It also rhymes with the grey, misty long-shot that earlier established the 'Goblin House', a Gothic pavilion in the grounds of Clive's family estate, filmed at the neo-classical Wilbury Park in Wiltshire, a place appropriately renowned, Ivory notes, as 'the first Palladian house in England' (Pym, 1995: 60). Although the architectural reference point of the Goblin House was classical, as the two men steal a kiss amid the columns that ring the building, the setting proves not quite so idyllic (as its name suggests), for the couple are spotted by Simcox, the deeply disapproving head-servant, as he cycles past. Simcox was played by Patrick Godfrey, who had previously played the prudish Mr Eager in *RWAV*. In that film, Eager's disapproval of the intimacy with which an Italian driver was embracing his lover was met by fellow picnicker Eleanor Lavish's (Judy Dench) elegant retort: 'I cannot see that you should object in such a landscape'. Through Lavish we hear the perfect enunciation of Forster's desire for the Italian (and later, by association, English) landscape to function as a theatre wherein any number of sexual possibilities might be 'legitimately' performed. However, the Goblin House offers little cultural protection to the protagonists in their search for intimacy; it is a rather too self-conscious edifice of neo-classicism or, perhaps, just not 'neo' enough.

The same cannot be said for the lively spectacle of the Bermondsey boxers, and whose subsequent nudity (a few scenes later, as Maurice tempers his spirit in this sporting arena and grows sexually confident after his 'split' with Clive) echoes with that of the celebrated Sacred Lake sequence in *RWAV*. In the full-frontal spectacle of the working-class male body – foreshadowing that of Maurice's future lover, the under game-keeper, Scudder (Rupert Graves) – it becomes clear that life can only be experienced in the present. Maurice embraces a Whitmaesque poetic reality rather than what Robert Martin terms a 'false vision of an idealised homosexuality', which Clive naively seeks in Greece (Bredbeck, 1997: 33).[6] The ancient world is exactly that, misty, remote and anachronistic, little more than a disillusioning and sexually enfeebling relic. Unlike the poetic smoggy 'haziness' Higson observes in 'That Long Shot of Our Town from That Hill' and other overt 'views through a camera' in Kitchen Sink dramas, the misty visions in *Maurice* and other films discussed here (even the dazzling golden sheen that bathes *RWAV*) foreground rather than mask their realist impossibility (Higson, 1996: 150, 153). These shots are meant to stand out in incongruity from the normative environment through which they are reached and, like the patinated surface of a coin or faded photographic grain, the authenticity of antiquity is only apparent in its mediating and distancing flaws. Classical conceptions of sexuality are liberating only in application. Clive needs to lift his eyes from the textbook in order to embrace the present and thereby transform it.

The classical past will appear once more in the British Museum, where Maurice and Scudder contemplate their relationship in the Assyrian gallery before spending the night together. This is their first public appearance as a couple, underscored by the reappearance of Simon Callow's Mr Ducie, with whose awkward prophecies of reproductive heterosexuality the film began. Maurice denies being the boy Ducie once knew, for indeed he has changed, but the presence of Callow, combined with his observation that the museum is 'not just a collection of relics' but a place in which to 'ask questions', restores a value to the classical past of which Ducie is completely unaware. Forster himself asked seeking questions on his early visits to the Greek sculptures in the museum, one in particular seeming to sexually intoxicate him: 'He simply radiates light. . . . Right across the Assyrian transept he throbs like something under the sea. He couldn't have done it in Greece' (Aldrich, 1993: 94).[7] Clive's abortive trip abroad proves that Maurice couldn't have done it in Greece either, Robert Aldrich highlighting the novel's attitude to such relics: 'Classical studies may awaken a person's homosexuality, but too much book-learning can stifle sex. Antiquity provides a model of homosexuality, but modern Greece and Italy do not provide bed-partners for Maurice' (Aldrich, 1993: 99). It is thus no coincidence that Forster transposes the sculptural vocabulary of his encounter onto the physical form of his classical emissary in *RWAV*, George, as he stands 'Barefoot, bare-chested, radiant' in the sunlight of the Sacred Lake (Forster, 1987: 152).

Classical mythology and an Arcadian setting thus 'allowed Forster to draw upon a world of desires otherwise unmentionable in an Edwardian context' (Martin and Piggford, 1997: 4). However, as one commentator in the *Financial Times* put it, Merchant Ivory's *Maurice* 'does not, definitely not, have the sunny Arcadian feel' of *RWAV* (Andrews, 1987: xvii). Although some kind of utopian possibility is glimpsed by Maurice and Scudder in the gloom of the boathouse where they meet at the end of the film, given their renegade identities as 'known homosexuals' the film's closure seems rather fragile. A similarly tentative closure is found in Stephen Frear's *My Beautiful Laundrette* (1985), where the film's protagonists are left, as the screenplay puts it, 'washing and splashing each other in the sink . . . both stripped to the waist' amid the glass-strewn ruins of the laundrette (Kureshi, 2000: 69). The men's watery playfulness is distracting pleasure from the reality of Thatcher's Britain outside, but as in *Maurice*, we are left wondering what will happen next. Filmed in a location described by James Ivory as a 'pseudo-Gothic "cottage" circa 1890' (Pym, 1995: 63), the boathouse looks both quaintly rustic in its mock-Tudor beams and glowing fire, but also rather grotty in its green-tinged darkness and dripping water.[8] However, Alan Hollinghurst celebrates Forster's ending as a 'visionary' 'romantic-pastoral' challenge to 'believe in the new possibility of happiness' for the protagonists (Hollinghurst, 1987: 1225). At least Scudder and Maurice seem destined for more happiness than the dutifully married Clive, who stares mournfully through the bars of his window at the end of the film, borne back into the past once more.

The Sacred Lake

If only the men had moored their boats upon *RWAV*'s Sacred Lake, although it's admittedly more of a pond than a lake. It is a liminal place of trees, ferns and water and should be reached unclothed. The lake is thus more of an idea than a reality, existing for an ephemeral moment, and as such it is utopian, or rather, in looking back to the classical, Arcadian. The utopian Sacred Lake setting seems the perfect place for Forster to shake off the shackles of a society from which he, and others of the Bloomsbury Group, wished to escape. Indeed, two of Forster's contemporaries at King's College suggest that Forster would have '"rejoiced"' to see Merchant Ivory's version of the scene: '"If only Morgan could have seen that"', one of them playfully observes (Lelyveld, 1986: 621).

Part of the Platonic doctrine of Oxbridge outlined by Dowling cites 'homoerotic friendship as a remembered dream', quoting Oxford scholar Hallward's contemplation whether 'in some antenatal experience I had lived the life of a philosophical Greek lover' (Dowling, 1994: 127). The sense of memory and cultural inheritance is crucial here. Even in a film like *Get Real*, whose Basingstoke setting seems a cultural world away from ancient Greece, there are fleeting touches of wistfulness that somehow echo the tone of Hallward's words, for example, the scene in which head-boy and athlete John (Brad Gorton) appears in Steven's (Ben Silverstone) bedroom to come to 'face up to' his sexuality and the teenagers spend the night together. Here, John recalls a geography field trip to a 'quite wild' Cornwall, where he and a male friend had got drunk sitting on rocks by the sea before stripping off to go swimming, one thing leads to another as his companion dries him off. John wasn't ready for this, so the moment swiftly passes and the boys never spoke of it again, yet the experience was clearly transformative for John in awakening hitherto unexplored feelings. More significantly, he is only fully able to 'act' upon his rather aching memory in the process of it becoming a 'scene' recounted to Steven, enabling them to sleep together. Cornwall, relatively speaking, is an exotic location within the UK, and it is perhaps no coincidence that it was along its temperate coast that British painter Henry Scott Tuke (1858–1929) created many of his homoerotic artworks; naked youths bathing in apparently Mediterranean waters being the primary trope appropriated from his classical muse. Fred Davis explains that the term nostalgia, which loosely applies to the kind of memory-haunted landscapes evoked here and elsewhere, derives from 'the Greek *nostos*, to return home, and *algia*, a painful condition' (Davis, 1979: 1). Here, the nostalgia isn't for 'home' or necessarily anything that the individuals have experienced themselves, but for a kind of transformative cultural memory that can be 'painted' over the present.

This queer parenthesis is placed on the Sacred Lake scene in *RWAV* as George meets Freddy for the first time on the stairs of the Emersons' villa (which Forster named 'Cissie Villa', no less), and his eyes widen visibly and remain fixed on him for the majority of the scene. The homoerotic agenda of Freddy's invitation here to 'come and have a bathe' is a little more explicit in his role as Scudder in *Maurice*. There, he asks Maurice if the men playing cricket (which Clive dubs 'the Olympic games') 'would like to bathe between innings'. The parallel would have been even stronger if the central casting was repeated in the films as planned. Unfortunately, Ivory informs us that Sands '"got frightened of the role"' two weeks into filming (Davis, 1986: 9).[9] In its 'natural' architecture, the woodland oasis echoes the classical topography of the Piazza in Florence, this time with trees forming a boundary of columns; the marble icons that had looked down in cold silence in the Piazza now plunge into the invigorating waters, as if realising that latent sexuality in a Roman bath. The moment appears spontaneous and curiously timeless, its elements Forster lists as 'water, sky, evergreens, a wind', things 'not even the seasons can touch', and in George a figure that stands 'statue'-like and 'Michelangelesque' on the flooded margin of the pond as he gazes at Freddy (Forster, 1987: 148–9). This reference could describe George's statuesque appearance; after all, Mr Beebe does appreciatively exclaim 'Italian art!' as he slaps George on the chest as they walk to the lake (Forster, 1987: 148). Indeed, George could be compared to Michelangelo himself, the Renaissance figure whose work epitomises the conflation of homosexual desire with aesthetic sensibility. The imagery of the scene clearly draws from nineteenth-century homoerotics. Aside from Walt Whitman, a poet described in 1877 as being 'more truly Greek than any other man of modern times', there is John Gambril Nicholson's 1892 verse, 'Clothed only in his wondrous loveliness / He stands upon the margin of the stream', which almost precisely describes the figure above (Meyers, 1977: 90; White, 1999: 324).[10]

With the cry 'I'll race you' as the trio climb out of the waters, the historical backdrop alludes to an Olympian sports field, another device to legitimise nudity along with the odd subtext. After all, Thomas Waugh suggests: 'nude bathing has been one of the most obsessive motifs of gay male narrative since its beginnings' (Waugh, 2000: 187). Even Oscar Wilde reportedly attempted to seduce young men at the Café Royale with tales of the Greek Olympic games and men 'nude, clothed only in sunshine and beauty' (Dowling, 1994: 45). There, Dover notes, 'athletic success' was both a 'powerful stimulus' to potential male lovers and helpful abjuration of effeminacy (Dover, 2002: 28). No wonder Steven is drawn to athlete John in *Get Real*, an '18-year-old with the looks of a demigod' according to the *Gay Times* (Parkes, 1999: 22).

Queer oases: Beautiful downtown Basingstoke?

Get Real's location is 'Beautiful downtown Basingstoke', *Time Out* notes with a sense of disbelief shared with *The Times*'s exclamation that 'the place really doesn't look that bad at all' (Johnston, 1999: 24; Cliff, 1999: 43). Tensions around social authenticity and homoerotic licence emerge, with Alexander Walker exclaiming that the film is 'more of a daydream than a document' and that it ignores the exigencies of real life by having no mention of safer sex (which isn't true) (Walker, 1999: 31). Basingstoke's New Town identity, a place 'people drive past on the M3', as director Simon Shore notes, appears to be a provocative move towards a location *Village Voice* perceives to be 'significantly posher than the South London flats of *Beautiful Thing*, though arguably more stifling' (Lim, 1999: 113). Posher or not, it is a step away from both city and country heritage, as the film's official website argues: 'The filmmakers saw Basingstoke as an opportunity to move away from the gritty social realism prevalent in British films today', Shore adding that the town has a 'very American' and therefore 'universal' quality about it.[11] While one might question the prevalence of gritty realism today, the film is drawn back to a shifting landscape of woodlands, parks and pools as well as the concrete precincts with which Basingstoke is generally associated. And perhaps, like its urban counterpart *Beautiful Thing* (Hettie MacDonald, 1995) – which discovered queer rainbow oases in high shots looking down on the monochrome urban geometry of Thamesmead – this very contemporary locality is one reason for the abundance of fan-fiction that inundates the websites for the film, where queer audiences can vicariously inhabit the spaces of the films through their characters, and even attend pilgrimages to their

Figure 7.2 The beautiful young things of Basingstoke: Steven (Ben Silverstone) consoles his not so 'gay' boyfriend John (Brad Gorton) in *Get Real* (1998).

Source: BFI Stills, Posters and Designs (Graphite Films).

locations. Though what they might find there, like Clive in *Maurice*, is of course another matter.

Near the beginning of the film Steven is seen cycling away from school through an underpass to then emerge 'in the woods' in search of sexual encounters. He is soon seen sitting on a park bench outside a public toilet, which does strangely resemble a rustic if rather dishevelled 'cottage'. Surrounded by trees and the sound of wildlife, the public lavatory appeared 'seedy' to *Time Out*, while *Gay Times* thought it looked 'like a sunny little homestead' (Parkes, 1999: 22). The cottage provides a vital social space for Steven, as he explains to the girl-next-door, Linda (Charlotte Brittain): 'where else am I supposed to meet other blokes like me?' It is also where he encounters John, the boy-in-the-cubicle-next-door. However, one of the most striking images in *Get Real* is that of the huge red-brick arch that frames the scene in which the boys negotiate a transitional point in their relationship following their first night together (John appearing Scudder-like in Steven's room).

A wide-shot through a railway arch introduces the location, presumably part of a Victorian viaduct on the fringes of the town. Its glowing red hues rise up the vertical borders of the frame to encapsulate a mise-en-scène of lush green trees swaying along the dusty path that meanders beyond and along which the two protagonists are approaching. While the summer sunshine is bright and direct, the light is photographed with a slightly diffuse glow, another of those shifts in cinematic register that renders a strangely ethereal air to the image, not unlike the scenes discussed in *Maurice* earlier. With the warm red walls against the sunlit trees, it is bizarrely as if this were the kind of picturesque ruin of a Roman palace or bath that would have intrigued Forster on his tours of Italy and that we see in the etchings found on the wall in Clive's home in Merchant Ivory's film, as he tries to consign his relationship with Maurice to the distant past of youthful misadventure, never to be mentioned again.[12] The shade under the arch gives a sense of seclusion, yet John's cry of alarm as Steven threatens to 'tell everyone' about their relationship suddenly echoes out, amplified by the architecture. The security of the setting is thus illusory, underscored by the vigorous breeze that blows the background foliage, reminding us that the radiant hues belie the decidedly cool air of a British summer. Cutting to a medium close-up in which the men are half-silhouetted in shade against the bright landscape behind, the men declare themselves a couple. The path behind them has been visible throughout this shot, and as they exchange a furtive kiss, a woman is seen glancing at them before she moves on, while they run out of the frame laughing. It is notable that each of the queer 'oases' under discussion are structured as to allow the possibility of interruption, though that does add that extra *frisson* of excitement to the activities undertaken therein.

'A passing benediction'

Also at a pivotal point in their relationship, the two protagonists of *Like it Is* (Paul Oremland, 1997) discover themselves at the shores of a secluded lake after driving their stolen Nissan out of the dark streets of London. Despite Matt's (Ian Rose) unsporting remark that it is 'too fucking cold for a swim', young bare-knuckle boxer Craig (Steve Bell) begins to strip and run towards the water in the early morning sun. The couple soon find refuge in a small boat that lies stranded on the shore next to the trees, and as the camera roves around their bodies we glimpse what appears to be semi-derelict boathouses beside them. This ramshackle landscape, where Craig finally comes to terms with his sexuality after an earlier, abortive attempt, might resemble the wreckage of Maurice and Scudder's love-nest, if it had been washed up in some outer London backwater. If the boathouse looks a little grubbier these days, times and landscapes have changed. Even when Forster looked back at unpublished work through two world wars in 1960: 'There is no forest or fell to escape to today', he notes, no 'deserted valley' either, 'people do still escape, one can see them any night at it in the films. But they are gangsters not outlaws, they can dodge civilization because they are part of it' (Forster, 1972: 221).

There seems to be a certain nostalgic impulse to recreate the greenwood environment to which Forster wistfully alludes and construct a discrete space to facilitate and 'legitimate' the homoerotic. There is evidently a need to avoid the gaze of a culture that would look upon it with the kind of disapproval embodied by Simcox, and those with considerably more power, too. Thus the very abstraction of these masquerades into the imaginative vestments of older and at least theoretically more tolerant cultures is hardly surprising. But as Tom Hutchinson argued in the case of *My Beautiful Laundrette*, such moments of 'surreality only emphasise the reality of the truth', that the titular laundrette is being shaped by the 'arid, acid world which is its context' (Hutchinson, 1985). The characters in these films make defiant performative gestures towards a mythically liberal classical past in order to transform and *dis-place* the cultural boundedness of the present. The dream-like spaces thus enacted through the (physical and imaginative) landscape disturb 'reality' as hysterical, but picturesque, reactions to intolerance.

As queer daydreams and not documents, the transient moments offered to characters and audiences alike in these films are obsolescent, much like the Sacred Lake itself. In Forster's novel the pool disappears almost as soon as the frolicking men leave it and return to 'civilisation', as if echoing its own detumescene with theirs: 'That evening the pool had shrunk to its old size and lost its glory. It had been a call to the blood and to the relaxed will, a passing benediction whose influence did not pass, a holiness, a spell, a momentary chalice for youth' (Forster, 1987: 152). Forster regretted the public's apparent contempt for homosexuality once it had come out into the open; if only 'it could be slipped into our midst unnoticed', he wrote (1972: 222).[13] I would suggest that the Sacred Lake scene did exactly that in creating a space in which one could obliquely fantasise, escape and even romp for a moment, but definitely not forget. As Dyer has argued, many heritage films demonstrate that gay 'identity had a past', and have used costume and the trappings of heritage to elucidate its constraints and contradictions (Dyer, 2002: 206). But it is also true that the queering of contemporary urban and suburban filmic spaces is no less contingent on the classical past than its Victorian and Edwardian literary antecedents. Indeed, all the more, as their classicism remains implicit and un-spoken, discovering a living, rude subterfuge in the vestiges – the bitter-sweet nostalgia – of the past. If only Forster could have seen it.

Notes

1 See Monk (1995) and Higson (2003) for a discussion of the Heritage debates and *RWAV* and the sexual 'radicalism' of the text. See also Williams (2004) for a more detailed discussion of the film's queer reception, particularly in respect to the Sacred Lake sequence.

2 A similar setting is also key to *Bedrooms and Hallways* (Rose Troche, 1998), as a group of men are led on a New Age camping exercise organised by Keith (Simon Callow), one man taking the opportunity to climb into another's tent and consolidate their developing queer relationship.

3 Dowling highlights that the ideal of martial virtue (the Latin 'Virtus' stems from 'Vir',

meaning male person) enjoyed a resurgence in fifteenth-century Florence, virtue celebrated by Uccello's romantic depiction of 'The Battle of San Romano' of 1432 which fascinates George in the short scene in the National Gallery.

4 In contrast, what we get in Cecil (Daniel Day Lewis), Lucy's fiancé, demonstrated in another scene by the lake when his heterosexual kiss is ridiculed, is a man who is inactive in his 'leisure', and consistently fails to participate in the homo-social pursuits of tennis or bathing. In Greek terms he is effeminate; Robert Aldrich goes so far as to call him 'an implicitly homosexual Wildean aesthete' (Aldrich, 1993: 95). By being pictured by Lucy only 'in a room', he is victim to the Greek prejudice towards women, whom society conspired to confine indoors.

5 Quote from Forster's 'Terminal Note' to the text, September 1960.

6 Bredbeck quotes from Robert K. Martin, 'Edward Carpenter and the Double Structure of *Maurice*' in *Journal of Homosexuality* 8.3/4 1983, 38.

7 Aldrich quotes from P.N. Furbank ed. (1977), *E.M. Forster: A Life* (vol. 1). London: Secker and Warburg, 110.

8 The boating motif is shared by Guy (Rupert Everett) in *Another Country* (Marek Kanievska, 1984), who spends a halcyon night lying in a punt in the Italianate grounds of his college with his blonde beau, James (Cary Elwes), his 'glorious vision'.

9 A. E. Housman's *A Shropshire Lad* and Samuel Butler's *The Way of all Flesh* are noted on the Emerson bookshelf at the villa, signposts, Eric Haralson notes, of Forster's 'own early readings' and a sign of the homoerotic parenthesis around the subsequent bathing scene (Haralson, 1997: 68).

10 John Gambril Nicholson, 'A Bather (for a painting by Edward Thomas)', *Love in Earnest: Sonnets, Ballades, and Lyrics*, 1892.

11 Paramount Classics official website for *Get Real*: http://www.paramountclassics.com/getreal/production_frame.html (downloaded 27 June 2003).

12 Italy also provides the final destination for self-destructive couple Oscar and Bosie (his 'golden youth', played by an Apolline Jude Law) in *Wilde* (Brian Gilbert, 1997), as Bosie fantasises about setting up a villa somewhere on the Amalfi coast after the playwright gets out of prison.

13 'Terminal Note', 1960.

Bibliography

Aldrich, R. (1993) *The Seduction of the Mediterranean: Writing, Art and Homosexual Fantasy*, London: Routledge.

Andrews, N. (1985) 'Britain, Washed and Spin-dried', *Financial Times*, 15 November, 23.

—— (1987) (review) *Financial Times* (weekend), 5 September, xvii.

Billsun, A. (1986) 'Just too Charming for Words', *Today*, 11 April, 24.

Bredbeck, G. W. (1997) '"Queer Superstitions": Forster, Carpenter, and the Illusion of (Sexual) Identity', in R. K. Martin and G. Piggford, *Queer Forster*, Chicago and London: University of Chicago Press, 29–58.

Cliff, N. (1999) Review of *Get Real, The Times*, 13 May, 43.

Davis, F. (1979) *Yearning for Yesterday: A Sociology of Nostalgia*, London: Collier Macmillan.

Davis, V. (1986) 'Lifting the Veil on a Dark Secret', *Mail on Sunday*, 9 November, 9.

Dover, K.J. (1978) *Greek Homosexuality*, London: Duckworth.

—— (2002) 'Classical Greek Attitudes to Sexuality' in Laura K. McClure ed., *Sexuality and Gender in the Classical World: Readings and Sources*, London: Blackwell, 19–33.

Dowling, L. (1994) *Hellenism and Homosexuality in Victorian Oxford*, London: Cornell University Press.

Dyer, R. (2002) 'Homosexuality and Heritage', in *The Culture of Queers*, London and New York: Routledge, 204–28.

Forster, E. M. (1972) *Maurice*, London: Penguin (completed 1914).

—— (1987) *A Room With a View*, London: Penguin (first published 1908).

Haralson, E. (1997) '"Thinking about Homosex" in Forster and James,' in R. K. Martin and G. Piggford, *Queer Forster*, Chicago and London: University of Chicago Press, 59–73.

Harvey, S. (1987) 'Men in Love', *Village Voice*, 22 September, 72.

Higson, A. (1996) 'Space, Place, Spectacle: Landscape and Townscape in the "Kitchen Sink" Film', in Andrew Higson ed., *Dissolving Views: Key Writings on British Cinema*, London: Cassell, 133–56.

—— (2003) *English Heritage Film*, London: Routledge.

Hollinghurst, A. (1987) 'Suppressive Nostalgia', *Times Literary Supplement*, 6 December, 225.

Hutchinson, T. (1985) 'Awash With the Way We Were', *Ham and Hide*, 15 November (unpaginated cutting, BFI library).

Johnston, T. (1999) 'Get Real', *Time Out*. 12–19 May, 24.

Kael, P. (1986) 'The Current Cinema: Twits, Turtles, Creeps', *The New Yorker*, 24 March, 112–15.

King, J. P. (1996) 'Crossing Thresholds: The Contemporary British Woman's Film', in Higson (1996), 216–31.

Kureshi, H. (2000) *My Beautiful Laundrette*, London: Faber and Faber (first published 1986).

Lelyveld, J. (1986) 'Forster's "Maurice" Becomes a Movie', *New York Times*, 12 November, 621.

Levine, J. P. (1996) 'The Functions of the Narrator's Voice in Literature and Film: Forster and Ivory's *Maurice*', *Literature/Film Quarterly*, vol. 24 n. 3, 309–21.

Lim, D. (1999) 'Get Real' (review), *Village Voice*, 4 May, 113.

Lowenthal, D. (1985) *The Past is a Foreign Country*, Cambridge: Cambridge University Press.

Martin, R. K. and Piggford, G. (1997) 'Introduction: Queer, Forster?,' in their *Queer Forster*, Chicago and London: University of Chicago Press, 1–28.

Meyers, J. (1977) *Homosexuality and Literature 1890–1930*, London: The Athlone Press/University of London.

Monk, C. (1995) 'Sexuality and the Heritage', *Sight and Sound*, October, 33–4.

Parkes, J. Cary (1999) 'From Reel to Real Lives', *Gay Times*, May, 20–6.

Pym, J. (1995) *Merchant Ivory's English Landscape: Rooms, Views, and Anglo-Saxon Attitudes*, London: Pavilion.

Quinn, A. (1999) Review of *Get Real*, 13 May, 10.

Robinson, D. (1985) 'Britain Cleans up at the Film Festival', *The Times*, 24 August, 7.

Sands, S. (1987) 'Maurice', *Vogue*, March, 12.

Schama, S. (1985) *Landscape and Memory*, London: Fontana Press.

Village Voice (1996) unattributed cutting, BFI library, 15 October, 72.

Walker, A. (1999) 'Coming Out in Front of the School', *Evening Standard*, 13 May, 31.

Waugh, T. (2000) *The Fruit Machine: Twenty Years of Writings on Queer Cinema*, Durham and London: Duke University Press.

White, C. ed. (1999) *Nineteenth-century Writings on Homosexuality: A Sourcebook*, London: Routledge.

Williams, M. (2004) 'Room For a Gay View?: Sexuality, Spectatorship and *A Room With A View*', in Jacqueline Furby and Karen Randell eds., *Screen Method: Comparative Readings in Screen Studies*, London: Wallflower Press.

8　Intermingling under controlled conditions

The queerness of *Prick Up Your Ears*

Kenneth MacKinnon

Presumably the term 'British Queer Cinema' derives ultimately from another, 'New Queer Cinema'. That label was created by B. Ruby Rich to describe the phenomenon in 1991 of a 'queer new wave', introduced at Toronto's Festival of Festivals that year. The year 1992 is taken by Rich to be a watershed for independent gay and lesbian film and video, for that was the year of Derek Jarman's *Edward II*, Christopher Munch's *The Hours and the Times*, Tom Kalin's *Swoon*, Gregg Araki's *The Living End* and Laurie Lynd's *R.S.V.P.* (Rich, 1993: 164).

A decade later, she alters her perception of a movement to that of a 'moment', one which caught a type of fresh, edgy film- and video-making. Her March 2000 *Sight and Sound* article takes New Queer Cinema as having transformed itself from radical impulse to niche market. Jarman is by now 'godfather' to New Queer Cinema. Her 2002 *Village Voice* essay goes on to declare that NQC lives on in all the gay film festivals around the world.

What, then, is or was queer about NQC? Is it reducible to films and videos about gay and lesbian 'issues', to homoerotic themes? Is it tantamount to largely independent, low-budgeted 'gay' moviemaking, however exactly defined? Michele Aaron talks of *Swoon* and *The Living End* as offering 'moving and powerfully seductive images of gay men and the aesthetic representation of passionate gay relationships' (Aaron, 1999: 68). Is that, then, the principal achievement of queer cinema?

The implicit invitation at times to see 'queer' as not only entirely sexual but tantamount to 'non-heterosexual' worries Pratibha Parmar, for example, who, wary of the tendency in queer discourses to create an essentialist 'queer gaze', declares, 'My sensibility comes as much from my culture and race as from my queerness' (Parmar, 1993: 175).

The Internet's *Qcinema* claims to review 'films which contain main or supporting characters who are identified as gay, lesbian, bisexual or transgender'. Yet, against this not infrequent tendency in many other such areas to conflate 'queer' with 'gay and lesbian', notice must be taken of Mark Simpson's determined opposing of 'queer' to 'gay'. Simpson claims to have liked the liberating strain of punkish aggression running through queer. Gay, on the other hand, did with queer what it had long accused the so-called straight world of doing, he believes. It suppressed the threatening elements. For Simpson, the gay/straight dichotomy is a cul-de-sac (Simpson, 1996: xv–xvii). Queer marks a distinct departure from both of these supposed binaries.

Queer theory, so-called, deriving ultimately from Michel Foucault through such gurus as Judith Butler and Eve Kosofsky Sedgwick, packs a considerable punch by undermining such old certainties as that dichotomy. It does so by its radical questioning of the 'reality' of such categories as 'gay' and 'straight' and by its emphasis on gender (and sexualities?) as *performative*, representing a set of learned behaviours rather than an immanent essence. Deborah Hunn identifies the critical and aesthetic trend of the 1990s to be towards 'queering sexuality', by, for example, the disarticulation of the homo/hetero binary (Hunn, 2000: 112). Thus, as it is challengingly described elsewhere, queer theory 'is no more "about" lesbians and gay men than Women's Studies is "about" women'. Rather, queer theory attacks the notion of the 'naturalness' of gender 'and by extension the fictions supporting compulsory heterosexuality'. Thus, in turn, queerness is located 'in places that had previously been thought of as strictly for the straights' (Burston and Richardson, 1995: 1). This theme is taken up with particularly striking effect by Alexander Doty, in relation to mass culture in general, rather than queer cinema, however identified. Typically, he questions 'the cultural demarcations between the queer and the straight' by pointing out 'the queerness of and in straights and straight cultures, as well as that of individuals and groups who have been told they inhabit the boundaries between the binaries of gender and sexuality' (Doty, 1993: xv–xvi).

One question to be asked therefore of British Queer Cinema, as it must be of New Queer Cinema, is whether one of its organising principles is a dismantling of the categories of 'gay' and 'straight'. Is its queerness radical enough to be recognisably Foucauldian? Or is the title just another example of the tendency to 'reclaim' the symbols and terms of gay oppression, as the wearing of pink triangles on the sleeves of the 'out and proud' is meant to achieve?

Subsidiary questions, inspired by the short history of New Queer Cinema, might include whether the sorts of film- and video-making embraced by the category extend to the commercial and mainstream. Again, is there something about the special use of 'queer' that highlights filmmaking of the 1990s as opposed to that of earlier decades? If so, concentration on Stephen Frears in the 1980s might seem unhelpfully contrary. Yet, his *My Beautiful Laundrette* (1986) takes a recognisably queer attitude to its central themes by handling the same-sex love affair between a Pakistani and ex-National Front white Brit in a highly unusual way. This unusualness could be boiled down to a refusal to foreground the categories of homo/hetero any more than those of Pakistani and white-British 'identities'. As one of the main characters declares, he is a professional businessman, 'not a professional Pakistani'.

Figure 8.1 A 'professional' love: Omar (Gordon Warnecke) and Johnny (Daniel Day-Lewis) in *My Beautiful Laundrette* (1985).

Source: Courtesy of Stephen Bourne (Working Title/Channel 4).

Laundrette partly fulfils Hanif Kureishi's wishes: 'I wanted the story to be about Asians, not about gays, so the gay relationship had to seem perfectly natural' (see Levy, 1999: 447). The film turns out indeed not to be about gays. Perhaps it is not about Asians either, at least with the implication of the distinctness of an Asian 'identity' or 'essence'.

Evans and Gamman, in attempting to come to grips with a notion of queer cinema, suggest, 'we want to make the case for identifications which are multiple, contradictory, shifting, oscillating, inconsistent and fluid' (Burston and Richardson, 1995: 45). Importantly, these multiple identifications are meant to unseat the confident primacy of heterosexuality. More crucially in the present context, a queer cinema by this description unseats the confident primacy of the so-called 'queer gaze' if that gaze be equated with a gay, lesbian, bisexual or transgendered perspective – straightforwardly so, because the categories of gay, lesbian and so on are themselves identifications with the oscillating tendencies listed above.

Michele Aaron takes as a significant aspect of *Heavenly Creatures* the film's refusal to pin down – or even to have its heroines offer a definition of – their meaning. The girls do not seem to find their meanings puzzling enough to investigate them. For Aaron, they 'can speak a language which the film and its viewers struggle to hear' (Aaron, 1999: 77). This is not to say, however, that other characters in the film do not in some other respects puzzle over and try to pin down the girls' meanings. They observe and try to make their own sense of them, much as their real-life murder trial inevitably had – literally – to judge them and thus venture an inter-pretation of them. The film's queerness resides less in having protagonists who are yet another queer couple who kill, to borrow Aaron's article's subtitle, than in its relating such categories as those it deals in to those who need to deploy them – the observers of the girls rather than the girls themselves. The film ultimately refuses to participate in the constructions placed by others on its heavenly creatures. Yet, it does not offer its own construction. It goes so far as to undermine confidence in the straightforward-seeming, and in that sense 'straight', categories of 'lesbian' as much as 'murderess'. It is on this understanding a very queer film, rather than just a film about queers.

This last example is useful as an explanation for the analysis of Stephen Frears' *Prick Up Your Ears* (1987) in ways that take it to be one of the queerest films ever made in the United Kingdom. If it deserves that title, it is not because it is about a male queer couple who kill (one apparently provoking the other to murder him and then himself). Its queerness resides in its opacity, the way that it keeps refusing to authenticate any one vision of Joe Orton and Kenneth Halliwell as the real McCoy. At the end of the film, truth remains elusive, half glimpsed. If problems of interpretation exist in relation to the central couple, their observers (Orton's literary agent, his sister, his biographer), those who seem to be our identification points if we are to reach the point of confident interpretation, are not allowed to be authoritative voices. This is true even though they do much of the speaking and

Figure 8.2 'Refusing to authenticate any one vision': Gary Oldman as Joe Orton in *Prick Up Your Ears* (1987).

Source: Courtesy of Stephen Bourne (Civilhand/Zenith Films).

allow the putative subjects' voices to be heard only through themselves. Born into an age which was yet to decriminalise homosexuality and whose conception of it depended largely on medical and juridical 'truths', Orton and Halliwell in this film create meanings for themselves, if they trouble to do so at all, from the impoverished models available to them. The meanings bestowed on them by their several observers are no more authenticated in the film than those that they see (and often fail to see) in their own lives.

If *Prick Up Your Ears* is at first glance the story of Joe Orton and of his life and death with Kenneth Halliwell, it is a story which is nearly always told by others, and above all by Orton's literary agent, Peggy Ramsay (Vanessa Redgrave). Whenever the tale appears to be sourceless and to be unfolding 'objectively' on screen, there will usually be a sudden comment on the soundtrack, reminding us that not just the details selected for the telling but the manner of the telling reflect the attitudes of a teller.

Early in the film, Orton (Gary Oldman) ceases listening to complaints from Halliwell (Alfred Molina) on the lift of a London tube and moves off to a quiet stairway with a young man he has just been eying up. At that point, the music turns as 'dark' as the shadows on the stairs. It reflects the restrained disapproval in Peggy's voice commenting on this moment as it happens in the film: 'According to the diary, a daily occurrence.' The couple's near embrace, which borders on the romantic, is swiftly brought down to the merely physical by the sound of a zip being lowered as tubes rumble by in the distance. The visuals are not exactly qualified and corrected by the soundtrack. All the same, that track reminds us that the visuals too are projections from others' imaginations.

Peggy clearly wishes to appear worldly-wise when she later uses the insider gay-British term, 'cottages' in conversation with Orton's future biographer, John Lahr (Wallace Shawn), in reference to men's public lavatories. Each resolutely refuses to let any discomfort with the information show. Instead, Lahr informs her that in the USA the word is 'T-room'. Peggy asks if he has ever noticed 'anything going on'. No answer is given. The brief exchange suggests perhaps that her confidence on the topic of cruising grounds and rituals is less justified than it appears to be. If she is to be the biographer's, and then our, best information source, then that source is uncertain and flawed.

In an earlier scene where she is dining with Mr and Mrs Lahr, Peggy tells them of Joe's first sexual encounter in a cinema at the age of 14. 'He came all down the man's raincoat', she remarks, and adds as if she had just offered the most matter-of-fact observation, 'Lovely melon!' This is not the equivalent of Orton's insouciance about his sexual promiscuity, whether that be interpreted as innocence or amorality. It sounds like self-conscious daring. Her adamant refusal to be shocked means that she projects on to her silent auditors so that she can disavow any discomfort by making it theirs.

Whether or not this is a persuasive analysis of these sequences, it is surely uncontroversial to suggest that in this film neither Orton nor Halliwell speaks for himself but is largely spoken for, scripted and authored by other figures. Moreover, these figures who comment on their relationship, on Orton's fleeting sexual encounters, Halliwell's physical unattractiveness and neurotic nagging, do not appear to have had homosexual experience. (At this juncture, it could be noted that

Kenneth Williams, for example, is strikingly absent as a character although he might have been a credible spokesperson for the Moroccan holiday.) They learn what they believe that they know about homosexuality from such sources as Orton's personal journal – which seems on this evidence to be less sober authority than Wilde's notion of something sensational to read on the train. Why else would Orton keep expressing surprise that Halliwell has not secretly read his diary? Why would Halliwell expect the final bludgeoning of his long-term partner to be 'understood' if the diaries were read?

As if underlining the flawed authority of the narrative's sources, the structure is unusually complex. The recounting starts at the end, with the discovery of the corpses and Peggy's snatching of the diaries. Rapidly thereafter we are in 1964, with Peggy narrating her first encounter with the writer, then in 1967, when London, according to her, was 'still quite exciting'. We may be deluded into thinking that we are eavesdropping on Halliwell and Orton bickering in their flat until suddenly Peggy's voice on the soundrack tells us, 'They lived in Islington.' – 'An apartment?' asks Lahr. – 'Hardly. It was a cupboard.'

We go to Leicester with John Lahr and suddenly we hear Orton's sister Leonie talking to Lahr about his earlier life at home. We are back in the 1950s, with John Orton (not yet christened Joe) entering the Royal Academy of Dramatic Art, meeting Kenneth, taking in the Festival of Britain with a night on the South Bank still with his girlfriend of the time, finally settling into Kenneth's rented flat and 'beginning a new era' in bed with him to the sounds of Elizabeth II's Coronation on a tiny flickering black-and-white television. Even then, we return to Leonie's home for an argument from her husband about the imagined origins of his brother-in-law's homosexuality: 'He couldn't have learned it in Leicester. He was corrupted.' Then back to Islington on Coronation Day. The speed of some transitions is dizzying.

Even at the end of the convoluted tale, the last words are given to Peggy and to Leonie's husband. The ostensible subjects of the film are reduced literally to ashes. Leonie is trying to conjoin the ashes of the separately cremated pair and worries that she has 'too much of Joe' in the mixture. 'It's a gesture, dear, not a recipe', Peggy comments archly. As if to remind us that understanding of both these figures has been handed over to well-intentioned but partial observers, this exchange is preceded by an official intervention of a kind trenchantly satirised in Orton's plays. A literally faceless bureaucrat – faceless in that he keeps his back to the camera – pronounces: 'Strictly speaking, we would have preferred it if both the deceased had been cremated on the premises. Intermingling would then have been carried out by experienced personnel under controlled conditions.' The protagonists who up till then have had their actions, speeches and motivations interpreted and thus controlled by Peggy, Leonie, Lahr, are now distanced from us still further by the voice of officialdom, which apparently has authority even over these interpreters.

This is a productive metaphor for the way that the then criminal status of male homosexual activity rested on 'understanding' of 'the homosexual condition' by psychiatrists, and that that understanding was in turn disseminated among those that here tell their story. The absurd library 'detective' who lands the pair in court where they are given a jail sentence recognises with revulsion that one (!) of them is 'a nancy . . . a ho-mo-sexual . . . a shirt-lifter'. An only slight less caricatured prison psychiatrist imparts to Orton the shocking news, 'I suspect your friend may be a homosexual.' – 'Jesus,' the prisoner responds, 'and there I am sleeping in the same room as him.' – The psychiatrist unhesitatingly believes whatever fictions Joe, the presumed heterosexual, tells him. 'Your friend's not like that,' he explains to Halliwell while in prison. 'He's married. He's got a child.'

When the experts and authority figures are as gullible and prejudiced as these men, surely Frears's film signals the unwisdom of trusting anybody who claims to speak for the pair, and in particular for their sexuality.

The complaints about unfairness in the film's depiction of Halliwell may be off the point. The film sows doubts about its own apparent refusal of credibility to Halliwell's claims that he inspired the successful playwright. What, for example, seems like proof of Orton's wit and originality when he tells Peggy, 'Cheap clothes suit me. They always have. It's because I'm from the gutter', later proves to be no such thing. It is exactly what Halliwell says of Orton early in their relationship.

The collages which the couple make when they deface library books, or which Halliwell attempts to sell as examples of his art, are what they themselves become in the film. A detail is taken from one person and affixed to another from another until a composite is built up. Hal Hinson, in his review of the film for the *Washington Post*, complains because the filmmakers 'seem not to have known exactly what to make of their subject. He remains the sum of what he's not.' The analysis is spot on, although the value judgement is not. It may be precisely the strength of Frears's film that in a pre-legalisation epoch both Orton and Halliwell cannot be authenticated, because the prism through which they are observed by those who would express them for posterity is their believed sexuality, and that sexuality is defined by a world that takes care to declare that it is untainted by it and paradoxically has no knowledge of it. Is it any surprise that not the filmmakers but the experts within the film fail to know exactly what to make of their subjects but insist nonetheless on the sense that they do make of them?

Alan Bennett has chosen to gift his figures of authority, particularly the police, with Ortonesque speech or behaviour. 'If there's damage to be done, call the police. That's their job', the landlady Mrs Sugden (Janet Dale) is told by her husband when she suggests breaking the flat door down. 'Dear oh dear oh dear. Somebody here's been playing silly buggers', one of the police says on discovery of the bodies.

Mrs Sugden is repeatedly rendered as a figure of Orton farce. 'You're halfway to being a household word,' she gushes to the celebrity, adding, 'Don't look at me. I'm not washed.' When asked if one of the dead men is bald, she responds, 'No. He wears a wig.' 'My vagina came up like a football', she recalls while telling her tenants of an accident with a spilled hot drink. Mrs Orton (Julie Walters) is recognisably kin to this character. 'This is my husband,' she tells her visitor from the council. 'Ignore him.'

When Joe first joins Kenneth, he expresses himself with naïve formality. 'Can you spell?', he is asked. – 'Yes, but not accurately.' 'Hotels are a closed book to me', says the Festival of Britain Joe. At this stage in his life, he prefers 'sexual intercourse' to Kenneth's 'fucking'. The film seems here to authenticate the notion that later is treated with such disdain – that Joe had a mentor, of language and style, in Kenneth. Even when Halliwell has entered his depressed period, his command of sardonic wit is admitted by Orton himself. Tersely ordered to masturbate when he seeks some form of physical satisfaction from Joe, he remonstrates as follows: 'Have a wank?! I need three days' notice. . . . Forces have to be assembled, magazines bought, the past dredged for some suitable unsavoury episode which can still produce a faint flicker of desire. It would be easier to raise the Titanic.' His command of rhetoric casts doubt on the way that the tellers of Joe's story try to depict Kenneth as a drag on the writer's spirit. He even tops Joe on occasions. At the wig-fitting, for instance, Joe says, 'This is on me', in reference to the cost. 'And this is on me', adds Kenneth, referring to the wig itself.

The casting of Joe as the free-spirited 'original' to Kenneth's clinging, dowdy second-rater is not the film's work, then, so much as that of the story's tellers. The mystery of their life together seems to be oversimplified, unsatisfactorily explained. Perhaps that is unsurprising when their sexuality is treated as a repulsive no-go area by bureaucrats and, at best, a source of titillated fascination by their acquaintances and would-be biographer. Lahr follows Peggy's lead in this. For them, Kenneth is the wife, Joe the husband – and, in a moment of unreflecting hubris, Peggy goes so far as to cast herself as the widow.

Left to himself, by contrast, Joe is supremely confident about the rituals of casual sex. The moment of cottaging at the Hampstead terminus of the 24 bus route becomes almost magical, balletic, enticingly low-lit rather than sleazily dark. There, and against the sunlit vistas of Moroccan beaches, homosexuality is allowed to be exhilarating and uncomplicated in the way that it presumably must have seemed to Orton when it was not being mediated by or to Peggy Ramsay and company, and not being argued about (corruption or collaboration?) by such 'experts' as his brother-in-law or John Lahr. His ridicule of the whole edifice of the law on homosexuality as criminal is encapsulated in the scene where he informs Kenneth that he alone should be imprisoned since Joe himself, being under age at the time, is 'the innocent party'. Their laughter at this mode of thinking is by implication at the expense of the po-faced outsiders who presume to judge them and their pleasures. Yet, the scrutinised are infected by the stereotypes of the scrutinisers. 'We girls must stick together', opines an effusively camp art critic. When Joe and Kenneth are reduced to physical fighting, their open-handed slaps are notably 'girlie'. Joe catches himself uncomfortably reflected in multiple bedroom mirrors, when Leonie casually mentions, 'It's amazing how many writers are queer.' His subsequent dalliance with a 'rough trade' workman, in which he can play whatever part he chooses to adopt for himself, is experienced as a relief, a juxtaposed antidote to the prescriptions that his family seems to need when contemplating him.

If Peggy insists on attempting to understand Orton's relationship with Halliwell and indeed with herself in terms of conventional marriage, it is remarkable how heterosexual marriage is debunked and hollowed out within the same film. The Lahrs in particular are a somewhat dysfunctional pair, she always on the point of explosive resentment, he bumbling along, failing to notice the obvious clues as to his wife's exasperation. When the film first takes the audience down the stairs into their kitchen, it looks for a moment as if it is the Islington flat that we are entering. Mrs Lahr (Lindsay Duncan) is apparently taken for granted as cook and house-keeper, much as Kenneth complains that he is. 'Any calls?', her husband enquires. Notably, he receives no answer. Later, she seems to relax visibly with Leonie and to share her amusement at her husband's bizarre thinking on sex. 'I don't care what men get up to', Leonie declares. Anthea Lahr adds, 'I don't care where they put it', to which Leonie responds, 'As long as they don't put it here'.

In voiceover in relation to the award evening, Peggy tells John Lahr, 'At moments of triumph, men can do without their wives'. Lahr agrees: 'They cramp our style.' 'But,' continues Peggy, 'sharing is what wives want.' So they demean Kenneth Halliwell with their 'understanding', and enter into complicity to lessen Anthea Lahr too. These experts on Halliwell's 'wifely' psychology have earlier taken turns to patronise Mrs Lahr. While she is preparing and serving dinner, she is largely ignored. Peggy's only genuinely interested question of her is, 'Do you type?' Later, when Anthea telephones Peggy for help with the diaries' shorthand, the latter gives her none.

In fact, it is hard to understand the general critical consensus, inspired possibly by nostalgic affection for Redgrave as, in her *Blow Up* period, one of the most enduring icons of the 1960s, that Peggy is a warm, wise character. The evidence is rather that she is a misogynist, casting blame unfairly on her secretary, whom she later characterises as 'slut' for no clear reason, patronising Halliwell ('This is our Be Kind to Ken evening') as readily as she ignores Anthea Lahr. Her insincerity to Ken – she automatically lies to him about Orton's whereabouts when the latter seeks temporary sanctuary with her – is matched by the picture she paints of herself as understanding 'other woman'. 'Ken was the first wife', she confidently pronounces. – 'What does that make you?', Lahr asks, not unreasonably, since we are given no insight into Peggy's personal life throughout the film even though she keeps interpreting the central pair to anybody who will listen. 'The second wife?' – No such modest role for her, though. 'Better than that, dear. The widow.'

A mark of the film's inscription of distance between subject and receivers is the sense that the story seems to take place in a period and place different from London of the 1950s and 1960s. Brian Epstein and the Beatles are figures in Orton's life as recounted here, and there is a quotation from the Sergeant Pepper album's 'A Day in the Life' on the soundtrack as the final credits roll. Yet, what might be the expected recreation of a much-filmed period to emphasise the 'swinging London' to which Orton manifestly contributed in actuality seldom happens.

The movie opens with the title, bracketed by double inverted commas, in white lettering against a black background. The music behind the opening credits is more Kurt Weill than Burt Bacharach. Coupled with the expressionist lighting – pools of darkness contrasted with blinding light from under the Noel Road flat's door – the opening of the movie suggests both a period and place (Isherwood's Berlin?) other than the expected, and seems also to promise a film noir. Noirish visuals reappear in the behind-the-scenes sequences at the Islington public library, 1930s' saxophone music is heard in some of the cruising scenes. When they travel to Morocco, where the blinding light becomes the whiteness of young men's jellabas, the soundtrack song appears to be culled from the beach sequences of Billy Wilder's *Some Like It Hot* with its 1920s setting.

The refusal to participate in the 1960s' chosen self-image of neocracy and liberation is a mark of the Frears film's clear-eyed recognition of the power that that period, with its authority figures and attitudes, has to interpret what it has chosen to focus on – and at the same time of its refusal to grant any easy access to objectivity or truth. It queers the tale and the telling.

In one of the most poignant moments of the film, Halliwell calls out, after the murder, 'Joe? – John?' Orton has told him just prior to his violent demise, 'I'm not John. John's dead.' Yet, at this point, when it makes no sense for his killer to invoke either persona, he still wonders which is the real Orton. We too are left asking questions about the man in John Lahr's biography, the versions of him created by Peggy Ramsay or Leonie Orton, and even the version of himself penned by Orton in those diaries.

The triumph of *Prick Up Your Ears* is that it is less a film about queers than a pervasively disorienting narration that has fully earned the description of 'queer'.

Bibliography

Aaron, M. (1999) ''Til death us do part: cinema's queer couples who kill'. In Aaron, Michele (ed.), *The Body's Perilous Pleasures: Dangerous Desires and Contemporary Culture*, Edinburgh: Edinburgh University Press.

Burston, P. and Richardson, C. (eds.) (1995) *A Queer Romance: Lesbians, Gay Men and Popular Culture*, London: Routledge.

Doty, A. (1993) *Making Things Perfectly Queer: Interpreting Mass Culture*, Minneapolis: University of Minnesota Press.

Gever, M., Parmar, P. and Greyson, J. (eds.) (1993) *Queer Looks: Perspectives on Lesbian and Gay Film and Video*, New York: Routledge.

Hunn, D. (2000) '"It's not that I can't decide: I don't like definitions!": queer in Australia in Christos Tsiolkas's *Loaded* and Ana Kokkinos's *Head On*'. In Alderson, D. and Anderson, L. (eds.), *Territories of Desire in Queer Culture: Refiguring Contemporary Boundaries*, Manchester: Manchester University Press.

Levy, E. (1999) *Cinema of Outsiders: The Rise of American Independent Film*, New York and London: New York University Press.

MacKinnon, K. (1992) *The Politics of Popular Representation: Reagan Thatcher, AIDS and the Movies*, Madison, NJ: Fairleigh Dickinson University Press.

Parmar, P. (1993) 'Queer questions: a response to B. Ruby Rich'. In Cook, P. and Dodd, P. (eds.), *Women and Film: A Sight and Sound Reader*, London: Scarlet Press.

QCINEMA (n.d.) *Qcinema: Queer Film Reviews and Queer People in Film.* http://www.qcinema.com/.

Rich, B. R. (1993) 'Homo Pomo: the new queer cinema'. In Cook, P. and Dodd, P. (eds.), *Women and Film: A Sight and Sound Reader*, London: Scarlet Press.

Rich, B. R. (2000) 'Queer and present danger'. *Sight and Sound*, March.

Rich, B. R. (2002) 'Vision quest'. *Village Voice*, 20–26 March.

Sedgwick, E. K. (1991) *Epistemology of the Closet*, Harmondsworth: Penguin.

Simpson, M. (ed.) (1996) *Anti-gay*, London: Freedom Editions.

Warren, S. (2003) 'Queer go deeper in "02"'. *Southern Voice*, 8 January.

9 Terence Davies and the *Unheimlich* home movie

Jim Ellis

Even though I'm the youngest of ten children and loved my mother, especially, and my sisters and brothers very much, I still felt as though I was looking in on something. And that was exacerbated by the fact that I then discovered in puberty that I am gay and hated it – I will go to my grave hating it. And then I grew up listening to my family talk about the way my father had treated us, and so I became actively passive, someone who was always observing.

(Terence Davies)[1]

For most gay men, the home movie is a gothic genre. This is not so much because it records the violence of the family, physical or psychological, or any of the other terrors of childhood. On the contrary: for the most part, the home movie produces the effect of the uncanny precisely because it does not record these torments, or even simple unhappiness. At the centre of the movie stands an unrecognisable version of the self, typically smiling: 'the double is "the same as me," yet totally strange; his sameness all the more accentuates his uncanniness.'[2] This distance between childhood as experienced or remembered and childhood as recorded is analogous to the distance often felt in childhood between the gay child and its own family. Some inchoate knowledge of difference prevents the child from feeling fully part of the events that surround it; family activities are viewed with a partial sense of detachment, as if they were unfolding cinematically, 'as though I was looking in on something', as Davies says. This is the case even when, perhaps especially when, participation and belonging are enthusiastically performed. In that regard, the uncanny home movie renders gay childhood perfectly.

In this chapter, I will be looking at Terence Davies's home movies, although I'm using the term 'home movie' rather loosely. Davies's frequent returns to his childhood, while occupying the same psychic terrain of the genre, are not documentary, at least not in the usual sense. Moreover, the home movie was a middle-class genre, while the life recorded in Davies's films is resolutely working class. The true working-class genre, at least according to these films, is the Hollywood musical or melodrama. Nonetheless, in the fragmentary, non-narrative structure of the films and their attempt to convey unmediated experience of family life, Davies offers us an aesthetically sophisticated meditation on the appeal (in both senses) of the more humble genre.

Davies's first three short films, *Children* (1976), *Madonna & Child* (1980) and *Death & Transfiguration* (1983), collectively known as *The Terence Davies Trilogy*, follow the life of Robert Tucker who, like Davies himself, is a working-class gay man from Liverpool. *Distant Voices, Still Lives* (1988) is a non-narrative portrait of a working-class Liverpool family in the 1950s; in this film, it is the camera, rather than a particular character, that is a stand-in for Davies. *The Long Day Closes* (1992) returns to the same terrain and a similar family, but is now centred on the youngest son in the family, Bud. This film, which lacks the physical violence of the earlier films, has occasionally been characterised as sentimental, particularly in its retailing of certain stereotypes of working-class life;[3] other critics have questioned whether Davies's approach to history is conservative or not, post-modern historiographic metafiction or nostalgic pastiche.[4] These questions about history are to some degree misplaced. While Davies is certainly interested in a kind of history, it is a 'memory realism' (as designer Christopher Hobbs puts it) that the films strive for, not an accurate documentation of post-war Liverpool working-class life.[5] In other words, Davies's films are set in the past because that's when his childhood happened, not because he's making a period film; the trappings of the past – the songs, the movies, the dresses – are important only insofar as they were, for that child, the material supports of fantasy, the elements of the particular psychic terrain that the films are interested in exploring. This attentiveness to the way in which material culture figures so profoundly in psychic life is, indeed, what makes Davies's psychological explorations so acute and so compelling.

Thomas Elsaesser remarks that *Distant Voices, Still Lives* 'is quite a complex "psychoanalytic" narrative, insofar as it is a drama of identifications, of a subjectivity refusing to settle into an identity and hence pervasive and unfocused on a single character'.[6] Following Elsaesser's insight, I will be looking at the fable of subjectivity that this group of films offers. Focusing on the brutality in the films, critics have looked at such things as trauma and masochism, particularly in relation to individual characters;[7] few, surprisingly, have focused on gay identity, although Armond White calls *The Long Day Closes* 'the first great movie about an explicitly gay child'.[8] The violence of family life is certainly central to these films, but they are equally interested in the role of popular art, particularly film and song, in the everyday. Moreover, the films themselves are highly formalistic attempts at rendering the fabric of consciousness; they are, to use Christopher Williams's terms, 'social art films', rather than social realism.[9] While Davies's evocations of memory offer a portrait of working-class family life, more crucially they tell a general story about the role of fantasy both in the construction of subjectivity and in the fabric of the everyday.

'I want my dad'

The split between the remembered and the pictured, or between family life as lived and the fantasy of the happy family, is dramatised in the opening sequences of Davies's *Distant Voices, Still Lives*. A family group stands facing the camera, dressed in black. The camera tracks towards them as they stand to leave, and then continues tracking in on a picture of the father, whose funeral they are about to attend, on the wall behind them.[10] After an exterior shot of them leaving with the hearse, the initial grouping is echoed in a shot of the same family on the morning of a wedding; the two scenes are linked by the soundtrack, on which Jessye Norman sings 'There's a Man Goin' Round Takin' Names'. The bride, Eileen, says 'I wish me dad was here'. We then hear her sister Maisie's thoughts in a voice-over, saying 'I don't. He was a bastard and I bleedin' hated him!' In the following sequence we see why, as he beats her with a yard brush while she scrubs the cellar floor. Her screams carry over into the next shot, where we have returned to the wedding party, with Eileen turning to her brother Tony to say, 'I don't half wish me Dad was here'. This is followed by some of Tony's horrific memories of his father.

The brutal father of *Distant Voices*, who we see beating both the mother and Maisie, throwing his young son out of the family home, and slapping the young

Figure 9.1 'Please say that you love me, Dad': the fantasy of the loving father, Pete Postlethwaite, in *Distant Voices, Still Lives* (1988).

Source: Courtesy of Stephen Bourne (BFI/Channel 4).

Eileen, is another version of the father we see in *Children*, the first film in the *Trilogy*. This father, who is similarly called Tommy, is also seen beating his wife and heaping scorn on his young son. Much like Maisie, the boy Tucker in this film declares after his father dies, 'The bastard's dead . . . we're free, Mam'. Nevertheless, not much later in the film the adult Tucker, ten or fifteen years older, is heard in a voice-over saying, 'Dad . . . Dad . . . please say that you love me, Dad'. In spite of whatever evidence memory might offer, the fantasy of the loving father still holds promise.

Childhood in Davies's early films (up to and including the non-autobiographical *Neon Bible* [1995]) is marked by two traumas: a brutalising father and the appearance of adult sexuality. The first line uttered in *Children* is a schoolyard taunt, 'Hey . . . who's a fruit then? . . . hey?' which sets the tone for much of what follows. This fusion of sexuality and torment will run like an electrifying current through all of Davies's films, principally through the twinning of the central traumas – the father and sexuality. We first encounter the father when the boy Tucker returns home after being chased by bullies. The father's groans are heard from off screen, and it is at first unclear whether he is having sex or is in pain. We then see the father rolling around the floor in agony, as Tucker looks on in horror. A nurse wrestles him onto the bed, undoes his underwear, and savagely jabs an injection into his buttock. As the father howls in outrage, he notices Tucker watching and shouts, 'How long has he been there? GET OUT'. The nurse ominously replies, 'He'll see worse'. The script reads that Tucker is 'both horrified and fascinated'.[11] This, at least for the *Trilogy*, would appear to be the Freudian primal scene, in which the primary elements of Tucker's sexuality coalesce; sex will for him be bound up with brutality and humiliation, split off completely from his romantic idealisation of muscular young men.[12] Significantly, the mother is absent from this particular primal scene, and thus is left untouched by the taint of sexuality. In Davies's films, the trauma of the father *is* to some degree the trauma of sexuality.

Because Davies's films are structured as memories, the father here is the father from the perspective of the child. It is no doubt significant that he is identified in the credits as 'Father', just as the mother is 'Mother'. He is a fantasy figure, in other words, although *Distant Voices, Still Lives* gives us occasional glimpses that he had an autonomous existence beyond the terrifying role he most often plays in the context of the family. In one scene, for example, we see the children hiding, watching in fascination as he whistles and grooms his horse; Eileen's friend Monica, because she is outside the family, can tease 'Mr D' and get the girls permission to go dancing.[13] For the most part, however, he is the Father. Although he is dead from the beginning of the film, he haunts the two marriages that frame it, Eileen's and Tony's, his photograph in the parlour looming in the background of the two wedding groups. Both Eileen and Tony are seen crying on their wedding days, both apparently for the same reason. In Eileen's case, she sobs repeatedly, 'I want my dad'; while Tony is crying on the step, 'Oh Mein Papa', is heard on a record from inside the house. In a line from the script, which is cut from the film, Eileen revealingly says: 'I know my dad was bad – I know that – but I always try and think of the good times – like Christmas'. In the film, we see him inexplicably destroying Christmas dinner. What the children in the films mourn, then, is not the father that they had, but the idea of a father, one that corresponds to the home movie fantasy of the happy family. What they are mourning is not the loss of the actual father, but the loss of a fantasy that made the traumas of existence more tolerable. Not coincidentally, this mourning occurs not with the death of the actual father, but with the arrival of sex, in the form of marriage.

The split between the father as remembered and the father the characters long for alerts us to the fact that there are two distinct paternal fantasies in play. The father in Davies's films does not function as what Lacan terms the 'paternal metaphor', a representative of the Symbolic Father. This is the figure that is the guarantor of the law, 'whose fundamental feature is not an open display of power but the threat of potential power'.[14] Far from being a bar to reproduction, the intervention of the paternal metaphor is necessary for there to be any relation between the sexes. (The longing in the films for this particular figure is what no doubt accounts for the charges of conservatism on the part of critics.) On the contrary, the father here is spectacularly lawless, violent and brutal. He figures instead as what Slavoj Žižek calls the obscene father, the perverse figure of enjoyment who, unlike the paternal metaphor, is excessively present. It is the decline of the paternal metaphor in Davies's films that renders sexuality traumatic: haunted, as it is, by the obscene father.

The death of the actual father in the films does not effect his disappearance from the realm of fantasy; his death, far from healing wounds, results in a further fracturing of reality. We see this, for example, in the split between Maisie's silence at Eileen's wedding and the voice-over in which she professes her hatred for her father. A more frequent version of this splitting is seen in the use of songs. In this film, as in most of Davies's, song is used to carry much of the emotional and narrative burden. In the pub, Eileen sings 'Brown-skinned Girl', a song about murdering one's husband, while sitting beside her domineering husband Dave. (Dad, as it turns out, was at the wedding after all.) Later, rather than continue an argument with him, she sings a sad, defiant version of 'I Want To Be Around [to pick up the pieces, when somebody breaks your heart]'. This kind of split occurs in relation to more positive emotions as well; a shot of Tony looking lovingly at his mother while she scrubs the front step dissolves into a scene of him singing 'I Want a Girl [just like the girl, that married dear old dad]'.

This is not to suggest that Davies is writing a musical, in which the characters express their emotions in song (although in fact it has been called 'the first realist musical').[15] In the sequence just mentioned, there is a break in time between Tony looking at his mother, and Tony singing in the pub. Except for the violent or abusive husbands and fathers, the characters in these films for the most part experience emotions only in a displaced way: through the songs they sing, the radio dramas they listen to, or the films they watch (Maisie and Elaine are seen sobbing at the conclusion of *Love is a Many-Splendored Thing*). It is the film that makes the connections between their lives and these emotions, not the damaged characters themselves, who cope with their lives through a form of dissociation. The film mimics this process of dissociation both through the songs, which continue on the soundtrack after the scene has shifted, and also through one of the most characteristic of Davies's formal devices, a long, slow tracking shot. These two elements are often connected: the scene shifts, the song continues, and the camera tracks across the exterior of a building. These often work as point of view shots, but in a particular way. Because the structure of the films is suggestive of the operations of memory, these shots suggest a detachment from the events they are witnessing. The camera's attention drifts away from an emotionally charged scene, preferring instead to calmly contemplate artefacts of the material world.

'Take us in, Mister?'

The separation between the image and the soundtrack is used to fullest effect in *The Long Day Closes*. This is the last of Davies's returns to his Liverpool childhood, and it acts as a culmination of many of the elements of the previous films. The family configuration has changed in this film: in addition to the twelve-year-old Bud, there are two older brothers and two older sisters in their late teens or early twenties. The father is completely absent from the film, which accounts for the generally sunnier tone of the film. Whereas *Distant Voices, Still Lives* did not make explicit whose memory it was, this film clearly acts as the memory of the central character, Bud, who is another version of Tucker from *The Terence Davies Trilogy*. In *Distant Voices* the songs on the soundtrack cannot always be tied to a particular character or moment; in *The Long Day Closes* they function as aural fragments from Bud's childhood. At the same time, the connection between the soundtrack and the image is generally looser in the latter film; when we hear Debbie Reynolds singing as he swings on a bar in front of the house, we understand that it is from a movie he heard at some other time.

   Although the father is absent from the film, there are moments when he seems to haunt it. Bud sits in his mother's lap as she sings a song that she says her father used to sing; that night, Bud has a nightmare in which a man's hands reach out from the wall and grab his head. He wakes up screaming, 'It was a man. It was a *man*!' In the script, the man's hands are identified as those of a labourer Bud has earlier been gazing at; in the film, they cannot be so clearly identified and seem instead to refer back to the absent father (or, the two simply are fused: 'a man'). The father's arbitrary cruelty in the earlier films is in this film displaced onto a series of authority figures, from the teacher, Mr Nicholls, who beats the boys 'to show [them] who's boss', to the sadistic Games Master, who shouts at Bud in the changing cubicle, 'Come on! Hurry up! We all know what you're trying to hide!'

It is not clear that Bud is fully aware of what it is he is trying to hide; like the young Tucker, he is obviously uncomfortable with his dawning sexuality, which evokes in him the same responses of horror and fascination. Bud's discomfort is established early in the film, when we see him watching a muscular, shirtless labourer through a window. The labourer notices him and winks, and Bud's face registers a queasy look as he slowly averts his eyes and slides away from the window. A few scenes later we see him inside the house watching another muscular young man at a bonfire on Guy Fawkes' Day, the flames colouring both Bud and the man. Further on in the film, when praying in church, Bud has a vision of Christ on the cross who, it turns out, is the shirtless labourer. Sexuality comes to be quite literally associated with torture, violence and sins of or against the Father. And as for Tucker, for Bud the torments of sexuality are not merely psychological. In the schoolyard, Bud is bullied and beaten by other boys, one of whom taunts him with the jibe from *Children*, 'who's a fruit then, eh?'

As in the earlier films, sexuality is experienced as trauma, connected with the father. As Wendy Everett observes, it is sexuality that threatens to divide Bud from his childhood, his cherished mother, and his brothers and sisters.[16] In this film, heterosexuality is, for the most part, shorn of the tragic elements that dog it in *Distant Voices, Still Lives*. Bud's older brothers and sisters are frequently seen preparing for dances, walking hand-in-hand with dates, or bicycling off on trips, literally and figuratively leaving Bud behind. For the film, childhood is a brief Eden. We see this established early on in a communal New Year's Eve celebration on the street: over the dancing and singing we hear Orson Welles intoning from the soundtrack of *The Magnificent Ambersons* that 'this pageant of the tenantry was the last of the great remembered dances that everybody was to talk about'. What remains for Bud is decay. After his siblings depart for one of their courting rituals, he descends to the coal cellar. On the soundtrack we hear a montage of sound clips including Miss Haversham from *Great Expectations* talking about her mouldering wedding cake, Orson Welles relating the decline of the Ambersons, and a fragment from Mr Nicholls's lecture on erosion ('life also cooperates in the work of destruction', he has told the boys earlier). The long day that is closing is Bud's childhood, and what follows for the gay child, the film suggests, is as grim as Tucker's solitary end in *Death and Transfiguration*.

Bud responds by holding himself apart from his family and the world. He is frequently filmed framed in windows or doorways, observing rather than participating in the action. This separation is taken even further when he catches sight of his own reflection in a window, and we see him watching himself watching his sister. In one of the few scenes where he joins in a sing-a-long with the adults, he is separated from the crowd by performing his song in the doorway, accompanied by his protective sister Helen; the doorway functions as a miniature proscenium arch, and the reverse shot further divides Bud and his sister from the rest of the room. An early shot of him with his arms folded on the window ledge, looking out

Figure 9.2 'The tormented adolescent who lives life vicariously through the arts'? Leigh
McCormack as Bud in *The Long Day Closes* (1992).

Source: Courtesy of Stephen Bourne (BFI/FilmFour/Palace).

of the window, is echoed by a later one of him in the cinema, arms crossed on the
edge of the balcony. This works to suggest that Bud's relation to the world around
him is not much different than his relation to the movies that he watches; if the
soundtrack is any indication, it is in the cinematic fantasies where his fullest
emotional life is lived.

  This relation to the world is brilliantly evoked in one of the film's tour-de-force
sequences, a series of tracking shots that dissolve into each other. From directly
overhead we look down on Bud swinging back and forth on a bar that hangs over
the cellar steps outside his house. The camera tracks left, and the image dissolves
into that of a cinema, where the camera continues to track in the same direction,
directly above the heads of the spectators. It follows, appropriately enough, the
beam of projection. We move in a similar fashion from the cinema, to the church,
to the classroom, and finally back to the stairwell, now empty. On the soundtrack
throughout the sequence Debbie Reynolds is singing 'Tammy', on which is over-
laid fragments of film dialogue, which offer ironic commentary on what is being
shown. The exhilarating beauty of the sequence, the combination of Reynolds's
soaring song and the sense that one has transcended the mundane, is completely
at odds with what the sequence suggests about the dull conformity of the life facing
Bud and the rest of the characters. When viewed through the lens of fantasy and
projection, however, the everyday is transformed. This echoes other moments in

the film, such as when the camera holds on a piece of carpet while sunlight plays across it, and we hear on the soundtrack swelling movie music that would normally accompany moments of high emotional drama. While on the one hand this kind of shot challenges us to look for the beauty in the mundane, it also pushes us towards a consideration of the role of fantasy in the construction of reality.

This brings us to one of the clichés, which is nonetheless frequently accurate, of the gay child: the tormented adolescent who lives life vicariously through the arts, whether this is theatre or opera or Hollywood film. But Davies's films make a subtler point about the role fantasy plays in everyone's life. The tracking shot that equates church, school and cinema makes a familiar observation about the ideo-logical institutions that fabricate reality for us. Bud is not the only character whose investment in fantasy makes life tolerable. We see this in the communal preparations for the dance, as the brothers wash and dress, and the sisters and girlfriends finish their elaborate and pleasurable rituals. Bud, meanwhile, has been sent out to acquire a series of purchases for his sisters, principally cosmetics and movie magazines, two key supports of 1950s heterosexual fantasy. A married couple, Edna and Curly, shows us one possible outcome of these courtships; Curly's talent is doing impressions of Hollywood actors, and the couple's interactions are a finely honed comedy routine, played out for those around them but also, most crucially, for themselves.

The fragility of this collective performance of reality is witnessed when a black suitor, looking for a woman named Mona, arrives at their door while they're preparing for the dance. Bud screams when he sees him, Helen tells him in a scared and angry voice that this is Kensington Street, not the main Kensington road, and John aggressively tells him to 'frigg off'. Although the insularity of the community pictured in the film would suggest they have little experience with racial others, this still does not quite account for their extreme reaction to this older, polite, soft-spoken man. The scene has something in common with Bud's two other moments of terror, the nightmare appearance of 'a man', and the vision of the labourer on the cross, which suggests that the visitor is another version of the monstrous, obscene father of enjoyment. The collective reaction suggests that this visit is what Žižek would call the answer of the Real, the terrifying return of the otherness of adult sexuality, literally out of place. This 'intrusion of enjoyment into reality' threatens to disrupt or overwhelm their collective hallucination of reality, inter-rupting most immediately the pre-dance rituals that both point to and efface, or perhaps domesticate, sexual desire.[17] The black suitor is what must be excluded or denied in order for life to function as normal (but is also that upon which, paradoxically, this functioning depends).[18]

But if the black suitor threatens to disrupt the functioning of reality for the family, there is also a way in which he threatens the viewer's nostalgic investment in a particular fantasy of the 1950s, one imagined as untouched by the racial traumas which would mark the decades that followed. The family screams on behalf of us:

the black man is in the wrong movie; he does not belong in a period film. Our discomfort at their racist reaction is quickly transformed into a discomfort at our own pleasurable investment in this racially homogeneous scenario. Like Bud caught looking at the labourer, we queasily slide away from our own guilty longing. The film catches the audience in a moment of uncanny and estranging self-recognition, reproducing in us the psychic structures it is so interested in exploring.

Fantasy, whether manufactured by Hollywood or collectively hallucinated, thus figures in a number of ways in these films. In the first instance it serves as a defence, most immediately against sexuality, which in the films is associated with the psychotic raging of the father. Fantasy offers a retreat or displacement, which makes existence tolerable. In its domestication of sexuality, fantasy also acts as both a lure and a compensation, coercing us to accept the demands of civilisation ('be fruitful and multiply') and offering us pleasure in return. It is important to recognise that although displaced, the pleasures of fantasy are nonetheless real (psychoanalysis would argue that they are, in fact, the only pleasures). If Davies offers us this knowledge in terms that, if not tragic, are at least melancholic, it is because of the particular relation of the gay child to fantasy.

Although both Bud and the heterosexual characters depend on fantasy, the key difference is that Bud sees the performance of reality for what it is. His face continually registers the discomfort of this self-consciousness, the sense that every gesture is a performance that could fail and potentially shatter the collective illusion. Both the fragility of this illusion and its necessity are registered in the opening sequence of the film: we see a derelict cinema in the rain, and the camera pans around to look at an equally derelict street. It is only when Nat King Cole starts to sing 'Stardust' and fantasy begins to infuse the image that we move back in time, to when the street housed a thriving community. Without fantasy, represented by the cinema, 'reality' is shattered, reduced to the meaningless rubble of the Real.

This, then, is the knowledge that haunts the gay child, the knowledge that renders the home movie uncanny. Because the child's sexuality makes it impossible to fully identify with the fantasy of the happy family, it necessarily identifies with other, more displaced fantasies. As we see in *Distant Voices, Still Lives*, trauma may temporarily separate heterosexuals from this fantasy, but they can return to it with a renewed fierceness. This return is not possible for the gay child without engendering the severe splitting evidenced in *The Terence Davies Trilogy*. But while the self-consciousness of the gay child may be alienating, it is not without its compensations, evident in the soaring beauty of the Debbie Reynolds sequence in *The Long Day Closes*. If for Davies, the pleasures of fantasy are a replacement for a more immediate experience of life, the films themselves suggest that this is not a bad bargain.

Notes

1 Davies quoted in Graham Fuller (2001) 'Summer's End', *Film Comment* 37, 1: 55.
2 Slavoj Žižek (1992) *Enjoy Your Symptom! Jacques Lacan in Hollywood and out*, New York and London: Routledge, 126.
3 John Caughie (1992) 'Half Way to Paradise', *Sight and Sound* 2: 10–13.
4 For opposing views on the question of history, see Susannah Radstone (1995) 'Cinema/Memory/History', *Screen* 36: 34–47; Martin Hunt (1999) 'The Poetry of the Ordinary: Terence Davies and the Social Art Film', *Screen* 40, 1: 1–16.
5 Christopher Hobbs quoted in Pat Kirkham and Mike O'Shaughnessy (1992) 'Designing Desire', *Sight and Sound* 2: 14.
6 Thomas Elsaesser (1988) 'Games of Love and Death, or an Englishman's Guide to the Galaxy', *Monthly Film Bulletin* 55: 292.
7 See, for example, Tony Williams (1993) 'The Masochist Fix: Gender Oppression in the Films of Terence Davies' in *Fires Were Started: British Cinema and Thatcherism*, ed. Lester Friedman, Minneapolis: University of Minnesota Press, 237–54; Geoff Eley (1995) 'The Family is a Dangerous Place: Memory, Gender, and the Image of the Working Class', *Revisioning History: Film and the Construction of a New Past*, ed. Robert A. Rosenstone, Princeton: Princeton University Press, 17–43.
8 Armond White (1993) 'Remembrance of Songs Past', *Film Comment* 29, 3: 14. One signal exception is Wendy Everett's (2004) comprehensive study *Terence Davies*, Manchester: University Press, which appeared after these lines were written.
9 Christopher Williams (1996) 'The Social Art Cinema: A Moment in the History of British Film and Television Culture', in *Cinema: The Beginnings and the Future*, ed. Christopher Williams, London: University of Westminster Press, 190–200.
10 Phil Powrie (2000) makes the photograph of the father central to a discussion of trauma in the film in 'The "Family Portrait", Trauma and the *Punctum* in *Distant Voices, Still Lives* (1988)', in Wendy Everett, ed., *The Seeing Century: Film, Vision and Identity*, Amsterdam: Rodopi, 20–35.
11 Terence Davies (1992) *A Modest Pageant*, London: Faber and Faber, 13.
12 Freud (1976) elaborates the concept of the primal scene in relation to the Wolf Man case history: the infant witnesses his parents engaged in *coitus a tergo*, which establishes for him (in retrospect) certain truths about sex. 'From the History of an Infantile Neurosis (The "Wolf Man")', *Case Histories II*. Freud Pelican Library 9, Harmondsworth: Penguin, 227–366.
13 This illustrates Žižek's assertion that we relate to people only insofar as they correspond to positions in fantasy: 'the "real father" is a miserable individual obliged to sustain the burden of the Name of the Father, never fully adequate to his symbolic mandate' (*Enjoy Your Symptom!*, 6).
14 Žižek, *Enjoy Your Symptom!*, 158.
15 John Rathall quoted in Martin Hunt (1999), 'The Poetry of the Ordinary: Terence Davies and the Social Art Film', *Screen* 40.1: 4.
16 Everett, 92–4.
17 Žižek, *Enjoy Your Symptom!*, 119.
18 The black suitor thus also functions as what Žižek calls the Thing: 'the Thing is not simply a foreign body, an intruder which disturbs the harmony of the social bond: precisely as such, the Thing is what "holds together" the social edifice by means of guaranteeing its fantasmatic consistency.' *Enjoy Your Symptom!*, 123.

10 More jiggery than pokery
Derek Jarman's *Edward II*

Raymond Armstrong

In the pantheon of Queer Cinema, Derek Jarman (1942–94) sits aloft and unchallenged as the most important gay filmmaker ever to have come out of the UK. Indeed no other British artist in any medium – and Jarman's creative activity was by no means limited to his output on celluloid[1] – has portrayed the conflict between the totems of the Establishment and the taboo of homosexuality with such restless fury and imagination. Of the dozen or so features that comprise his cinematic legacy, *Edward II* (1991) remains 'Jarman's most commercially successful and perhaps widely seen film'.[2] This no doubt has much to do with the fact that it is also the most formally accessible and emotionally absorbing of his pictures. The ideal starting-point for those unfamiliar with the director's work, *Edward II* is a kind of kaleidoscopic compendium of all the key thematic elements that distinguish Jarman's *oeuvre*. Depending on what angle you approach it from, the film could be variously categorised as: (a) a revisionist biography of a putatively gay historical figure – like *Sebastiane* (1976), *Caravaggio* (1986) and *Wittgenstein* (1993); (b) an idiosyncratic adaptation of a classic text from the canon of English literature – like *The Tempest* (1979), *The Angelic Conversation* (1985) and *War Requiem* (1989); (c) a polemical treatise on the state of contemporary Britain – like *Jubilee* (1978) and *The Last of England* (1987); or (d) a defiant celebration of gay love under the shadow of death – like *The Garden* (1990) and *Blue* (1993). Moreover, it even includes a kind of pop video, with Annie Lennox performing 'Every Time We Say Goodbye', and thus reminds us of the director's notable collaborations with the likes of Marianne Faithfull, Bryan Ferry, Pet Shop Boys and The Smiths.

A shocking-pink triangle of passion, poetry and politics, *Edward II* qualifies as a queer text on three separate counts. First, it is about a reckless gay king who was martyred in the early part of the fourteenth century; second, it is based on a play written by a swashbuckling gay dramatist at the end of the sixteenth century; and third, it was brought to the screen by a radical gay artist in the last decade of the twentieth century. As a result of this combination of subject matter, source material and stylish *mise-en-scène*, the film offers a unique triply distilled representation of gay experience in England throughout the ages.

Figure 10.1 'A shocking pink triangle of passion poetry and politics': Edward (Steven
        Waddington) and Gaveston (Andrew Tiernan) in Derek Jarman's queer
        Edward II (1991).

Source: Courtesy of Stephen Bourne (Palace).

   The filmmaker was attracted to Christopher Marlowe's 'dusty old play' (iii)[3]
chiefly because of its latent topicality rather than the quality of its blank verse (26).
Just as 'Marlowe outs the past' (iii) by dragging this royal skeleton from the closet
of English history, so Jarman purposefully refurbishes the story of Edward II
in order to lift the lid on current events, and expose the homophobia and hum-
buggery at the very heart of British society. Famed for his decidedly quirky use
of anachronistic devices, the director employs such elements more extensively –
and indeed more effectively – here than ever before. Through an eclectic range of
costumes, props, sound effects and music, he contrives to criss-cross the centuries
between the Medieval, Elizabethan and modern eras. The fibres of past and present
are thus ingeniously woven together, and bristle with a palpable sense of their
mutual relevance.

   In order to foreground the gay subtext, Jarman and his co-screenwriters,
Stephen McBride and Ken Butler, have stripped the play down to its bare essentials.
Several of the *dramatis personae* have been conflated into composite characters and
much of the action has been restructured. The film begins with the eponymous
sovereign (Steven Waddington) being held captive in a dungeon at Berkeley Castle,
where he is watched over by Lightborn, his stealthily appointed executioner. The
story of how Edward came to be in this predicament is then teased out through a

series of telling flashbacks. As the drama unfolds, we learn how the King's peculiarly intimate association with the Gascon squire Piers Gaveston (Andrew Tiernan) had aroused a tremendous amount of hostility from both the Church and the aristocracy; how Queen Isabella (Tilda Swinton), her wifely affections brusquely scorned, had entered into a lethal alliance with the ambitious Mortimer (Nigel Terry); and how together they had plotted the downfall of Edward and his 'sweet friend' (22).

Throughout *Edward II*, Jarman parallels the tragic plight of the Plantagenet King with the insidious persecution of the gay community under the successive Conservative governments of Margaret Thatcher and John Major. Time and again, the focus returns to the corridors of power in Whitehall and the palace of Westminster. Near the beginning, for example, Big Ben – the bell in the clock tower at the Houses of Parliament (which incidentally was not even cast until the middle of the nineteenth century) – can be heard chiming, almost disapprovingly, as Edward holds out his arms to embrace Gaveston on his return from exile; and, moments later, its sonorous striking of the hour sternly coincides with the two men kissing each other on the lips. Further on, in a scene that has the air of a modern-day ministerial meeting, we see Mortimer and his confederates sitting around a replica of the Cabinet table, whereupon the form that will authorise the renewal of Gaveston's banishment is delivered in a red despatch box. When Edward himself is subsequently coerced into signing this document, we notice that the paper is headed with the symbol of a crown on top of a portcullis – which would only become the official emblem of the British legislature six centuries later – and that the words 'Issued at Westminster this year of our Lord 1991' are inscribed underneath.

It is not just the machinations of Parliament that are represented in the film, but also the voices of dissent that were being raised by those outside. This constituency emerges from the shadows when the killing of Gaveston provokes OutRage – that is, the militant gay-rights group of which Jarman himself was a prominent member. Spurred on by a rampant Edward, legions of gay activists, many of them blowing whistles, wearing white t-shirts with slogans and carrying banners, march in protest at this murderous act of queer-bashing. They are confronted by police in full riot-gear, and, just as the director intended, the scene quickly begins to resemble one of the violent demonstrations against the Poll Tax (another detested piece of Tory legislation) that had rocked Central London in the spring of 1990. It is a mark of their significance to the film that the final shot should require the camera to move slowly through the huddled ranks of these gay campaigners, who remain silent and motionless, as Edward's elegiac last words reverberate ethereally down through the ages. According to Jarman, 'all the OutRage boys and girls are inheritors of Edward's story' (1991: 146); and, as such, they must persevere in their struggle for liberation and equality. Nearly seven hundred years after the fact, those elements within the Establishment – like 'the lordly peers' (1991: 10) and ecclesiastical bigwigs – who had denounced and destroyed Edward and Gaveston are the very same reactionary forces who continue to oppose the gay-rights movement today.

* * *

Some historians have sought to deny the homosexual nature of the bond between Edward and Gaveston, but the fact that we are dealing with a gay relationship is spelt out loudly and clearly in Jarman's film, when Isabella, lamenting how her husband dotes upon the affections of Gaveston, asks Mortimer, 'Is it not queer, that he is thus bewitched?' (1991: 38). The emphatic 'queer' has been substituted here for the word 'strange', which is what appears in the corresponding line of Marlowe's text.[4] The movie also elaborates on the play's suggestion that the two men are attracted to one another because of their sameness. At one point, Edward asks his lover: 'Knowest thou not who I am?/Thy friend, thy self, another Gaveston' (1991: 18). This aspect of similarity is duly reflected in their matching blond hairstyles and also in the way that they often appear together in clothes that are either identical or subtly co-ordinated. It should perhaps be noted here that neither Steven Waddington nor Andrew Tiernan is actually gay. Still, their sexual orientation notwithstanding, the characters they portray are certainly not the kind of stereotypical 'limp-wristed lisping fags' (1991: 30) so often depicted in the tabloid press and TV sitcoms from the 1970s; but neither are they presented as saintly paragons of gay manhood. Jarman deliberately refuses 'to make this an easy ride' for the viewer (1991: 46). If we are inclined to sympathise with Edward and Gaveston, then it is not because there is anything particularly admirable or heroic about these characters in themselves; rather it is because of the truly transcendent passion with which they love each other. Twice Edward is asked, 'Why should you love him whom the world hates so?' (1991: 50, 66). His response is immediate and categorical in its assurance: 'Because he loves me more than all the world' (1991: 50). What mattered most to Jarman was that the forbidden romance between Edward and Gaveston should itself be seen as something noble and wonderful. Granted, some queers are not very nice people; but the bottom line is that 'you don't have to like somebody to accept their right to have a love affair'.[5]

Although Gaveston himself boasts of his ability to 'draw the pliant King' (1991: 10) whichever way he pleases, the love between the two men does seem to be both genuine and deeply felt. When viewed outside of this relationship, however, Gaveston generally comes across as a rather cynical and unpleasant individual. Cocksure of his position as the King's darling, he swaggers around the court and never misses an opportunity to rub his adversaries' noses in it. 'Andrew is not playing Gaveston in a way that will endear me to *Gay Times*', remarked Jarman wryly (1991: 20). Indeed, at several points in the opening half of the film, Gaveston is presented in an almost demonic light. First, there is his thuggish and sacrilegious humiliation of the Bishop of Winchester, in the course of which, to the whistled strains of 'To Be A Pilgrim', the lofty cleric is literally defrocked, beaten, sexually molested, and finally 'blessed' with his own dentures. Next, there is the episode in which Gaveston – bearing a curious resemblance to the crouching incubus in Henry

Fuseli's famous painting 'The Nightmare' (1781) – squats naked on the throne, and then begins to hop about, making 'a frightful clucking' sound and gesticulating wildly at the scandalised Mortimer (1991: 30). Soon after that, we witness Gaveston's fiendish pseudo-seduction of Isabella, which appears to be what finally pushes her over the edge and triggers her transformation into a vengeful homo-cidal vampire. Even though our attitude to Gaveston softens quite considerably as the film progresses, the unfavourable impression created by these earlier images is much too vivid to be erased.

A far less abrasive and *louche* character than Gaveston, Edward posed quite a different problem for the director. 'I don't want to make Edward weak or vacillatory', said Jarman, 'I want to be on his side, make the love affair noble'.[6] Yet, in spite of that, the King still tends to come across as a rather quixotic figure, who is so blindly infatuated with Gaveston that he fails to notice his swain's more knavish and diabolical traits. On the other hand, a much darker side to Edward emerges after the killing of Gaveston, when he becomes a virtual outlaw in his own kingdom. Hell-bent on exacting retribution and effectively criminalised because of his desires, his actions take on a more desperate and even ferocious quality. This is evidenced most strikingly in the scene where a policeman – the same one who had earlier garrotted Gaveston with his truncheon – is crucified on a couple of sides of beef and then vindictively eviscerated by Edward. During this sequence, the regal slaughterer (like his accessary Spencer) wears a red apron, a white coat, and a dark blue shirt and trousers – an ensemble that schematically evokes both the colours and to some extent (especially when viewed from the rear) the geometric patterns of the Union Jack. The spattering of the policeman's blood all over the King's apparel here can thus be directly related to the moment in Marlowe's play when Edward declares that he wants to see the royal standard stained with the blood of the villains who have slain Gaveston.[7] Dubbed 'the butcher's apron' by Irish nationalists and sundry other anti-Brits, the once supremely iconic but now increasingly anxious ensign of the United Kingdom had itself been spectacularly sullied in several of Jarman's other films, including *Jubilee, The Queen Is Dead* (1986)[8] and (most memorably) *The Last of England*, where the flag is draped across a huge bed on which a naked Bacchanalian youth and a hooded man in combat-gear ruttishly lock horns and roll around together with gay abandon. It would be hard to imagine a more punkishly unpatriotic illustration of how homosexuality has always been conspicuously at odds with the symbolic trappings of the British state.

Ever the maverick, Jarman not only set out to 'violate' (1991: iii) an esteemed Elizabethan text, but – much to the displeasure of the Marlowe Society and highbrow traditionalists everywhere – he also claimed to have dramatically 'improved' it.[9] By far the most significant of these 'improvements' centres on the fate of the protagonist. The one thing that most people know about Edward II is the peculiarly gruesome way in which he was killed; that is, by having a red-hot poker thrust into his anus. The manner of this assassination, perhaps more than anything, is what brands Edward as a queer. The point was driven home with a malignant lack of subtlety: at once a crude parody of and an infernal punishment for the act of sodomy. If indeed it is the case that 'Real men take it up the arse' (1991: 156), as the slogan proclaims just before this sequence in the screenplay,[10] then Edward II must surely be considered the very apotheosis of masculinity.

Prior to 1991, the only notable cinematic treatment of the notorious poker scene had been in Sidney Lumet's Cold War spy thriller *The Deadly Affair* (1966), where David Warner, as the hapless Edward, is heinously shafted on a West End stage, while a Hitchcockian sequence of murderous intrigue is simultaneously being played out in the midst of the theatre audience. There can be no doubt that Jarman also wanted his dramatic account of Edward's tribulation to mirror what was being done to certain members of his audience; however, he was, at the same time, becoming increasingly sick of telling sad stories about the death of queers.[11] Consequently, impelled by an audacious mixture of iconoclasm and wish-fulfilment, he decided to rewrite the history books and 'rescue' Marlowe's play by incorporating a 'happy ending' for the misprized King (1991: 162). By way of a rationale for this decision, the director gave some credence to an unlikely 'conspiracy theory', which maintains that Edward had somehow managed to escape from the dungeon in Berkeley Castle and then fled to the Continent, where he lived out his days as a prayerful anchorite (1991: 158).

Rather than dispense with the poker altogether (as Bertolt Brecht had done in his version of the story), Jarman recognised that its impact as a visual motif was much too powerful to lose. Accordingly, the sight of an iron rod being heated – by everything from a blazing furnace to an acetylene torch – recurs ominously throughout the film. Haunted by this insistent image, a distraught Edward suddenly finds himself seized by the horrific moment of his own doom. We watch as the searing action proceeds, virtually in slow motion, against a hazy scarlet backlight; meanwhile, an obscenely jubilant plainsong blares out on the soundtrack, only to be punctuated by the insuppressible screams of the squirming pathic. However, no sooner has this sequence drawn to a close than we see the lifeless monarch begin to stir and realize that it was all just a nightmarish 'premonition' (1991: 160). Shortly thereafter, Lightborn approaches Edward with the hot rod in his hand; but just when it looks as if the infamous insertion is actually about to take place, the executioner unexpectedly throws the salamander into the cesspool. He then turns to his liege and silently pays homage, before kissing him gently on the mouth. Fittingly perhaps, the part of this affectionate angel of death is played by Kevin (Keith) Collins, Jarman's real-life companion and the man who was helping him to face the grim reality of his own impending demise.

Although 'dedicated to the repeal of all anti-gay laws' (1991: iii), *Edward II* is essentially a product of Jarman's seething indignation at Section 28. Introduced by the Conservative government in 1988, this swingeing statute not only made it illegal for local councils to 'promote homosexuality', but also decreed that all state-maintained schools should teach the view that homosexuality was abnormal and therefore unacceptable 'as a pretended family relationship'. In effect, this encouraged a virtual embargo on the works of all gay and lesbian artists – from classic writers and composers to contemporary dancers and photographers. With representations of homosexuality having been rendered so problematic and the threat of prosecution a constant concern, municipal authorities were being instructed to play safe and keep anything that touched on gay issues out of school classrooms, public libraries, civic theatres and galleries.

Queers were being pushed out of the picture in all areas of everyday life. Those who turned to the escapist realm of the cinema found that it offered them precious little succour, let alone sanctuary. 'It is difficult enough to be queer, but to be a queer in the cinema is almost impossible', complained Jarman. 'Heterosexuals have fucked up the screen so completely that there's hardly enough room for us to kiss there' (1991: iii). Securing more room for queers in the cinema not only required gay characters to be more visible on the screen, but also meant that there had to be better funding and distribution for the works of gay filmmakers. *Edward II* was itself a case in point. The film may only have cost a very modest £750,000, but it was easily Jarman's most expensive production, and it took him several years to scrape together the finance to make it. Moreover, despite attracting his largest-ever US audience and winning prestigious awards at both Venice and Berlin, he was unable to find anyone who would agree to distribute the movie theatrically in Great Britain.[12]

The idea of queers being denied a space is arguably the central theme of *Edward II*. What we have here is, after all, the story of two gay men who are repeatedly torn apart just to prevent them from being together under the same roof. Furthermore, during those brief times that they are able to enjoy each other's company, their happiness is invariably compromised by the prying eyes of spies and the intrusive echoes of noises-off. Just how far society is prepared to go in its relentless hounding of the couple is vividly illustrated when the chorus of disgruntled earls bursts into the King's bedchamber with a pack of beagles.

History records that Gaveston was expelled from England several times because of his inappropriate relationship with Edward. In Jarman's film, we watch as, on the last of these occasions, the King's paramour is forced to take his leave by walking down a narrow corridor lined on either side with spitting priests. Later, having been lured back with specious assurances about his safety, he is hunted down like a wounded animal, systematically boxed-in and battered by police riot-shields; until finally, denied even the space to breathe, he has the life choked out of him. A similar fate befalls Spencer – Gaveston's sometime bedfellow and Edward's loyal aide-de-camp – who is subsequently throttled to death because he too is, what Mortimer calls, a 'Girlboy' (1991: 142).

Edward himself is overruled and undermined on all sides. When he tries to prevent his sphere of influence from shrinking any further, he is taken captive and shut up in an oubliette. At one point we see him standing waist-deep in the cesspool, paralysed by his complete lack of manoeuvrability. In a sardonic twist, his executioner is even seen stroking a ferret – an animal specifically bred to harry gentler creatures out of their natural habitats. The uniquely invasive nature of Edward's designated execution further highlights the fact that no place is safe for him. Those determined to poke their noses into other people's private affairs are prepared to target even the innermost recesses of the body.

The reality of having to operate within an enclosed space is also reflected in Jarman's *mise-en-scène*, which, as always, makes a virtue of the necessity of having to do things on a shoestring. The film was in fact shot entirely indoors over five weeks at Bray studios. Moreover, it is worth noting that the screenplay deliberately emphasises that every sequence is an 'interior' – even, paradoxically, those that are supposed to be alfresco; such as the one in which Gaveston stands howling on a rock at the edge of the sea on a stormy night. The actual 'rooms' are cavernous affairs; empty of all but the most minimal of furnishings, and linked by a maze-like network of dusky passages and doorless portals. Whatever light there is emanates largely from artificial sources, causing shadows to loom up and flicker across the sheer stone walls and dirt floors. All of this goes to create an oppressive, almost sub-terranean sense of confinement, and its claustrophobic impact was felt by everyone who worked on the film: 'The set became a metaphor for the trapped country, the prison of our lives, "the closet of our heart"', in Edward's words.'[13]

In the world of *Edward II*, Heterosoc[14] has not only conquered space, but also regulates it with a rod of iron. The situation for the queer in the street could scarcely be more depressing or familiar. As a filmmaker, however, Jarman prefers to celebrate defiance rather than succumb to defeatism. Fundamentally transgressive in terms of both style and content, his is a cinema that recognises no boundaries, repudiates all inhibitions, and seeks to rise above any constraints. Each of his films is flamboyantly choreographed around his determination to exceed the limits of what might reasonably be expected of him, whether because of his meagre financial resources or his terminally declining health. The title of his first volume of autobiography *Dancing Ledge* (1984) – named after a beauty spot on the Dorset coast – perfectly encapsulates this notion of the artist's indomitable spirit determined to express itself despite being stuck on a perilously strait platform.

It is indeed through the ritual of dancing that the gay lovers in *Edward II* are able to make the most of both the space and time that they share with one another. Dancing becomes a way of celebrating their intimacy and togetherness; a means of demonstrating their mutual attraction and physical compatibility. It allows them to move their bodies freely in harmony and rhythm, and to side-step anything that stands in their way. Under the queer logic of dance, all of the mundanely hetero-sexist codes and conventions that have been designed to cramp their style can be flouted with impudence and impunity.

There are four instances of dance featured in the film: three of them involve a *pas de deux* between Edward and Gaveston, while the fourth is a solo outing for Edward's juvenile successor. The key factor is that every one of these dance sequences purposefully evokes a sympathetic connection with some famously gay or sexually ambiguous third party.

The first dance is a somewhat vicarious exercise, since it merely involves the pair frolicking on the throne, while watching two male hoofers (from the internationally renowned experimental dance troupe DV8) perform an athletic high-energy ballet, which rather inauspiciously seems to recount the tale of a tragic love affair.

The second dance is a much more earnest encounter, given that it forms the centrepiece of the scene in which Edward bids a poignant farewell to the outcast Gaveston. According to Jarman, the 'best lines in Marlowe sound like pop songs' (1991: iii); therefore it is entirely appropriate that this most lyrical moment in the film should magically combine the playwright's words with those of a Cole Porter standard. A spotlight shines on the sad-eyed, pyjama-clad lovers as they shuffle barefoot to 'Every Time We Say Goodbye', sung here by the androgynously angelic figure of Annie Lennox who observes them benignly from the wings.[15] The result has to be one of the most exquisitely romantic interludes in the whole history of the cinema.

The third dance marks the joyous occasion of Gaveston's final return from exile. As he and Edward are reunited, a Mozart string quartet segues into a jaunty piece of organ muzak, reminiscent of the type that used to be played in cinemas during the intermission. The tuxedoed partners then launch themselves into a gleefully camp cha-cha-cha, in the course of which they even manage to negotiate the toothy transfer of an ersatz rose-stem. Jarman has acknowledged that this skit is a homage to Billy Wilder's *Some Like It Hot* (1959), with its gender-bending tango between Osgood (Joe E. Brown) and Daphne (Jack Lemmon in drag). He actually wanted to use the same music for this little pastiche, but the copyright costs turned out to be prohibitive (1991: 88). The quasi-erotic dancing of Edward and Gaveston, which has become ever more dynamic since they first stepped out together, thus reaches a carefree climax in this exuberant Latin-American routine, not least because they assume – albeit quite wrongly – that all threats to their relationship have now receded.

As well as importing aspects of a wider gay tradition into the film to lend support to the beleaguered lovers, Jarman also subverts and impugns the 'normal' credentials of their principal antagonists. As the scene where a group of young men practise a rugby scrum in the nude demonstrates, the director is always looking for a way to queer the pitch. In the case of Isabella, we are struck by the fact that the more icy and implacable she becomes, the more Hollywood-style glamour she seems to acquire; so much so that, with her increasingly fabulous wardrobe and accessories, she appears to be deliberately modelling herself on such celebrated gay icons as Greta Garbo, Joan Crawford, Audrey Hepburn, and even Evita Peron (1991: 148, 124). Meanwhile, the soldierly machismo of the moustachioed

Mortimer is gloriously vitiated when he is seen parading around in the night wearing nothing but a tart's leopard-skin coat. This sartorial confusion is also evident in the behaviour of Edward's filial namesake and heir apparent, who, after being removed from the 'unnatural' (1991: 130) influence of his father and placed in the ostensibly more orthodox custody of his mother and Mortimer, soon begins to exhibit signs of growing transvestism.

It is indeed the young Edward III who triumphantly affirms the terpsichorean motif at the close of the film. With the tables having been turned on the nefarious heterosexuals, Isabella and Mortimer find themselves incarcerated together in a sturdy cage, where – still dressed to kill, but now caked from head to toe with white flour – they don't even have enough room to stand up. There they are left to ruminate and rot, literally under the high heels of the girlish boy-king, who sways majestically above them as he listens to 'The Dance of the Sugar Plum Fairy' on his Walkman. The choice of such an instantly recognisable and dainty piece of music neatly underscores the symbolic victory of the sprite-like gay dancers; especially since the composer of this tune, a certain Piotr Ilyich Tchaikovsky, was himself (like Cole Porter) a 'fairy' of some note.

Several years before he directed the ultimate 'blue' movie, Jarman had toyed with the idea of making *Edward II* as a kind of porno flick[16] – 'More of an Elizabethan lay than an Elizabethan play' (1991: 16) – with lots of gratuitous sex and violence. All such notions were immediately abandoned, however, once the BBC came onboard as the project's principal financier.[17] Jarman knew that he was now going to be heavily restricted in terms of how much explicit material he could get away with showing, and that clearly had an effect on the way the film turned out. While *Edward II* does offer a fairly frank and open portrayal of gay sexuality, with 'much flaunting of male flesh',[18] there is nothing here as contentious or as graphic as some of the scenes that are to be found elsewhere in Jarman's *oeuvre*. Consider, for example, the grotesque priapic pantomime at the start of *Sebastiane*, or the blasphemous disco-*cum*-orgy in *Jubilee*, or the aforementioned romp on the massive Union Jack in *The Last of England*. Given the director's reputation for crafting such wilfully provocative images, the BBC (who were obviously anxious to avoid the kind of rabid controversy that had followed the TV premieres of *Sebastiane* and *Jubilee* on Channel 4) had decided to cover themselves for all eventualities by making sure that Jarman was contractually obliged to deliver a slightly 'softer' version of *Edward II* for broadcasting purposes. As it transpired, there was only one scene that fell foul of the Corporation's own in-house watchdogs. The sequence in question occurs immediately after the opening credits, when we are first introduced to the character of Gaveston. Clad in a long white nightshirt, the King's favourite walks towards a large bed while reading aloud from a postcard that he has just received from Edward. On the edge of the bed sits the figure of Spencer, who is in the process of getting dressed. During the ensuing conversation between these two men, a pair of naked 'hustlers' – both of whom claim to be sailors – 'fuck without a blush' alongside them (1991: 6). In truth, however, this coupling is much tamer than Jarman's colourful description here would seem to suggest; and, even in the un-expurgated theatrical and home video editions, the scene is notable not for any flagrant exhibitionism, but rather for its tenderness and intimacy. Furthermore, the amorous mariners themselves are featured only in profile, their bodies are intermittently obscured by the foreground figures of Gaveston and Spencer, and we never catch even a glimpse of their private parts. Nevertheless, when it came to airing the film on TV, the BBC rather cravenly chose to transmit a censored version of this scene, in which a number of shots had been substituted and re-framed. To add insult to injury, they also deemed it necessary to have the continuity announcer caution viewers that the movie they were about to see was 'uncompromising and explicit in its language and depiction of male homosexuality'. It is interesting to note that all of the film's many disturbing and violent scenes – including one involving (heterosexual) sadomasochism – remained intact. The sight of two queers gently making love was evidently considered too dangerous for British TV audiences in the early 1990s, yet it was perfectly acceptable for us to see a straight man trussed up and lying naked on his belly, with a trio of vicious wenches half-strangling him and grinding their stiletto heels into his flesh. With *Edward II*, the BBC had com-missioned a film that expressly set out to challenge the Establishment's programme of discrimination against gays; but ironically, by applying such egregious double standards to the production, the Corporation itself had ended up exemplifying exactly the same kind of institutional bias. Still, concerns about editorial duplicity notwithstanding, the decision to bowdlerise the gay love scene certainly did not weaken the subversive thrust of the film; on the contrary, the very fact that the BBC had allowed themselves to be cowed into taking this action – rather than risk incurring the wrath of their already grudging paymasters in the Conservative government – only made the film's message all the more urgent and compelling.

Notes

1 He also produced a great many paintings and drawings, wrote a number of books, and designed sets for the theatre, opera, ballet and several of Ken Russell's films, including *The Devils* (1971), *Savage Messiah* (1972) and the unrealised *Gargantua* (1972–73).
2 'Introduction', Lippard, p. 8.
3 All page numbers in parentheses refer to Jarman, Derek, *Queer Edward II*, London, British Film Institute, 1991.
4 Marlowe, *Edward the Second*, 1.2.55.
5 Derek Jarman, quoted in Chedgzoy, p. 213.
6 Derek Jarman, quoted in Peake, p. 382.
7 Marlowe, *Edward the Second*, 3.2.138–45.
8 A short film featuring three songs by The Smiths.
9 The headings 'EDWARD II' and 'improved by DEREK JARMAN' run on alternate pages throughout the screenplay.

10 In *Queer Edward II*, the text for each sequence is typographically emblazoned with an OutRageously homosexist slogan by Greg Taylor.

11 Jarman discussed this frustration during a special edition of Channel 4's *The Media Show* on the making of *Edward II*.

12 'Interview with Derek Jarman', Lippard, p. 168.

13 Derek Jarman, quoted in Chedgzoy, p. 206.

14 'Heterosoc' is a term coined by Jarman 'for the systematic domination of the queer subculture by the hetero-oppressive majority that continues to control the offices of the state and the institutions of civil society'. Martin Quinn-Meyler, 'Opposing "Heterosoc": Derek Jarman's counter-hegomonic activism'. Lippard, p. 119.

15 This version of the song had previously appeared in the AIDS-benefit project *Red Hot and Blue*, where it was accompanied by a video of Lennox watching some old home-movie footage of Jarman as a boy with his family.

16 O'Pray, p. 184.

17 *Edward II* was actually the second of three Jarman films to receive funding from the BBC. The first was *War Requiem*, and the last was the posthumously released *Glitterbug* (1994).

18 Peake, p. 469.

Bibliography

Chedgzoy, Kate (1995) *Shakespeare's Queer Children*, Manchester: Manchester University Press.

Jarman, Derek (1991) *Queer Edward II*, London: British Film Institute.

Lippard, Chris (ed.) (1996) *By Angels Driven: The Films of Derek Jarman*, Trowbridge: Flicks Books.

Marlowe, Christopher (1909–14) *Edward the Second*, Vol. XLVI, Part 1, The Harvard Classics, New York: P.F. Collier & Son.

O'Pray, Michael (1996) *Derek Jarman: Dreams of England*, London: British Film Institute.

Peake, Tony (1999) *Derek Jarman*, London: Little Brown.

11 Beyond the pale

The politics of Neil Jordan's
The Crying Game

Andrew Moor

Jody: You lack imagination Fergus. Think of something more alluring . . .

Dil (Jaye Davidson), the dark-skinned, extravagantly feminine hairdresser in Neil Jordan's *The Crying Game* (1992), is a man, not a woman, as we discover when, midway through the film, he disrobes in preparation for sex with Fergus (Stephen Rea), Jordan's heterosexual protagonist. Fergus has likewise been duped. Dil's penis is briefly displayed in crotch-level close-up, and the abruptness of the display heightens the shock we share with Fergus. Frontal male nudity is still surprisingly taboo (except in the rarefied traditions of classical art, or in pornography). This film broke out of the limited confines of the art-house, where explicit treatments of sexuality are more commonplace, and crossed over to multiplex popularity by trading on its 'secret', especially in the USA. The dramatic significance of its revelation scene is very much bound up with the mainstream audience it sought out. The spectators' focus is centred on the heterosexual male protagonist's distressed reaction to the sight of Dil's penis. We watch him lash out and vomit in shock. The politics of this, one of the most significantly queer moments in our culture, are thus questionable. Jordan's liberal fascination here with transgressive sexuality, and with race, has a touristic flavour: he floats a cast of flattish stereotypes in order to take depth soundings on white, straight masculinity. Is this dismissal of tourism not too easy though, ignoring as it does the progressive potential of the mainstream tourist's encounters beyond the pale; and is a film which centres on softening the psychology of a white male inevitably conservative? And is queerness itself not, by definition, a shifting, nomadic phenomenon, fleeing the safe haven of gay identity politics to subvert terroristically the value-laden assumptions defined and defended by the centre? *The Crying Game* demands that we reassess the histories of Dil and Fergus after the revelation scene. Our lazy assumptions are attacked. Paradoxically, Dil's identity is made less fixed by the sudden, sensational spectacle of his genitals, and Davidson's playful performance of gender continues to tease. The meaning of his penis is, as it were, up for grabs, and the fact that the film's narrative twist is

Figure 11.1 'I kinda liked you as a girl': Fergus (Stephen Rea) ponders the meaning of his
relationship with Dil (Jaye Davidson) in *The Crying Game* (1992).

Source: Courtesy of Stephen Bourne (Palace/Channel 4).

mediated through its impact on a straight protagonist actually raises its queer
capital. The film may be a white male liberal fantasy but at least it does not preach
to the queer-converted, and in raising the possibility of an erotic frisson between a
gay man and a not-entirely-resistant straight one it also caters to the gay taste for
that most forbidden of fruits.

We use the certainties of popular culture to anchor ourselves. 'When a man loves
a woman, he can't keep his mind on nothing else.' 'Sometimes it's hard to be a
woman, giving all your love to just one man', especially when 'after all, he's just a
man'. Romance is a 'crying game'. Better times are shifted into an imagined future
with bluebirds over 'The White Cliffs of Dover'. On one level, these popular songs,
heard and performed throughout the film, reaffirm some of our guiding clichés: the
utopian faith of Vera Lynn, and our various narratives of love (the distracted male
suffering of Percy Sledge which forms an overture to the film, the resigned fatalism
of Tammy Wynette, or the sentimental masochism of the song which lends the film
its title). Things are not quite so pedestrian though, because the ironic pitch
of Jordan's screenplay tweaks these well-loved, mainstream platitudes. The songs
are worked over, and this is symptomatic of the way the film uses performance
to dissolve other firmly held positions and to reassess the familiar. 'The White Cliffs

of Dover' is sung in a run down London bar, 'The Metro', by a crowd of misfits crooning along with a glitzy pub-chanteuse: this nostalgically evokes the community spirit of the Home Front (and the sense of community in 'The Metro' is important, given its apparently oddball clientele), but the song's connoted evocation of a racially pure island race of Albion is mismatched with the film's multi-ethnic, permeably bordered, post-colonial terrains. The abrupt appearance of same-sex desire in the narrative retrospectively quizzes the heterosexual assumptions of Percy Sledge's lyrics. Music and mixes by The Pet Shop Boys and Boy George (who sings the title-song over the closing credits) mark a genuinely gay contribution to the soundtrack, and while 'Stand by your Man' inevitably recalls Tammy Wynette, it is sung by Lyle Lovett, his male voice unexpectedly queering the pre-feminism of Nashville's recipe for wedded perseverance.

   This playful intertextuality and the privileging of performance are signs of the film's postmodern register, part of the 'game' of its appropriated title. It would be wrong, though, to read its ludic quality as trivialising or denying real, historical conditions. The film politicises its treatment of romance by offering a purview of 1990s sexual and racial politics: masculinity in crisis; traditions of stereotyping; heterosexism, various transgender issues, gayness and queerness: 'tick where appropriate'. Little wonder then that, especially in the USA, academic publications on the film could constitute a small library on their own. Just as pressingly, though, Jordan plays out his love plots within the conflict in northern Ireland. These 'Troubles' are the crying game the film addresses. The gender issues imaginatively allegorise the politics of the six counties. Sexual boundaries, the film suggests, are as artificial as the border dividing Ireland, and crises of category in the realm of sex and gender are connected to other crises in the realm of nationhood. As Carl Dahlman usefully puts it, 'Rather than abandon the geopolitical problematic, the film calls into question the ethics of oppositional politics and its attendant identity categories, beginning with the heteronormative relationship' (Dahlman, 2002: 129).

   In the opening sequence, a group of IRA volunteers, cold-blooded Peter (Adrian Dunbar), Jude (Miranda Richardson) and Fergus, kidnap Jody, a black British soldier serving in Ulster (played with winning charm by Forest Whittaker). Fergus is more emotionally responsive than the others – a 'gentle gunman' to echo the title of an earlier British film dealing with Irish politics (Basil Dearden, 1952). He establishes a rapport with the prisoner, growing fonder of him while on guard duty. Jody shows Fergus a photograph of his 'girl', Dil. Anticipating his death, he asks Fergus to visit Dil to pass on his last regards. The killing is bungled by Fergus, who cannot shoot Jody in the back when he tries to escape. Jody then runs straight into the path of a British Saracen truck and is killed by those hurrying to rescue him. In a suspect narrative manoeuvre, then, Fergus is absolved of direct guilt for Jody's death, helping us to associate our feelings with Fergus as he crosses the water to London, to 'lose himself' as he puts it. Having forged this unlikely bond with a

British soldier (Stockholm Syndrome reversed, the captor here identifies with his captive), Fergus seeks out Dil, possibly motivated by guilt, by shared grief for Jody, by honour or by desire, although his motives — other than his need to disappear after his botched job — are unclear. This second encounter with cultural difference leads Fergus into yet more challenging psychological territory, and his personal development allegorically signals, in microcosm, a way out of the Ulster problem.

Jody is kidnapped from a tacky fairground, lured by the promise of sex with Jude. The film's opening tracking shot skates over a river mouth, dwelling on a revolving ferris wheel before it descends to find Jody and Jude, with Fergus slyly following them. From *The Cabinet of Dr Caligari* onwards, fairgrounds are the dark carnival of expressionism, subjective spaces jeopardising fixed identities. Jordan had already essayed the erotic potential of fantasy spaces in *Company of Wolves* (1984) and would do so again with *Interview with a Vampire* (1994). In *The Crying Game* a fairground seduction initiates another psycho-sexual journey. In an odd reversal, it is the kidnapper Fergus, doleful, hangdog, hapless and initially reckoned by his prisoner Jody to 'lack imagination', who is shipped into an exotic underworld. The spinning fairground wheel proleptically maps out Fergus's dizzy trajectory. Other key motifs in the film's mise-en-scène include windows, glass-houses, walls being demolished (by Fergus), half-open blinds (at 'Millies', the hairdressing salon where Dil works), semi-transparent drapes (in Dil's apartment), and journeys over water. These signify Jordan's major theme: crossing boundaries, going beyond the pale, envisaging difference, or, in the geopolitical terminology which the film allegorises, the importance of pluralism, a postmodern politics of multiple truths, a trans-territorialism, genuine interface and dialogue: in a word, multiculturalism.

Fergus: He's a good soldier: He believes in the future

The queered (postmodern?) relationship between Fergus and both Jody and Dil cannot be understood without recalling the roots of Ireland's disputed national territory. Modernity seeks to rationalise the world, categorise it and to impose a sense of hierarchy. Nationhood is one of its chief expressions, and the state its chief agent, ensuring that the nation's acknowledged boundaries contain a politically centralised community. While the industrialised economics of modernity account for the appearance of nations, nationalism may try to legitimise itself by harking back to pre-modern bonds based on religion or ethnicity. There is no reason why these pre-modern alignments should be expected to observe the margins of the nations superimposed upon them. Ireland was polarised when Irish nationalism, in the nineteenth century, chose not to secularise the emergent nation but instead tried to foster an Irish consciousness by appealing to Roman Catholicism, thereby failing to recruit those who defined themselves differently or against the Catholic

Church. Jordan is Irish, of course, and his film, which fulfilled his stated aim to 'make something that comes out of the nationalist point of view' (Burke, 1993: 17), similarly occludes the voice of pro-English/Ulster Protestantism, focusing instead on Republicanism and the English. The struggle to emerge from a colonial past into modern nationhood exacerbated and then kept alive Ireland's pre-modern ethic/religious tensions, which were reinvigorated by partial independence and the drawing of a national border around Ulster.

The new economic conditions of late capitalism, consumerism, virtual reality, and of supra-national or sub-national structures such as the European Union have, political postmodernists argue, begun to erode the authority of the nation state and to loosen the rigid territorialism which attends it. In Cathal McCall's words, this 'has shifted the focus for politics from the emphasis of modernity on establishing a dominant truth as the basis of socio-political order to a postmodernist concern for the accommodation of communal difference' (McCall, 1999: 7). Within this pluralism, national identity endures as but one point in a shifting network of configurations (familial, local, regional, metropolitan, continental, global) which themselves combine with other forms of consciousness and practice drawn from all manner of cultural relationships, not least gender and sexuality. In these latter fields, the notion of 'identity', which implies depth and fixity, is still politically valuable (think of community action groups), but it has had to accommodate itself to ways of thinking that highlight more contingent and tactical choices such as performativity, masquerade and queerness. After the dominance of Unionist rhetoric in the six counties precipitated the modern Troubles in the late 1960s, contemporary Irish politics has begun to shift in focus towards postmodernism, with a recurring emphasis on an 'Irish dimension' in Ulster politics, the power-sharing executive (1972), the Anglo-Irish Agreement (1985) with its cross-border co-operation, the multi-party talks and agreement (1998), and the possibility of multi-level arrangements fostered through Europe. It would be naïve to forget the persistent modernist, national claims of Sinn Fein and of Ulster Unionists (both of their identities are rooted in territorial claims), but the paradigm shift which is postmodernism does offer some possibility for the future, or at least some way out of the deadlock of the crying game.

It is a dawning sense of this possibility which leads Fergus to say of his doomed prisoner Jude that 'he's a good soldier: he believes in the future'. We might rightly be troubled by any film which donned one of postmodernism's more frivolous guises simply to reject history, particularly a film about Ireland. Here though, the lesson Fergus learns from his encounter with Jody is that we are better served by fresh adjustments to the present which are founded on an awareness of historical change, than we are by monological perceptions which are so transfixed by the values of modernity that they rely on rigid, naturalised and pure demarcations. The sense of possibility goes hand in hand with a sense of play. During the long sequence where Fergus guards Jody, an ironically polite banter develops:

Fergus: It's not 'Paddy'. It's Fergus.
Jody: Nice to meet you, Fergus.
Fergus: My pleasure, Jody.

This playful civility is important. Fergus, the volunteer, still holds to his political cause, which he summarises succinctly to the British soldier: 'you guys shouldn't be here'. While Jody's admission that he just 'got sent' to Ireland, and that he joined the army because 'it was a job' exposes the limited choices available to him in London, his very physical appearance vexes Fergus's view. A cultural kinship might be drawn between Irish Catholics and Black Britons – they share parallel class histories of marginalised disadvantage, as black Jody seems to recognise when he tells white Fergus 'you wouldn't shoot a brother in the back'. Jody's post-colonial presence mocks Fergus's adherence to a discourse of pure Irish nationalism. Jody was born in Antigua, where his beloved cricket is 'the black man's game', and migrated with his father to London as a boy, where the sport is for 'toffs'. Jody's enthusiasm for cricket mimics, democratises and surpasses the sporting skills of his erstwhile colonial rulers.[1] But it is when Jody attacks the provincial racism of Ulster that the ironies of his presence are fully clear: 'I get sent to the one place in the world where they call you nigger to your face. [In an Irish accent] "Go back to your banana tree nigger!" No use telling them I come from Tottenham.' Whittaker's fake Belfast accent underscores the constructed and provisional status of national identities. While the migrant, racial histories of Black Americans and Black Britons are simultaneously evoked by Whittaker's presence, his London accent, though boldly attempted, has 'mockney' echoes of Dick Van Dyke's pearly-kingdom, and when filtered through this hazarded cockney the Belfast accent is doubly artificial. Fergus's sense of what the performative, post-colonial condition might have to offer disengages him further from the fixed fanaticism of Peter and Jude.

In London, Fergus changes. He acquires a new haircut (like Henry Fonda's Wyatt Earp, the wild man is barbered to fit a civilised future) and a new name – 'Jimmy' (Dil thinks he is Scottish – another separation of the man from his roots, and a sign of Fergus's incipient performativity). He visits Dil at the 'Metro' and a traditional, romantic interest develops. The sight of Dil's biological sex strips away a false consciousness, triggering a response which rehearses the larger cognitive reprocessing with regard to Irish history which it also aims to provoke. Jody's heterosexuality had seemed unquestionable when he was lured into the fairground by Jude's promise of sex. Was he bisexual? Fergus then meets Dil at Jody's behest: a practical joke, or a sign that Jody recognised a latent homosexuality in Fergus? Certainly the Jody-Fergus sequence can be read for signs of homosexual attraction. Jody calls Fergus 'the handsome one', and in a moment of embarrassed male-bonding, Fergus helps Jody (whose hands are tied behind his back) to urinate by gingerly holding his off-screen penis for him. The sight of Dil's penis later on recollects this earlier moment of homoerotic potential. After Jody's death Fergus dreams of him, radiant in cricket whites and bowling towards him. One such image occurs while Dil is performing oral sex on him (before the revelation of Dil's biological sex). This is a classically triangulated moment of repressed male homosocial desire – Fergus's unconscious wish for Jody mediated through the black 'woman' Dil – and, in hindsight, queered further by the knowledge that the black 'woman' is a man. Yet this is too easy an explanation. The dream may signify Fergus's guilt, his grief, or may be purposefully enigmatic, dramatising his barely articulated sense that something about Jude will help him 'find himself'. After Dil reveals his sex, Fergus dreams of Jody again, this time laughing at the successful googlie he has posthumously bowled to his erstwhile enemy-friend.

Dil: **Are you pretending yet?**

Fergus: **I'm working on it**

Despite the retrospectively visible homosocial signs in the Fergus–Jody relationship, the film (in keeping with its rejection of fixity) refuses to confer a new homosexual identity onto Fergus. Male heterosexual assumptions are mocked by his (and our) failure to discern Dil's sex, but there is no real attempt to develop or consummate a gay relationship. The potential of sexual interaction between a heterosexual man and a gay man, whose performance of femininity troubles the easy allocation of gender to him, is a marker of the film's queer credentials. As a transvestite, Dil is well used to performing. His performance, though, is a form of 'passing', his clothes and outward appearance hiding his manhood. Marjorie Garber (1993) argues that manifest transvestism can be subversive because it foregrounds the constructedness of gender and sexuality (it is a hyperbolic form of 'gender trouble', to use Judith Butler's phrase). While Shantanu DuttaAhmad suggests that Dil's 'transvestic performance' goes unseen and is therefore robbed of its transgressive potential (DuttaAhmed, 1988: 64), Davidson's performance has a differently subversive purpose. Rather than parading a mismatch between nature and culture from the first reel, Dil's passing capitalises on the queer tactics of concealment and revelation. His penis is the film's Trojan horse, catching hegemonic masculinity off-guard, almost with its pants down.

    After the unforeseen genital epiphany, Dil's extravagantly feminine performance takes on new meanings. Dil and Fergus next confront each other in the 'Metro', and its previously disguised status as a gay/transvestite bar is now made honestly clear. Dil's optimistically romantic pursuit of the straight Fergus is clearly stalemated by the truth of his own biological sex. The disagreement between them, though, is mediated through a third person, Col the barman, played with his customary sardonic detachment by Jim Broadbent. The triangulated discourse between them (because Dil refuses to speak to Fergus directly) echoes their early, tentative courtship at the 'Metro'. The same three-way verbal game was played then, with Dil's flirtation filtered through Col. The film's ironic rhetoric knowingly casts Col as a film cliché: the all-seeing bartender, uninvolved yet commenting on and orchestrating the world wisely. Symmetrical shots with Dil and Fergus at opposite edges of the screen and Col in the centre emphasise his importance as an external referee, a 'third way' through whom productive dialogue can be sustained between what would otherwise be two polar opposites. We are implicitly invited to map the allegory into Irish politics.

Dil next appears, cross-dressed to kill, at the building site where Fergus is working, play-acting a role which combines levels of cheery optimism, ironic banter and defensive denial: 'Darling', he says, 'Never let the sun go down on an argument . . . Let's kiss and make up honey'. The role he plays is a mask, a camp show, which, like the sunshades he wears, hides his emotional and physical bruising. His camp-ness here is stereotypically gay (the labels 'old trooper' / 'such a survivor' might be applied). Stereotypes are generally held to be crudely reductive and negative phenomena, but the codes they offer can, like the homely chestnuts Dil recites, be appropriated usefully. Here, Dil's 'stiff-upper-lip' performance is a valuable coping mechanism, and he deploys it productively and intelligently. Even the 'cuppa' which Dil politely offers Fergus is significant, casting this black, gay transvestite as a suburban, English housewife, but also nodding to the nation's ritual recourse to tea-drinking in times of crisis. As with the playing to stereotype, the enacting of ritual in this postmodern world offers a ready-made social script for Dil to draw on. Fergus still functions in a traditional, chivalric way, using threats of violence to defend Dil's honour on the building site, but camp performance gives Dil the upper hand. He twice prompts Fergus to ask to meet him again until, after minor reluctance, he consents.

These codes of campness allow Dil enough irony to accommodate the gap between reality and his desire for Fergus. This would seem like desperate denial were it not for the seductive comic register, and for Dil's optimistic faith in pretence. To Fergus's hesitant 'I kinda liked you as a girl', Dil replies 'Well, that's a start': evading the issue perhaps, but admirable nonetheless. The film repeatedly promotes the pragmatic politics of play. Fergus resents being wrong-footed about Dil, and regrets the truth of Dil's sex. 'You can always pretend', Dil suggests, and Fergus seems to soften his position: it 'won't be quite the same' but he's 'working on it'. Disavowal is a powerful mechanism, and the way Fergus starts to acclimatise to the knowledge of Dil's sexual sameness queers the classically Freudian scenario of the heterosexual male's recognition of sexual difference. The film, though, only toys with the chance of reciprocated same-sex desire. While Dil can extract a goodnight kiss from Fergus, sex is off the menu. As Fergus says, he 'can't pretend that much'. This signifies a nervous heteronormativity at the film's heart, a policing of the borders of straight masculinity, but the metaphorical bedroom door between Dil and Fergus is nevertheless kept ajar.

Jude: 'Keep the faith'

Fergus's fluidity contrasts with his rigid IRA past, which catches up with him when Jude, with a new tough look, arrives from Ireland. She threatens his 'wee black chick' to recruit Fergus in a suicidal mission to assassinate a British judge (on his way out of a brothel – another sexual-political blurring). Tellingly she instructs Fergus to 'keep the faith'. Fergus transforms Dil's appearance 'into' a man, dressing him in Jody's cricket gear, and cutting his hair, ostensibly to protect him. This is no simple reinstatement of a 'true male biology' though, for the male clothing Dil wears is an ill-fitting masquerade. Our memory of Dil's appearance as a woman confuses our sense that he is not. When Fergus tells Dil he would like him better as a man, the possibility of same-sex desire is again foregrounded, and Dil, deprived of make-up, is unenthusiastically metamorphosed towards a 'straight-acting' category (one of the more paradoxical of gay identities). In redesigning Dil, Fergus is resurrecting an image of Jody, whose death he partly caused, and this obscures his motives, with the film re-enacting the necrophiliac obsessions of Hitchcock's *Vertigo*.[2] Fergus's involvement with Jude causes Dil to grow hysterical, and the film then thrusts yet another stereotype onto Dil: the self-destructive, emotionally unstable queen. When Fergus finally tells Dil that he was involved in Jody's killing, Dil ties Fergus to his bed, making him miss his appointment with Jude (although it seems Fergus's intention is to escape the IRA altogether). The assassination of the judge is blundered. Jude appears in the flat, armed with a gun, and she is shot dead by Dil, in an excessive display of violence. Dil repeats 'She used her tits and that cute little arse to get him didn't she?' as he fills her with bullets. Fergus helps Dil escape and takes the blame for the shooting. In a brief closing coda, Dil visits Fergus in prison. The playful tone of pretended possibility returns, as Dil promises to wait for Fergus to be released in 2,335 days' time (the 'gay' consummation still deferred) and as the camera tracks away from them, we hear Lyle Lovett's 'Stand by your Man'.

Feminist readings object to the transformation of Jude into a monstrous *femme-fatale*, dressed in the tough look of 1940s film noir and overplayed jaggedly by Miranda Richardson. Her despised use of sex to lure Jody to his capture (a typical spy genre deceit), and the film's bloodthirsty annihilation of her, are undeniably problematic. In its defence, the film uses stereotype deliberately and self-consciously throughout. Fergus is offensively called 'Pat' by his two-dimensional yuppie boss, Jody was 'nigger' in northern Ireland, and Dil, too, is cast in various stereotypical roles. Dave, a minor character whom Dil is involved with, is a crudely drawn caricature of violent, shell-suited Essex-man, against whom both Fergus's and Dil's masculinity are to be measured, but no critic has leapt to defend the good men of Essex from this caricature of unreconstructed Neanderthal masculinity. The film wants us to see its demonised stereotypification of Jude as part of its rhetorical strategy to deconstruct traditional ways of seeing: it asks us to reflect upon the

Figure 11.2 The *Gender* Game: 'Monstrous *femme-fatales*' Dil (Jaye Davidson) and Jude
(Miranda Richardson).

Source: Courtesy of Stephen Bourne (Palace/Channel 4).

ethics of habitual modes of representation. Jude, of course, is the only biological woman in the film, and she is shot dead. Our rightful concern about this marks a weak point in the film's strategy. To say that Jude is actually a positive, strong woman's role is a moot point, but it is barely persuasive. What is in keeping with the film's anti-essentialist thrust, though, is Dil's horror that Jude used her 'tits and arse' to get Jody. The film stresses the performativity of gender and relationships, and what Dil's outburst expresses is not 'the TV's jealousy of the woman's natural endowments', as Mark Simpson maintains (Simpson, 1994: 170), but Dil's disgust at Jude's reliance on her biological sex, a metaphor within the film for her entrenched ideological fixity.

By focusing on Fergus's psychological development, the film occupies the hegemonic centre-ground, but it does so progressively to test the limits of liberalism. Arguably, this is to the detriment of the other characters, the representation of whom attracted much criticism. Yet these criticisms, as well intentioned as the film's own progressive liberalism, tend to expose their own partiality and etch out the boundaries of their competing systems of understanding. Feminist gender studies repeatedly appropriate Dil as a woman (he is usually called 'she'), and while this displays an understanding of the discourse of gender performance it also critically (and hetero-centrically) sidelines the possibility of same-sex desire between him and Fergus. It also erases the issue of Dil's undeniable biological maleness, yet the film never implies that Dil is either transsexual or is discontented with his manhood, and Dil's own references to himself as 'a girl' are dramatised with his characteristic irony. Kristin Handler argues that the film shores up Fergus's masculinity by allowing him to absorb feminine traits at the expense of women, and that it works to subordinate all those who are 'not-men', a category which includes the non-phallic, effeminate Dil (Handler, 1994: 36). Polemically reluctant to concede the possibility that masculinity might soften or adapt on its own terms, Fergus's gentler characteristics can only be accredited to the feminine; Dil is similarly stripped of his own constructed, camp, gay masculinity. To Mark Simpson, the transvestism is nothing less than a misogynistic appropriation of womanliness by a man. His observation that in Dil, 'the Good Girl is so "good" that she has a penis' wittily acknowledges the film's queer play with castration anxiety, but the wish to see the film as dramatising white patriarchy's assimilation of otherness dubiously undervalues the validity of transvestism itself by arguing that it 'has come to represent sympathetically the fantasy of doing away with women altogether' (Simpson, 1994: 168–70).

As with the charges of gender critics, it has also been argued that the racial representation in the film is controlled by Fergus's subjectivity, whose experience is favoured.[3] This charge of orientalism carries weight, but it overlooks the intelligence of Jody and Dil, downplaying the way they each use queer performative strategies to exercise power. Fergus is unsuccessful as a terrorist, wrong-footed by Jody and Dil, taken hostage by Dil, and then submits to British law by taking the blame for the killing of Jude. As an embodiment of cultural dominance he is more than a little compromised, while both Jody's and Dil's understanding of postcolonial multiculturalism is effective and full of possibility.

The film's liberal anchoring in white, straight, male subjectivity compromises its queer credentials, but this is to carp. It was marketed at, and achieved the very mainstream audience with most to learn from its queerness. It presents a contest between the rounded identity politics embodied by Fergus and a host of performative, masqueraded and ironic elements, and the ongoing relationship between Fergus and Dil signifies a constructive dialogue between the two (again, the 'Irish' dimension need not be laboured). Despite the politics of difference and marginality which the film alludes to, its centre of gravity is in the ethics of multiculturalism – a liberal aesthetic, a hegemonic structure, and one which does not eradicate inequality, but nevertheless one which demands respect and accommodates multi-accented, cultural variety. The centre tends to incorporate. Perversely, the progressive capital purchased here by the queer intrusion of Jaye Davidson's penis was acquired through a marketing campaign in the States which stressed the secret of the film, and which misdirected audiences by selling it as a noir-thriller (*femme-fatale* Jude holds a smoking gun on the poster, although she never holds one in the film). On the back of the film's success, its American distributors Miramax, standard-bearers of American independent cinema, sold out to Disney, while in Britain, the production company Palace Pictures went bust. While, to echo Dil's reassurance to Fergus, this may just be a matter of 'details baby, details', it is a sign of tactical queerness successfully impressing itself on mainstream culture.

Notes

1   Brian McIlroy notes the ironies of this debate: 'As Fergus leads Jody out to be shot, they argue over cricket and hurling, one a sport that has been co-opted, enjoyed and paraded by the former colonies, the other a sport only played seriously in Ireland and symbolic of a monochrome nationalism' (McIlroy, 1998: 58).
2   Peter N. Chumo II notes how these sequences resemble the cross-dressing in Hitchcock's *Psycho*, but more relevantly he charts the resemblances to *Vertigo*, where another failed man re-fashions a false woman to resemble a previous dead character (Chumo II, 1995: 247–53).
3   See, for example, Darrell Moore, 'Now you Can See It: The Liberal Aesthetic and Racial Representation in *The Crying Game*', *CineAction*, No. 32, Fall 1993, pp. 63–7, and Lola Young, '"Nothing is as it seems": Re-viewing *The Crying Game*', in Pat Kirkham and Janet Thumin (eds.) *Me Jane: Masculinity, Movies and Women* (London: Lawrence and Wishart, 1995).

Bibliography

Burke, M. (1993) 'Celtic Dreamer', *Film Ireland*, April/May, 16–21.

Chumo II, P.N. (1995) '*The Crying Game*: Hitchcockian Romance, and the Quest for Identity', *Literature Film Quarterly*, Vol.23, No.4, 247–53.

Dahlman, C. (2002), 'Masculinity in Conflict: Geopolitics and Performativity in *The Crying Game*', in Tim Cresswell and Barbara Dixon (eds.), *Engaging Film: Geographies of Mobility and Identity*, Oxford: Rowman and Littlefield.

DuttaAhmed, S. (1988) '"I thought you knew": Performing the Penis, the Phallus, and Otherness in Neil Jordan's *The Crying Game*', *Film Criticism*, Vol.23, No.1, 61–73.

Garber, M. (1993) *Vested Interests: Cross-dressing and Cultural Anxiety*, London: Penguin Books.

Handler, K. (1994) 'Sexing *The Crying Game*: Difference, Identity, Ethics', *Film Quarterly*, Vol.47, No.3, 31–42.

McCall, C. (1999) *Identity on Northern Ireland: Communities, Politics and Change*, Basingstoke: Palgrave.

McIlroy, B. (1998) *Shooting to Kill: Filmmaking and the 'Troubles' in Northern Ireland*, Trowbridge: Flicks Books.

Moore, D. (1993) 'Now you Can See It: The Liberal Aesthetic and Racial Representation in *The Crying Game*', *CineAction*, No.32, 63–7.

Young, L. (1995) '"Nothing is as it seems": Re-viewing *The Crying Game*', in Pat Kirkham and Janet Thumin (eds.), *Me Jane: Masculinity, Movies and Women*, London: Lawrence and Wishart.

12 'It's my nature'

AIDS narratives and the moral re-branding of queerness in the mid-1990s

Gregory Woods

a) The gay plague

The babble of hateful voices that worsened the first decade of the AIDS epidemic for gay men has been characterised by Lee Edelman as follows: 'in the case of AIDS, infection endlessly breeds sentences – sentences whose implication in a poisonous history of homophobic constructions assures that no matter what explicit ideology they serve, they will carry within them the virulent germ of the dominant cultural discourse.'[1] One major aspect of this 'poisonous history' was the system-atic demonisation of the 'AIDS carrier' as a deliberate serial killer, and the gay man as an 'AIDS carrier'. The immorality of gayness itself was but an early sign of the immorality that was playing self-indulgent games with life and death. In a seminal essay on vampiric imagery in the cultural unfolding of the epidemic, Ellis Hanson writes:

> Myths about gay sex serve to amplify myths about AIDS; and so when I speak of the vampire as the embodiment of evil sexuality, I speak of gay men and people with AIDS in the same breath. I am talking about the irrational fear of PWAs and gay men who 'bite.' I am talking about essentialist represen-tations of gay men as vampiric: as sexually exotic, alien, unnatural, oral, anal, compulsive, violent, protean, polymorphic, polyvocal, polysemous, invisible, soulless, transient, superhumanly mobile, infectious, murderous, suicidal, and a threat to wife, children, home, and phallus.[2]

Hanson identifies Randy Shilts' controversial history of the early stages of the epidemic, *And the Band Played On* (1987), as providing 'an archetypal instance of how the myth of the gay male vampire got superimposed onto people with AIDS and how the whole package was sold (by a gay journalist) to the American public' (p.331). In particular, in his portrayal of the supposed irresponsibility of a Canadian airline steward, Gaetan Dugas, the epidemic's 'patient zero', Shilts uses the stan-dard techniques of thriller fiction to embellish his sinister construction of gay promiscuity.[3] Shilts' defining, conclusive sentence on 'patient zero' states: 'At one time Gaetan had been what every man wanted from gay life; by the time he died, he had become what every man feared.'[4] For Shilts, not only does Dugas actively embody the sudden collapse of gay liberation and all the hopes it sustained, but he does so by shouldering the blame for our collective terror as the epidemic began to manifest itself in gay subcultures across the world. In effect, every gay man becomes his victim. His unrelenting search for pleasure inflicts not only multiple deaths but widespread fear in the face of pleasures that kill.

However, at the particular moment when a hostile press remembered the existence of bisexuality – no great secret since the two Kinsey reports, of 1948 and 1953, had convincingly posited a spectrum of sexualities rather than just a heterosexual majority and a tiny homosexual minority – this burden of blame was momentarily shifted from the gay man to the bisexual man. By contrast with the former – who, since gay liberation, had become relatively visible in his jeans and plaid shirts, with his earring and clone moustache – the bisexual was suddenly constructed as far more sinister because invisible – all the more invisible than any purely homosexual man had been because of his sickeningly deceptive behaviour towards women, which made him look straight. Like those reds America had found under its beds in the 1950s, the bisexual was regarded as especially threatening because he was already there, between the sheets, within the very tabernacle of the nuclear family. Even single women with active sex lives were presented as the passive, will-less victims of this marauding philanderer. By contrast with him, we could present ourselves – to an extent justifiably – as having responded to the epidemic with urgency (though Larry Kramer would not have agreed) and responsibility. Our media had brought AIDS to the centre of our concern, we had developed care networks, safer sex was our invention, and we had adapted our subculture to the requirements of the time.

It may be that, in future, gay historians will recognise this as the moment when the struggle for equal rights and social assimilation in Britain was, if not exactly won, brought within reach. In the first place, new drug therapies were proving successful at prolonging the lives of people with AIDS. Although the epidemic had caused a vicious backlash against gay men and lesbians, engineered by the popular media and hypocritically capitalised on by Tory politicians burning off their resentments of social reforms dating back to the late 1960s, it also, in the end, aroused massive amounts of productive sympathy. Despite demonisation, the fact became manifest that gay men were doing more than the government to combat the epidemic. It helped that the Major government looked increasingly unsteady as the decade progressed. John Major's 'back to basics' campaign drifted into laughable disarray as a sequence of Tory members of parliament and cabinet ministers were outed as adulterers and worse.[5] Derek Jarman's objection to Ian McKellen's acceptance of a knighthood from John Major in 1991 was understandable, indeed laudable in its vehemence. But the award did signal the fact that a consistently and actively homophobic administration no longer regarded open homosexuality (in an actor, at least) as a bar to formal honours. By the time Tony Blair's Labour administration was elected in 1997, the atmosphere was right for gradual (some would say, frustratingly slow and piecemeal) repeal and reform of Britain's archaic sexual laws.

After the combined onslaught of anti-gay propaganda consequent upon the AIDS epidemic itself and the Thatcher government's drive to censor affirmative expressions of gayness – all converging, in particular, on the year 1987, when a nationwide public information campaign made such claims as that 'AIDS is everyone's problem' and 'AIDS can affect anyone', and 1988, when Section 28 of Local Government banned the use of public money to 'promote' homosexuality – a liberal response of affirmative gay images reasserted that it could be good to be gay, and that in being gay one could also be good. Demonisation was met by canonisation. Simplistic stereotypes were answered with simplistic stereotypes. This is what happens in a crisis. The important distinction, though, is between punitive and progressive representations. As the bisexual man suddenly took the less threatening gay man's place as public enemy number one, out gay men seemed by contrast all the more safe for their visibility and the mistaken belief that they did not belong to, and therefore could not endanger, normal families.

b) The good gay man

In Stephen Walker's *Closing Numbers* (1993), the good gay man, who is open and honest and knows all about HIV transmission and safer sex, is contrasted with the irresponsibly secretive and promiscuous bisexual.[6] The film is about a middle-class family invaded by the threat of AIDS, via the body of the husband, Keith, who is secretly having an affair with a gay man, Steve. The victim of the piece is the wife, Anna, played by Jane Asher, an actress at that time best known for her wholesome image and cake-baking skills. The narrative minutiae are not important here. What matters is that on finding out that her husband is having an affair, Anna arranges to meet the person in question. She sets a date in a particular restaurant at a particular time. Assuming she is going to be meeting a woman, she is thrown into confusion when a man approaches her table.

> *Steve*: Hello. I'm Steve. [*He shakes her hand before she realises who he is.*] Do you think I could have a sip of your wine? I'm in a bit if a state.
> *Anna*: She sent you instead of coming herself? What are you? A brother? Friend? If it's a joke it's not a very good one.
> *Steve*: It's not a joke. I'm the person you want to talk to. [*The wine waiter interrupts.*] A bottle of dry house white, please. We'll order later. [*To Anna:*] You'd no idea, had you? I don't mean about me. I mean about Keith. I'd always assumed wives sensed when their husbands were bisexual. We met three months ago.

[*Spine-chilling soundtrack accompanies the look of horror on Anna's face. She bursts into tears.*]

The horror the film represents and generates at this moment is in response not to the messenger but to the message, not to gayness but to bisexuality. From the outset, Steve is represented as being civilised (even when 'in a bit of a state' he recognises a 'dry house white' from a quick sip) and speaking from a position of much greater knowledge of the ways of the world than the sheltered, though educated, housewife. In this crucial early sequence of scenes, a number of Steve's utterances identify him as the definitive good gay man. Jenni Olson describes him as 'one of the most level-headed gay characters you've ever seen on the screen', and even this is an understatement.[7] Steve and Anna continue their conversation in a park, Steve describing how he first met Keith:

Steve: He was sitting on his own in a gay pub one lunchtime: new face, wearing a city suit, clearly married. I knew at once he needed protecting – from himself, if nothing else. I recognised the look of someone who's inches away from being beaten up and robbed. [*Pause.*] Actually, I'm glad you phoned.

Anna: Why?

Steve: I've insisted we only do safe sex. He has to accept that. But not long ago he and I were talking . . . about ourselves . . . about the past. Keith told me about a promiscuous period three years ago. He was very down at the time. He behaved as if the risk of AIDS didn't exist. And anyway, I thought that you and he were sleeping apart – a convenient conclusion to jump to, I suppose. He rang you once from my flat, and from the way he spoke I guessed that you might still be sleeping together.

Anna: Is that a question?

Steve: It is important. More so for you, I think.

Anna: We're married. We do make love.

Steve: Unprotected?

Anna: Two, sometime three afternoons a week, for the last three months. Before that, not so often. Nowhere near so often. Very imaginative sex, too – most unusual for Keith. You should write a manual. [*Pause.*] You're trying to tell me I might be infected.

Steve: Two years ago I'd have said, What's the point of being tested? But now, if you were HIV-positive, there's a lot more help.

Anna: Why should you care about me?

Steve: I'm a carer. It's my nature.

Even in the face of a distraught wife's anger, Steve comes across not as a home-wrecker but, on the contrary, as some kind of defender of the sanctity of marriage and the family. The gay man is suddenly re-imagined as being capable of maturity

Figure 12.1 Married bliss? Anna (Jane Asher) realises the shocking truth about her husband
Keith (Tim Woodward) in *Closing Numbers* (1993).

Source: BFI Stills, Posters and Designs (Channel 4).

and restraint. In the face of death, he has become the master of his wayward
genitals, the gate-keeper of his rectum. Even as a married man's gay lover, he is
presented not as the embodiment of perverse adultery, but as a secular guardian
angel. Without his intervention, Keith would have gone off the rails.

By bringing up the topic of HIV, Steve raises the film's main point – that AIDS can affect anyone. Everyone is at risk. (Even Jane Asher? Yes, even she.) If her husband's bisexuality is a horrific discovery to an unsuspecting wife, the threat of HIV transmission makes it all the more so.

> *Anna*: You said I ought to get myself tested.
> *Steve*: Everyone makes their own decisions.
> *Anna*: Why warn me then, in the first place?
> *Steve*: How could you decide when you didn't know?
> *Anna*: Salve your conscience and it just might pay dividends . . .
> *Steve*: Who for?
> *Anna*: For you. If I'd left him.
> *Steve*: But you haven't.
> *Anna*: Yet. [*Pause. Close to tears:*] Why did he do it?
> *Steve*: Have you asked him?
> *Anna*: All this [?] talk of not being his true self. How the hell do you find the meaning of life groping some stranger in the dark?
> *Steve*: You don't. It's a strong compulsion, and like most drugs it only gives temporary relief.
> *Anna*: From what?
> *Steve*: One's self. One's situation. [*Anna sighs.*] Sorry.
> *Anna*: No you're not. You're safe. You know more about him than I do, and you were clever enough to protect yourself. Why should you be sorry? He isn't even your problem any more, is he?
> *Steve*: Is he yours?
> *Anna*: Oh yes, I think so, don't you? It may have been only a registry office but I agreed to every word. It was . . . it was an informed decision. [*Crying.*] Now I need another. I have to know. I'm so frightened. [*He holds her. She cries on his shoulder.*]

Paradoxically, even though gay sex brought HIV into the family, it also brought the greater intimacy of more imaginative sex between husband and wife; and even though it created estrangement between them, ultimately it is educating them both. Where earlier gay and AIDS films had supportive, heterosexual, female minor characters ('fag hags' like Lisa in Norman René's 1990 film *Longtime Companion*), it was now the gay character who supported the hapless straight woman. The 'fag hag' had been replaced by the 'hag fag'.

It is worth remembering the reality. Faced with institutional neglect and media hostility, it was gay men – but not, of course, all gay men – who founded what became the world's main AIDS organisations, and gay men who not only invented safer sex but quickly became involved in safer sex education. This life-saving innovation is usually attributed to Michael Callan and Richard Berkowitz's pamphlet

How to Have Sex in an Epidemic, published in New York in 1983. Inevitably, as it became clear that gay men were by no means the only group who were going to be substantially affected by the epidemic, the majority had to turn to this minority for advice and help. This situation resulted in the apparent paradox that some of the most sophisticated and innovative safer sex education materials for women and for hetero-sexual men were developed under the aegis of Gay Men's Health Crisis (GMHC) in New York City. GMHC swiftly went on to become the largest AIDS organisation in the world. And what started as a gay organisation named after a gay man, the Terrence Higgins Trust quickly achieved an equivalent pre-eminence within Britain.

The AIDS counter-discourse was fronted by gay men. This had a salutary effect. Against a background of hysterical and hostile voices it became possible to hear the dignified, rational and informed arguments of a small number of publicly visible gay men like Simon Watney and Tony Whitehead, the public face of the Terrence Higgins Trust. Both wrote indispensable regular columns for the gay press – Watney in *Gay Times*, Whitehead in *Capital Gay* – but they were often at their most effective in the more exposed arena of the public broadcast. If the epidemic had its positive role models in its fictional representations, they were not plucked out of nowhere. They were based on the resilient – indeed, in some cases, heroic – behaviour of actual individuals. It was impossible to watch such men's interventions, often under hostile fire, in televised interviews and discussions, without being profoundly humbled, impressed and moved. Something similar, in miniature, occurs in *Closing Numbers*. The gay man possesses and provides all the information and even much of the care.[8] It is not Keith but Steve who accompanies Anna to the clinic for her HIV test, and it is not Keith but Steve who drives her to collect her results. On the latter occasion, indeed, Keith leaves home, unable to face her at all. (Or rather, it may be that he selfishly cannot face the necessary deduction, should her results come up positive, that he himself is HIV-positive.) It is, of course, Steve who drives the son to persuade the father to return home.

Steve's eventual anger with Keith adds a much-needed third dimension to his character. When Keith self-pityingly goes to him for sympathy – they meet up in a gay bar – Steve explodes at last. As they leave the bar, Steve initiates this exchange:

Steve: What did you really come here for, eh? What do you want from me?
Keith: Nothing, I don't want anything.
Steve: Yes you do! You want me to comfort you, be gentle, kind, under-standing. You want me to tell you that it's all right to be scared.
Keith: Is that such a terrible thing?
Steve: I'm not Anna! And I'm not a fucking saint! I don't need to understand you or even like you. And I don't think you'd find my *pity* very helpful.

The word 'pity' is spat out with such unexpected venom that Keith is left with no response. He turns his back on Steve and storms off. The fact is that, up to this point, the audience has been led to believe – as, perhaps, Keith himself believes – that Steve is literally, indeed, 'a fucking saint'. His saintliness is confirmed by the very sanctity of his fucking practices, his insistence on safer sex. His has been the voice of reason in all circumstances: as interlocutor with the angry wife; with the self-absorbed and -indulgent husband; with the whingeing son; with Jim, the gay friend with AIDS. . . . The problem with this representation is that, by contrast, it threatens to make the developing dementia of the gay man with AIDS seem positively perverse.

c) The bad gay scene

It is hardly surprising that the positive gay role model was never allowed to prevail unqualified. While some individual gay men might be portrayed as caring, informed and responsible the gay scene as a whole was subjected to intensified representations as a location of disease. The reason for the bisexual's having become a carrier is that he frequented gay venues. The gay club, therefore, remains, definitively, a place in which irresponsible and dangerous sexual events are arranged. It follows that the clients of such a place will be identified as being irresponsible and dangerous themselves. Remember that, in *Closing Numbers*, even the blameworthy bisexual, Anna's husband Keith, is vulnerable in such a place. It is just a gay pub at lunchtime, but Steve takes one look at Keith there and recognises him as 'someone who's inches away from being beaten up and robbed'. It is only after acting on his bisexuality and going to gay social venues that the normal husband becomes an AIDS-carrier.

This apparent contradiction undermines the positive image *Closing Numbers* attempts to purvey. Mere virtue cannot save the good gay man from the reputation of the bad gay crowd. The same problem has always arisen in television news reports and documentaries about HIV transmission. No matter how many responsible gay men were individually interviewed – for instance, spokesmen for the Terrence Higgins Trust, before lack of government funding drove it to re-market itself as *not* being a gay organisation – there was always a general shot of a milling nightclub dance floor, all flashing lights and frenzied silhouettes, giving an impression of hedonistic anonymity. What we gay men on the scene may have thought of as a refuge from the crass values of hetero-Thatcherism, to other eyes, would have looked like Sodom regained. So, even while the individual gay man was getting a make-over as a caring secular saint, the gay subculture was still stigmatised as dangerous, immoral and diseased.

In Jean Stewart's *Nervous Energy* (1995), too, the gay scene and subculture are depicted as uncaring environments in which the most vulnerable get left to their own devices. The film's autobiographical screenplay, by Howard Schuman, seems to be burning off accumulated resentments in a vengeful sequence of negative representations of minor characters, the family and erstwhile friends of Tom, a gay man with AIDS.[9] None of Tom's gay friends in Glasgow have been in touch during his illness in London. Moreover, as a harrowing scene towards the end of the film spells out, aesthetic effeminacy might itself even be considered infectious. Tom, who has AIDS, is attacked by one of his oldest gay friends, Arnie, in the following terms:

> I'm angry at you, if you want to know the truth. I'm sorry. I'm just trying to be honest. But I told you, in '83, when I got back from the States, *be careful*. And when you were screwing around with that opera singer – I mean, he'd been performing in New York, San Francisco, Sydney – you said I was swallowing a line. . . . But I was right and you were out of control. And so you went and committed suicide, you stupid prick! That's what I can't stand.

Arnie will not give Tom and his lover Ira a bed for the night. Nor will another gay couple: the one who is at home reluctantly lets them in but when his lover returns home he wakes Tom and Ira up and throws them out. So much for community.

The patience of the caring gay man is tried by the PWA whose dementia is slipping into irrationality and bouts of self-threatening misbehaviour. In *Closing Numbers* Steve copes with Jim's mood-swings with hardly a harsh word. The danger in this manifestation of difference is that the sick gay man might come across as morally less controlled than the well gay man. A similar risk arises in *Nervous Energy* where, despite a bovine performance from Alfred Molina as Ira, the viewer's sympathy seems to be demanded as much in relation to the PWA's lover as to the PWA himself. Yet Ira's patience with his wayward lover soon comes to seem oppressive, his reason unreasonable. The dying man is trying to experience a few last pleasures; his lover is trying to defer his death. There are times these two aims seem incompatible. Ira, Tom's lover, and Ian, Tom's brother, are in dispute about the extent to which Tom's bouts of anti-social behaviour are caused by his illness and its treatments (Ira) or by an essentially perverse character (Ian). The debate is clinched for the brother when, having arrived to take Tom away, Ira noisily makes love with him in the brother and sister-in-law's shower. The homophobic elder brother's attribution of perversity is confirmed by what he regards as this reversion to type: neither Tom nor Ira knows how to behave in a family house; therefore Tom's waywardness has nothing to do with his HIV. His problem is a recalcitrant queerness which does not merit even the reluctant pity Ian has been granting his illness.

d) No sex, please, we're gay

The only sex actually shown in *Closing Numbers* is 'bad' sex, putting the suburban housewife at risk. The opening scene in which she and her husband make love – he going down on her – seems, on the face of it, conventional (and therefore safe) enough, until later developments reveal the husband's prolific gay infidelities. In one such scene, somewhat implausibly, Keith is vigorously buggered by a squaddie in one of the lavatories of an inter-city train. There being no sign of condom use, one assumes there is no condom in use. In relation to possible viral transmission, Keith's rectum is the anteroom to his wife's vagina. Although Steve is meant to be the fount of all virtuous wisdom on sexual matters, no sexual event involving him is ever shown. He and Keith share one hungry mouth-to-mouth kiss the first time we see them together, but that is the limit of what is made manifest. As a result, notwithstanding all evidence of his experiential knowledge and understanding, he comes across as curiously sexless. This appears to be the only way in which the filmmakers can feel confident of showing a virtuous gay man. Once gay men get together – unless one of them is dying – gay sex happens; once there is gay sex, there is vice and HIV.

In Kenneth Branagh's slightly earlier film *Peter's Friends* (1992) Peter is, as it were, bisexually celibate – and happy to be. He is played by Stephen Fry, an actor who was known to be a gay celibate and claimed to be happy as such. Peter's friends, all heterosexual, are all in such dreadful relationships – or, in the case of Maggie (Emma Thompson), so desperate to pair up with anyone – that he seems by far the most balanced of the lot. His sexlessness is a major factor in the conveying of this impression. He is placid to the point of blandness, but there does prove to be a limit to his patience. It is just before midnight on New Year's Eve that he finally snaps in the face of his friends' whining and bickering. In particular, the alcoholic Andrew (Kenneth Branagh) has spectacularly fallen off the wagon and has been haranguing Peter about why he bothered inviting all his friends in the first place. As in Mike Newell's later film *Four Weddings and a Funeral* (1994), gayness seems chastely tragic by contrast with the ubiquitous incontinence of heterosexual courtship and rutting rituals. Driven to the limit of his self-imposed discretion, Peter makes the following announcement:

> I invited you all here . . . because . . . you all mean a lot to me, as you know . . . and . . . I'm sorry, this is, um, this is not very easy, um . . . because recently . . . I, I had a blood test, and it turns out that I'm HIV-positive. [*Stunned silence.*] I'm sorry. I, I, I didn't mean to sober you up that fast. [*Clock strikes.*] Well, happy new year.

The effect of the contrast between Peter and his friends is to further isolate the gay man – the impressive house he has inherited from his family is usually empty – and characterise him as living an inactive and *therefore* blameless life. With no lover and no gay friends, he is beyond the reach of temptation and viral transmission. With little human connection beyond some pretty distant friendships – the New Year gathering is a reunion after many years' dispersal – Peter is, simply, less interesting than the people around him. His HIV announcement is his one dramatic coup, and all it can invoke in an audience is the formulaic pity due a character we have not yet learned to care for.

Not dissimilarly, in Brian Gilbert's *Wilde* (1997), Stephen Fry gives such a stolid, immobile performance as Oscar Wilde that Jude Law (Lord Alfred Douglas) and Tom Wilkinson (as his father, the Marquess of Queensberry), seem vibrantly attractive by comparison. The point being that the supposedly 'positive' version of gayness was becoming, by the mid-1990s, distinctly dull. It had hardly made any significant advance on, for example, the moral neutrality (the blandness) of Colin Russell (Michael Cashman) in the television soap opera *EastEnders* a decade previously. Although Colin was in a relatively respectable, monogamous relationship with Barry Clark (Garry Hales), the two of them could never be seen to do much more, by way of monogamously relating, than hug. Indeed, the relationship soon became so awkwardly inexpressible that Barry became heterosexual and Colin was left on his own. As a positive gay character, he could have neither sex nor HIV; as a purely tokenist representation, he could have no gay friends. This left him in a void of yuppy blandness which only illness could resolve: he was given multiple sclerosis and written out of the script in 1988.

Given the proliferation of dull gay role models I have been describing, it is hardly surprising that, in 1999, the ill-behaved central figure of Stuart Jones (Aidan Gillen) in Russell T. Davies' television drama *Queer As Folk* came as a blessed relief. His drug-using, car-smashing, schoolboy-screwing antics gave a fresh sense of the freedoms available to the freed. Those of us who once used to wear the early gay-liberationist lapel badge *Gay is Good* thought of it as meaning both that gayness felt good and that it was not morally evil. Indeed, the fact that it was pleasurable was a sign of its virtuousness. What we did not believe was that this should confine us to the hetero-hegemonic view of what was virtuous behaviour. In the 1990s, certain queer voices insisted on continuing to assert the right to behave badly. Derek Jarman's work consistently attacked the moralisation of disease, whether for liberal or repressive motives, and went on consistently celebrating the transgressions of queerness. Yet, ironically, Jarman knew that his own illness had radically altered the way people looked at him. Since announcing he was HIV-positive, he said, 'Reaction to me has changed. There is an element of worship, which worries me. Perhaps I courted it.'[10] Jarman was canonised by the Sisters of Perpetual Indulgence on 22 September 1991.

Notes

1 Lee Edelman, 'The Plague of Discourse: Politics, Literary Theory, and AIDS', in Ronald R. Butters, John M. Clum and Michael Moon (eds.) (1989) *Displacing Homophobia: Gay Male Perspectives in Literature and Culture* (Durham and London: Duke University Press), pp.289–305; p.303.

2 Ellis Hanson, 'Undead', in Diana Fuss (ed.) (1991) *Inside/Out: Lesbian Theories, Gay Theories* (New York and London: Routledge), pp.324–40; p.325.

3 Patient Zero was rehabilitated as the central character in the musical *Zero Patience*, released as a film by John Greyson in 1993.

4 Randy Shilts (1988) *And the Band Played On: Politics, People, and the AIDS Epidemic* (New York and London: Penguin), p.439.

5 Sadly, Major's own adultery was not revealed until he had long been out of office.

6 One of the cultural consequences of the hostile barrages to which gay men were subjected in the first decade of the epidemic was a requirement of authenticity in gay voices which addressed AIDS. We wanted to hear the truth, for a change. Therefore, if there was to be (say) an imaginative literature of AIDS, it should be based on first-hand experience. We wanted artists who spoke from an informed position. If there was to be fiction, in short, it should pretty much be autobiographical. (The model of Holocaust literature was often invoked.) The accusation of inauthenticity would be aimed at David Cook's screenplay for *Closing Numbers*, just as it would later be levelled at Ron Nyswaner's screenplay for *Philadelphia*. It was not enough that such writers were gay men – though that was, of course, a step in the right direction. They had to seem not to be pandering to the requirements of the heterosexist mainstream. And the best guarantee of that was personal involvement in the epidemic. Otherwise, such writers would be accused of cashing in on the suffering of their fellow gay men, and doing so from an uninformed position.

7 Jenni Olson (1996) *The Ultimate Guide to Lesbian & Gay Film and Video* (New York and London: Serpent's Tail), p.57.

8 Even Jim, the dying gay man, has Health Education Authority safer-sex posters adorning his bedroom wall. This is somewhat unconvincing, since he is supposed to be an aesthete.

9 Keith Howes attributes the first reference to AIDS in British television drama to Howard Schuman's play *Videostars*, broadcast late in 1983 – *Broadcasting It: An Encyclopaedia of Homosexuality on Film, Radio and TV in the UK, 1923–1993* (London: Cassell, 1993), p.16.

10 Jarman, *Modern Nature*, p.25.

13 *Beautiful Thing*

British queer cinema, positive unoriginality and the everyday

Ros Jennings

Hettie Macdonald's (1996) film *Beautiful Thing* did not sweep the board in terms of accolades and awards at the important international queer film festivals. Although it did respectable business, it did not make a particularly huge impression at cinema box offices either. It is an unassuming film that is competently made but which has none of the distinctive aesthetic and narrative strategies so apparent in the other queer films that burst on to our screens in the early 1990s.[1] Even within the British context of queer filmmaking, it has none of the art film credentials that we associate with Britain's leading queer filmmakers of the time such as Derek Jarman, Isaac Julien and Pratibha Parmar. As I will go on to explore in more detail in the final part of my discussion, the lack of new queer cinema credentials notwithstanding, I have an exceptionally deep affection for the film. Taken as a whole, the film is unoriginal and unsophisticated in its concerns and, as such, is an excellent example of genuine and ordinary everyday British fayre – it is jam roly-poly rather than crème brulée – and it is precisely because of its function as a kind of metaphorical 'comfort food' that the film has importance. *Beautiful Thing*'s filmic world is that of the everyday, of daily struggles and small triumphs. The politics of the film are lived and personal, taking place on a very human scale.

Although *Beautiful Thing* has quite earnest intentions about the positive affirmation of young white gay male identities, it uses humour skilfully to project its message and to create a film that is both touching and uplifting. Set in a working-class housing estate in east London, the story centres around two good friends: Jamie (Glen Berry) and Ste (Scott Neal). The opening scene, which takes place in a school games lesson, sets the tone of the film. It establishes the contrasting personalities of the two main characters and it also sets out the film's positive take on multicultural and gender relations with a bang, or more precisely a whistle (blown by Meera Syal[2] as the sari-wearing wise-cracking, games teacher for the girls' football lesson which is taking place on the adjacent pitch). Jamie hates sport and tries to get out of games lessons as often as he can. His interests are classical Hollywood films (particularly musicals) and he enjoys reading gossip and celebrity magazines such as *Hello*. Next to his bed a picture of Lucille Ball is on prominent display. With such credentials, he certainly does not measure up as one of the lads and as a consequence the other boys at school bully him. His discomfort with hegemonic notions of rough and tough active masculinity is, of course, enough to insinuate quite early on in the film that he is queer.[3] Ste on the other hand both likes sport and is good at it. He fits in well at school and unlike Jamie, is quite clearly one of the lads.

For Ste, it is in his home life where his difficulties lie. Both Ste and Jamie are children of one-parent households but their experience could not be more different. Since his mother left, Ste has been the object of his alcoholic father and elder brother's frustration, anger and violent abuse. Jamie, however, has had consistent and loving parenting from his mum, the formidable Sandra (Linda Henry). Sandra, like Ste's father, has not had an easy life but unlike him she is smart and has been able to cling on to sufficient self-esteem/self-motivation to constantly strive to make a better life for herself and her boy.

In what, refreshingly, turns out to be a classic romance narrative, the story develops around a set of tensions that result from the fact that at the outset of the film Jamie is in the process of realising not just that he is gay, but that he is also attracted to his long-time friend Ste. After Ste receives one beating too many from his father, Sandra intervenes in the situation and takes him into their home suggesting that he will just have to 'top and tail with Jamie'. They discover fairly quickly that they both feel the same about each other, but the plot twists and turns around the ways they experience their feelings and desires in relation to their private and public identities. Jamie's growing self-realisation and confidence is placed in relation to Ste's struggles and difficulties. For Ste, reconciling his awareness of his sexual identity relative to his public persona (i.e. as one of the lads) is fraught with difficulty for him. Not surprisingly, he is particularly anxious about what will happen when his dad and brother find out.

Too often when queer identities are theorised and when queer films are criticised, they are done in the abstract. In the following discussion of *Beautiful Thing*, I want to offer a more situated type of critique. One that tries to link an analysis of the film's core engagements (that of burgeoning queer identities and everyday/ordinary existences) to both its British production context and the specificities of a particular set of reading/viewing circumstances. I have chosen, therefore, to structure this chapter in relation to an examination of certain relevant key themes. As my starting point, I introduce my organisational device for analysis, that of 'positive unoriginality'. I use this concept initially to discuss the filmic style of *Beautiful Thing*, but I also utilise it as a much broader device to encompass a range of more politically inflected debates about ideas of the 'everyday', positive images, the formation of queer identities and notions of community. To conclude, I will attempt to draw these themes together by means of a situated personal and non-metropolitan reading of the film.

'Positive unoriginality' is a term that has come into being in relation to Australian cinema; circulating via the work of Meaghan Morris (1988) and, more especially

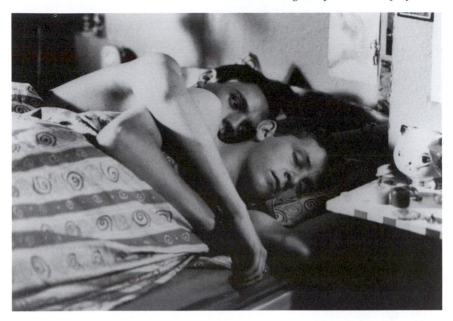

Figure 13.1 Who's 'top' and who's 'tail'? *Beautiful Thing*'s 'everyday queers' Jamie (Glen Berry) and Ste (Scott Neal) (1996).

Source: BFI Stills, Posters and Designs (Film Four).

for my own appropriation here in this article, through the thoughts and writing of Tom O'Regan.[4] At the heart of O'Regan's discussions is a reflection on the attempts of critics (mainly Australian) to position and define Australian cinema in relation to notions of distinctiveness and creativeness. As a medium-sized English language cinema unable to compete with Hollywood in terms of budgets and distribution, Australian cinema has been criticised for:

> a reliance upon social realism, docu-drama, social problem film-making, too much dialogue, emotional underachievement of actors, colourless 'ordinary' leading men and women.
>
> (O'Regan, 1996: 97)

British cinema can, of course, also be accused of exhibiting most if not all of these attributes on a regular basis. However, as O'Regan has argued in relation to Australian cinema, many critics have been able to convey these aspects positively, claiming that in their very unoriginality the films in question often provide a space of gentle subversion and resistance. In particular, O'Regan points to the ways that films displaying positive unoriginality have produced a 'tentative defiance of the codes' (1996: 232) particularly in relation to notions of genre (where an interesting balance between conformity and hybridity has often been achieved). In a similar vein, therefore, I wish to divert the concept of 'positive unoriginality' away from Australian cinema and, in this instance, apply it to the British-made film, *Beautiful Thing*. As I have suggested earlier, *Beautiful Thing* is unoriginal compared to many contemporary films that explore queer subjectivities and identities.[5] It is very much a mainstream film and, for a film made in the 1990s, it is also in many ways a kind of 'throw-back' in that it explores 'coming-out' as its major motif. Its representation of queer desire between its two young male central characters is neither explicit nor particularly sexy.[6] The expression of desire that we are presented with is both awkward and fumbling and therefore typical of the way that first sexual encounters are usually experienced. Formally, the film draws on but also plays with a recognisable aesthetic of British realism; the kind that can also be seen to span/ crossover with contemporary television in terms of both look and more particularly, characterisation. In the case of *Beautiful Thing*, the dominance of a television aesthetic gives the film an intimacy and also an accessibility to its characters that is often not the case in queer themed narratives. The overall association with television is especially strong in *Beautiful Thing* because of its connections with both Channel 4 money and its co-producer, Tony Garnett.[7]

The film's exploitation of realism is emphasised by a combination of factors such as: dialogue and regional accents, mise-en-scène (consisting of the dreary concrete uniformity of a working-class high-rise estate)[8] and, with no disrespect intended, it is also signified by the average-looking cast (including the two main characters Jamie and Ste, who are both rather sweet, cute even, but certainly not handsome or beautiful in the way that Hollywood would demand). Overwhelmingly, *Beautiful Thing* positions itself within discourses of ordinariness and the 'everyday'[9] and it is from this location that I want to start to unravel the notion of 'positiveness' in relation to the film. My interpretation of the O'Regan model of 'positive unoriginality' is that not only does it operate across the seemingly straightforward 'unoriginal' form, but it is also the product of a number of tensions, contradictions and negotiations that are embedded within the text. Sometimes these tensions are overt but quite often they are covert. The 'positiveness' of the film is enunciated as a product or, perhaps more precisely, as a set of tensions that infuse the text and which also generate the distinctive space or 'voice' of the text. The 'positiveness' of the 'unoriginality' is also based upon a 'critically positive' stance or disposition towards the material.

In *Beautiful Thing*, the majority of the film's strategies are overt and it is in its very 'overtness' that it makes infringements into the space of conventional genre expectations. To place two young men as the romantic couple at the centre of a comedy romance is still quite unusual, and although it is slightly more common to see same-sex desire handled sympathetically in mainstream genres these days, there are very few unambiguously happy conclusions and even fewer 'boy meets boy' romances given the blessing of a joyful narrative resolution. On the whole, mainstream genres still work to uphold the values of compulsory heterosexuality and family values. One of the most interesting aspects of *Beautiful Thing*, therefore, is that it also upholds family values but not in any specifically heterosexual/nuclear sense. Generically speaking, as a romantic comedy, the film falls within the conventions of a genre of integration and works towards the resolution convention of the embrace (which it achieves quite spectacularly in its final sequence). In terms of its construction, the film's main anxieties and potential disruptions to narrative harmony are not located in the two main characters' psychological acceptance, and self-realisation, of the fact that they are gay (though I admit that Ste experiences a little more trouble than Jamie and also takes more time in this respect), but are rooted in the consequences that their identities might provoke in relation to family and community. While it is true that the strong supporting cast is almost emblematic of British cinema, it also serves the purpose of emphasising the place of family and community in the film. The supporting characters are represented in the sort of depth that, in certain ways, actually makes them more interesting than Jamie and Ste. Particularly notable are: Jamie's mum Sandra, her well-intentioned, but rather vague[10] 'new man'/ex-hippy boyfriend Tony (Ben Daniels) and their feisty and often hilarious neighbour, Leah (Tameka Empson), a troubled young black woman, whose disillusionment with her life has put her beyond parental control and caused her to take refuge in a fantasy life. Unusually for someone of her age, Leah is obsessed by the music of former American West Coast group the Mamas and the Papas and in particular worships their most famous singer, the late Mama Cass. In her identifications with both Cass and the group's melodious, feel-good tunes, Leah both draws energy and takes comfort. The music of the Mamas and Papas not only weaves through the film as an up-beat soundtrack but read in the context of the film's narrative, songs such as 'It's Getting Better' and 'Make Your Own Kind of Music' become uplifting gay anthems.

Less vividly portrayed, but nonetheless essential to the creation of a particular milieu are the more incidental characters (the busybodies, almost seaside postcard caricature couples) who help 'police' the neighbourhood with their noisy presences and interfering ways. Together, these characters form the hub of a community. The physical dimensions of their environment enforce the sort of side-by-side living (either along the balconies of the blocks of flats or as their flats overlook each other) that necessitates interaction. Although the realist mise-en-scène reflects the look, location and spatial dynamics of an East End working-class environment accurately, the rainbow that appears in the sky over the titles immediately suggests that not all is as it might first appear. Throughout the film, Thamesmead is bathed in a golden light reflecting the sizzling sun of a summer heatwave. In this light, the blue doors of the houses on the balcony where Jamie, Ste and Leah live take on the look of a Mediterranean holiday complex (this is also emphasised by Sandra's hanging baskets of bright red geraniums). In *Beautiful Thing*, the exploration of a coming-out story within this solidly working-class community is particularly effective. Unlike some other key films which examine coming to terms with non-hegemonic sexuality and identity (e.g. *Desert Hearts* (Deitch, 1985)), *Beautiful Thing* does not sweep the viewer off to a really exotic location like the Nevada desert, but explores this theme in what is possibly a more meaningful way. *Beautiful Thing* exploits the concept of 'positive unoriginality' by 'queering' the familiar and the everyday.[11] As Robert Reynolds indicates: 'In imagining new ways of becoming oneself and belonging, queer might help re-address that crucial tension of late modern life – how to reconcile a creative invention of the self with the art of being in common' (2002:168). By focusing on the ordinary and the everyday from a positive dis-position, the film exposes the fragilities of a socio-cultural system that reinforces compulsory heterosexuality in some interesting ways. To those who were involved in the pre-queer politics of gay and lesbian liberation, Jamie and Ste's romance narrative, which achieves resolution in a public demonstration of their love, fulfils long-hoped-for dreams in terms of visible representation in a popular film. Since the advent of queer approaches to identities and sexualities, however, belief in the power of positive images to bring about acceptance and visibility of same-sex desire has declined. Indeed as Julianne Pidduck's consideration of popular film genres, queer cinema and queer theoretical criticism, suggests: 'Queer cultural criticism often explicitly differentiates itself from a more traditional politics of lesbian/gay representation that champions "positive images" within popular culture' (2003: 284). On the surface, *Beautiful Thing* could therefore be dismissed as a straight-forwardly and traditionally positive project in terms of its representing its two main protagonists and their relationship. Where the film departs from this model is in its representation of its supporting characters Sandra, Tony and Leah. *Beautiful Thing* does not embrace the 'in your face' tactics of most 1990s queer cinema but makes its intervention in a much more subtle way. The film attempts not just to validate choices about same-sex desire (as it does quite explicitly with Ste and Jamie), but through its construction it works to destabilise the available roles and desires of the community at large, making them both more plural and more contradictory. Its tactic is to emphasise the performative aspects of living, desire and human inter-action. Thus, although the 'disruptive implications of coming out' (Pidduck, 2003: 284) provide the structure of the narrative, the project of the film as a whole embraces a much more complex understanding of human sexuality. Consequently, if as Burston and Richardson argue that: 'part of the project of Queer is to attack . . . the fictions supporting compulsory heterosexuality (1995: 1) then *Beautiful Thing* is certainly engaged with the queer task of revealing how precarious the glue holding together heterosexual hegemony is. In addition, if as Burston and Richardson also suggest: 'Queer Theory seeks to locate Queerness in places that had previously been thought of as strictly for straights' (1995:1), the depiction of Sandra, Tony and Leah can be seen to playfully dispute heterosexual stability.

Sandra and Tony's relationship is one queer joke from start to finish. When Jamie asks Tony where he met his mum, Tony replies that they met at *Gateways*. The fact that *Gateways* was one of London's most famous lesbian clubs (immortalised in

Robert Aldrich's 1968 film, *The Killing of Sister George*) 'queers' the provenance of their relationship and adds a further layer of disturbance to their representation as heterosexual in the conventional sense. On the Thamesmead estate, Sandra has the reputation of being a sexual predator (and the fact that Tony is eight years younger does nothing but add to that reputation). She is direct in her approach to sex and she isn't afraid to ask Tony to 'sort [her] out'. In their interactions, Sandra and Tony can plainly be seen to flout stereotypical notions of heterosexual power relations. Even in her tightest shortest skirt, Sandra still comes across as powerful and unequivocally butch. No matter how heterosexually active Sandra is shown to be (or we are told she is), Sandra's heterosexuality is constantly positioned as open to question by the film's formal strategies. From early on it is clear that her most meaningful conversations and emotional support come from her friend and co-worker, Louise. On the surface there is nothing unusual in that. After all, this is the case for most heterosexual women. There is certainly also nothing unusual in their chaste parting kiss as they say goodnight after walking home from work together (after all, straight women greet and part from their straight girlfriends in this way all the time). What is unusual is signified by the following shot consisting of Sandra's lingering (almost smouldering) gaze at, the now off-screen, Louise.

If Jamie is queer because he doesn't like sport but likes musicals and Lucille Ball, then compared to the other adult men that we meet on the Thamesmead estate, Tony is queered by being middle class, relatively well educated and sensitive (not to mention by being seen in public in Sandra's pretty little blue dressing gown). Throughout the film, Tony is reactive rather than pro-active (which is finally what makes him superfluous to Sandra). He does, however, seem genuinely caring and he is the one character in the film that does not need to struggle to accept the news that Jamie is gay (he has obviously moved in more liberal circles than the Thamesmead estate). He has internalised the politics of the 'new man' and has certainly come into contact with feminist ideas (he tells both Leah and Sandra that they disempower themselves as women with their use of language). It goes without saying that a large part of his attraction to Sandra is the fact that she is unquestionably a strong woman.

In his discussion of stereotypes and positive images, Alan McKee (2000) points out that: 'In order to "do politics" we must always retain certainty about what is good and bad in culture, what is good and bad in representation.'[12] On the surface, *Beautiful Thing* embraces an easygoing version of the power of positive images (including the version of multiculturalism that is established from the outset). As the main focus of the film, Ste and Jamie's representation is the most 'positive' and possibly as a result of this, also the most one-dimensional. For the secondary characters such as Sandra and Leah (Tony much less so) their representations are more contradictory and less clear-cut. Consequently there is much less certainty in how we read their representations. Leah's presence as a rebellious but rather disturbed young black woman contributes some of the most exciting moments to the film but also provides some of the most disconcerting moments/images. For instance, when Ste's brother Trevor manages to get her to open her bedroom door and marches in to turn off the Mamas and Papas' song that is deafening the whole neighbourhood, her face is a grotesque reverse image of a minstrel show player with a thick layer of white cold cream covering her skin. She is wearing a colourful bathrobe reminiscent of Mama Cass's spectacular kaftan-style dresses and singing into her hairbrush (when not making sexual advances to Trevor). Although her appearance could justifiably be part of her nightly skin-cleansing routine, it is just as likely that it is a way that she plays out/performs her imaginary identifications with Cass Elliot.

Throughout the film, there are a series of abusive verbal exchanges between Leah and Sandra. Sandra's first words to Leah are 'slag' and Leah refers to Sandra as both an 'old slapper' and the 'black hole of Thamesmead'. Their interaction for the majority of the film revolves round sexual insults that serve to underscore both their antagonistic relationship and reinforce their status as heterosexual women. 'It's not natural', declares Sandra, 'a girl of her age into Mama Cass'. Indeed, Leah's representation constantly questions what 'natural' might be in terms of representation and identity. Leah brings a dynamic presence to the balcony. The antagonism between Leah and Sandra is hardly surprising as both characters are not afraid to get right in your face. Leah is the antithesis of well-behaved femininity and her rebellion brings her into extreme danger (nearly falling off the balcony and getting run over during a bad drugs trip). However, in the final sequence of the film, the unexpected truce between Leah and Sandra tips the scales from heterosexual to queer in a startling way. When Leah accepts an invitation to go for a night out with Ste and Jamie to a gay pub (*The Gloucester*), she seems to turn a psychological and emotional corner in her life. Though the truth of her assertion to Sandra that: 'I intend to find myself a nice dyke tonight because I tell you, I'm through with men!' is dubious, it does mark a moment that sees her look beyond the restrictions of life on the estate and also suggests a playful slip/shift in a previously presumed stable heterosexuality. When Sandra takes her hand (at Leah's instigation) and leads Leah down to the piazza to dance alongside Jamie and Ste in their act of queer defiance, Sandra and Leah's act of symbolic solidarity not only poses further questions about Sandra's already doubtful sexuality but also emphasises the performativity of desire (certainly in the ways that it can be represented through cultural and cinematic codes). In the clingy black dress that has become such a classic signifier of sexy femininity, Sandra is a powerful figure (her height and size emphasised in contrast to her dancing partner). Although this moment has been initiated by Jamie and Ste's public display of affection, the two young men are so lost in each other that they are oblivious to the onlookers. By contrast, Sandra is only too aware of the audience and surveys them with a defiant glare. Her body language signifies the protective demeanour of a lioness protecting her cub, daring anyone in the crowd to just try and say something about her son. At the same time, however, she is also decidedly sexy (especially in the sinuous movements of her dance with Leah). This conflation of the maternal figure and sexiness is a troublesome coupling for traditional conceptualisations of gender and heterosexuality. It becomes even more threatening to heterosexual stability when this representation then becomes tinged with associations of lesbianism. 'What is this dyke gonna be like?' she asks Leah. Leah's description is vivid reflecting that this representation already has an active place in her imaginary. According to her, the dyke will be big and butch. She will have green eyes and she will be tall 'so [I'll] have to look up to her', says Leah. 'Nice' replies Sandra, and as Mama Cass continues to sing 'Dream a Little Dream' we are left to gaze on Leah dancing with the green-eyed woman of her dreams. Significantly, the only member of the crowd moving to the music and looking at them with interest (rather than amazement) is Sandra's friend Louise.

In this climactic moment of the film we witness Jamie and Ste's act of coming out to their immediate community. This constitutes a significant personal journey for them. When Tony asks Jamie why his mother is upset, Jamie is able to produce a veritable tirade of derogatory names for being queer (shirt-lifter, knob-shiner, etc.). In his short life, the ideology of compulsory heterosexuality has permeated his everyday experience. Accordingly, if: 'The cultural matrix through which gender identity has become "intelligible" requires that certain kinds of "identities" cannot

Figure 13.2 'Dream a Little Dream': Sandra (Linda Henry) and Leah (Tameka Empson) show their support as Jamie and Ste publicly proclaim their love.

Source: BFI Stills, Posters and Designs (Film Four).

"exist" – that is, those in which gender does not follow from sex and those in which the practices of desire do not "follow" from either sex or gender' (Butler, 1990:17), then Jamie's growing self-realisation makes him only too aware of his deviant desire and his resulting outsider status. *Gay Times* becomes an instruction manual to non-heterosexual life, leading Jamie and Ste into the 'strange' world of a nearby gay pub, *The Gloucester*. Although Jamie and Ste live in London, the Thamesmead estate is constructed as a small and confined world where it is difficult to go unnoticed (e.g. Jamie can't even play truant from school without his mother catching sight of him). In many ways therefore, the filmic world constructed in *Beautiful Thing* can be seen to mirror (or act as a stand-in for) the non-metropolitan experience of trying to find a space/place/community where you can feel comfortable, once you realise that you might not be straight. Though this 'community' might consist of the queer 'scene' of pubs, clubs, gyms, cafes, bookshops, etc., as McKee has discussed, it is not necessarily either 'a physical space, nor even a conglomeration of individuals. It exists in a variety of non-physical states.'[13] As McKee continues, one of these non-physical states is that of the imaginary and it is, of course, the imaginary that film is able to explore so effectively because of its polysemic nature.

It is debatable whether positive images have the power to change the hearts and minds of those who have so internalised dominant ideological notions of sexuality that anything but heterosexuality is an aberration. Equally, it is similarly debatable as to whether the queer deconstruction of heterosexuality that takes place in *Beautiful Thing* would even register with such people. To be truthful, I'm not bothered either way. What does concern me, and what has caused the film to have a lasting and 'positive' effect on me, is the fact that the film charms its queer audiences with an open but direct address.

I first saw *Beautiful Thing* in my local art cinema in Gloucester, a small provincial city in the South-West of England. In this non-metropolitan viewing context where there is very little visible evidence of a physical community (seven years later there is still only one gay pub and no queer clubs in Gloucester [just a regular disco night on Mondays, the 'dead' night of the week]), living a queer life can be quite precarious. The way that *Beautiful Thing* constructed Thamesmead as a non-metropolitan enclave within Britain's biggest metropolis chimed strongly with the location where the film was being screened. The communal laughter at various parts of the film quickly identified the queer elements in the audience, cementing them in a temporary relationship with each other via their individual text/viewer relationships with the film. One mode of textual connection between the film and those viewers I was sitting with that night could not have been anticipated by the film's complex polysemic address. For Ste and Jamie *The Gloucester* pub becomes their safe haven. Ironically, for those of us in that audience who frequented Gloucester's only gay pub, we didn't feel very safe, as only a few weeks before someone had shot an air rifle pellet through the window of the pub (making Ste's statement that 'everyone wants to kill me' not seem that far-fetched). In this context, the appeal to positive images made as part of the film's address had a powerful effect and has contributed to my lasting affection for the film. Both its 'unoriginality' and its positive/uplifting tone made the beleaguered queer audience of Gloucester feel able to make connections to a (albeit temporary) 'positive experience' in relation not just to the film's textual construction but also with the other queers[14] in the room that night.

It would seem that while the notion of a queer address has generally been conceived of as being in opposition to the project of 'positive images', this need not always be the case. With its central 'coming out' narrative, *Beautiful Thing* employs one of the most typical strategies associated with positive images and traditional identity politics. This is, however, only one of its modes of address. In its 'positive unoriginality', *Beautiful Thing* shifts characteristically British cinematic modes of representation (e.g. the strong supporting cast, the concentration on dialogue rather than action) to offer the viewer some uncertain forms of viewing identification. From the outset of the film, the rainbow in the sky (framing the Thamesmead estate) signifies that there will be no certainties for the viewer to rely on (not only is the space and place of the film represented as both metropolitan and non-metropolitan at the same time, but key characters such as Sandra and Leah are also represented as heterosexual and non-heterosexual at the same time). In its combination of denaturalisation and 'positive images', *Beautiful Thing* works in the most queer of ways to invite its audiences to replace their certainties with questions.

Notes

1 See B. Ruby Rich (1992) and Amy Taubin (1992).
2 Meera Syal has since become one of the UK's most famous British Asian writers, performers and personalities with writing credits for *Bhaji on the Beach* (1993) and more recently *Anita and Me* (2002). She came to public attention as a regular member of the pioneering British Asian comedy team involved with BBC Radio 4 and the BBC television series, *Goodness Gracious Me* (1998–2000).
3 For instance, the false name that they make up for Jamie in order to play a prank on their substitute male games teacher is 'Hugh Janus'.
4 See O'Regan (1996).
5 As I have come to expect with her work, Julianne Pidduck's (2003) comprehensive survey of gay, lesbian and queer film since the 1980s in 'AFTER 1980: Margins and Mainstreams' (the concluding chapter to the second edition of Richard Dyer's *Now You See It: Studies in Lesbian and Gay Film*) presents a particularly thoughtful overview. In relation to the points that I make here, it also provides a particularly insightful contextualisation.
6 Sex never takes place on screen. It is always something that is alluded to or suggested rather than explicit in its depiction. It is also something that is represented tenderly or playfully rather than lustfully (on one occasion, a scene of Jamie and Ste in bed is accompanied by the soundtrack of 'Sixteen Going on Seventeen' from Rogers and Hammerstein's musical *The Sound of Music* (Wise, 1965).

7   Tony Garnett's pedigree as a television producer can be traced back to classics such as the famous 'Wednesday Play' *Cathy Come Home* (Loach, 1966).

8   These elements provide a recognisable or 'knowable' world for the film but as I will discuss later, these realist elements are manipulated and like everything else in the film not presented in a purely 'straight' manner. With the rainbow forming an arc in the sky over the estate and the prolonged heatwave resulting in the inhabitants donning their bright summer clothes, Thamesmead becomes a place of magical possibilities.

9   See O'Regan's discussion of 'positive unoriginality' (1996: 237).

10   Suggesting that he has lost more than a few brain cells due to too much dope.

11   Michel de Certeau's (1984) location of the tactics and strategies of resistance to the constraints of dominant ideology within the 'everyday' are extremely pertinent to those adopted in *Beautiful Thing*.

12   See 'How to tell the difference between a stereotype and a positive image: Reading *Priscilla, Queen of the Desert*', *Screening the past*, Issue 9, 2000, http://www.latrobe.edu.au/www/screeningthepast/firstrelease/fr0300/amfr09b.htm uploaded 1 March 2000.

13   According to McKee, community can be constructed and powerfully via the imaginary just as much as in physical spaces and human relationships. See http://www.latrobe.edu.au/www/screeningthepast/firstrelease/fr0300/amfr09b.htm uploaded 1 March 2000.

14   I use this term in its most fluid, diverse and inclusive sense and very much in the same way that *Beautiful Thing*'s mode of address is offered as both specific and open at the same time.

Bibliography

Burston, P. and Richardson, C. (eds.) (1995) *A Queer Romance: Lesbians, Gay Men and Popular Culture*, London: Routledge.

Butler, J. (1990) *Gender Trouble: Feminism and the Subversion of Identity*, London: Routledge.

De Certeau, M. (1984) *The Practice of Everyday Life*, Berkeley: University of California Press.

Jagose, A. (1996) *Queer Theory: An Introduction*, New York: New York University Press.

Morris, M. (1988) 'Tooth and Claw: Tales of Survival and *Crocodile Dundee*'. In *Pirate's Fiancée: Feminism, Reading and Postmodernism*, London: Verso, 241–69.

O'Regan, T. (1996) *Australian National Cinema*, London: Routledge.

Pidduck, J. (2003) 'AFTER 1980 Margins and Mainstream'. In Richard Dyer with Julianne Pidduck (2003) *Now You See It: Studies in Lesbian and Gay Film*. Second edition, London: Routledge, 265–306.

Reynolds, R. (2002) *From Camp to Queer: Remaking the Australian Homosexual*, Carlton: University of Melbourne Press.

Rich, B. R. (1992) 'New Queer Cinema'. *Sight and Sound* 2(9), 30–4.

Taubin, A. (1992) 'Beyond the Sons of Scorcese'. *Sight and Sound* 2(9), 37.

14 Taming Oscar Wilde
Queerness, heritage and stardom

Glyn Davis

Around a hundred pages into *Moab is My Washpot*, Stephen Fry's autobiographical recounting of the first twenty-or-so years of his life, he dwells at great length on his lack of musical ability – 'God's unforgivable cruelty in denying me the gift of music'.[1] Fry relates what he calls his 'tone dumbness' to enduring, and keenly felt, experiences of alienation:

> my passion for music and my inability to express it in musical terms stand really as symbols for the sense of separateness and apartness I have always felt. In fact they stand too as a symbol of love and my inability to express love as it should be expressed. [. . .] You see, when it comes down to it, I sometimes believe that words are all I have. I am not actually sure that I am capable of thought, let alone feeling, except through language. [. . .] It was years before Oscar Wilde was to shake me out of a feeling that this was a failure in me, when I read his essay . . . *The Critic as Artist*.[2]

This recognition of words as a powerful, potent resource – indeed, of the delights that language and its manipulation can afford – is not the only point of connection between Fry and Wilde, although it is an important one, and central to the concerns of this chapter. Both men also attained prominent positions of public and cultural visibility as witty, intellectual homosexuals. Perhaps most significantly, Fry, in his only lead film role to date, played Oscar Wilde in the heritage biopic *Wilde* (Gilbert, 1997). This was not the first filmic version of Wilde's life – *Oscar Wilde* (Ratoff, 1959) featured Robert Morley in the lead, and *The Trials of Oscar Wilde* (Hughes, 1960) starred Peter Finch as Oscar. However, whereas these two earlier examples are potentially most clearly described as costume dramas, *Wilde* is very specifically an instance of 'heritage film'.

Heritage cinema is a rather loosely defined genre. Although some critics have suggested that heritage films have been produced in a variety of European countries since the 1960s, the crucial template for the genre is usually assumed to be the body of work produced by the Merchant-Ivory stable in the 1980s and 1990s in Britain:

key examples include *A Room with a View* (1985), *Howards End* (1992) and *The Remains of the Day* (1993). The formal characteristics of the heritage genre, as Richard Dyer notes,

> include the following: the use of a well known literary source, and/or key historical moments . . ., periods . . . or occasionally the lives of writers and artists; these texts, moments and figures most often drawn from the past 150 years; a conventional film style, with the pace and tone of art cinema without its propensity for symbolism, intellectual talk or noticeable directorial styles; settings and costume based upon meticulous research, presented in pristine condition, brightly or artfully lit.[3]

Over the last fifteen years or so, academic debates regarding the heritage film have proliferated. Given the number of screen versions of books by writers such as Jane Austen, E. M. Forster, Thomas Hardy, Henry James and Edith Wharton that have been produced, it is no surprise that some critics have focused on the topic of adaptation, and of fidelity to the original source texts. Most often, however, it is the politics of the heritage film that have been subjected to scrutiny. With many main instances of the genre produced while Britain was under Conservative rule, heritage films have been criticised for offering up nostalgic, escapist spectacle, valorising the luxurious homes and possessions of the wealthy, and mourning a lost 'little England'. This position is clearly expressed in a 1993 essay by Andrew Higson:

> these key films in the *national* cinema of the 1980s are fascinated by the private property, the culture and values of a *particular* class. By reproducing these trappings outside of a materialist historical context, they transform the heritage of the upper classes into the national heritage: private interest becomes naturalized as public interest. Except, of course, these are still films for a relatively privileged audience, and the heritage is still refined and exclusive, rather than properly public in the sense of massively popular. The national past and national identity emerge in these films not only as aristocratic, but also as male-centred, while the nation itself is reduced to the soft pastoral landscape of southern England untainted by the modernity of urbanization or industrialization.[4]

In recent years, since the airing of alternative, more positive perspectives on the heritage film's politics and systems of representation (I will explore some of these opinions shortly, in the next section of this chapter), instances of the genre are most often interpreted as sending out ambiguous messages, and as riven by internal contradictions. Andrew Higson's book *English Heritage, English Cinema* (published in 2003), for instance, adopts a largely relativist perspective, and is reluctant to prioritise one reading of the genre over another.[5] In contrast, in the pages that follow, I intend to identify the limitations of the heritage genre with regard to its representations of queerness. Although queerness occasionally manages to break through the glossy skein of the heritage film's generic form, often using words as a battering ram, I will suggest that the genre is unable to accommodate the disruptive, radical potential of queerness. *Wilde* serves as a particularly useful focus for such an argument – in particular, because of the claims that have been made for Wilde, to which I will return shortly. Firstly, however, it is necessary to proffer a brief overview of the relationship between the heritage film and homosexuality.

Heritage cinema and homosexuality

In defiance of the pessimistic assessments of the conservatism, nostalgia and class bias of the heritage film put forward by Higson and others in the early 1990s, a number of critics have highlighted the manner in which the genre has afforded considerable screen time to characters that would normally remain in the margins. Women and gay men have often occupied prominent diegetic positions within instances of heritage cinema and television – an observation that partly explains the appeal of the genre to female and gay male audience demographics. Indeed, with regard to homosexuality, Richard Dyer has noted that, despite 'its middle-brow respectability and focus on a homophobic past, heritage cinema in general has been surprisingly hospitable to homosexual representation'.[6] Discussing a broad range of examples from a number of different countries, Dyer claims that heritage films featuring lesbian and gay protagonists, '[w]ith arguable exceptions . . . all take a broadly positive view of homosexuality'.[7] Thus, as examples, *Another Country* (Kanievska, 1984), *Maurice* (Ivory, 1987) and *Carrington* (Hampton, 1995) all focused their narratives on gay men. Lesbian characters, although appearing less frequently, have also been afforded screen time: lesbianism was a central ingredient of the BBC television serialisation of Sarah Waters' novel *Tipping the Velvet* (2002), and Patricia Rozema's film of *Mansfield Park* (1999) contained marked lesbian overtones.

Aside from overt characterisation, heritage cinema's form could be seen as offering up a range of other potential pleasures for gay male spectators. Andrew Higson, for instance, has suggested that many heritage films verge perilously close to self-parody, and thus are potentially open to camp interpretations and appro-priations.[8] In addition, and a little more prosaically, Higson has identified the genre's 'continual insistence on the pleasures of the male body'.[9] This latter point has also been made by Claire Monk. Writing about key examples of the genre, she noted that:

> The rarity of the spectacle of the male body, outside films specifically aimed at a gay audience, clearly places these movies somewhat outside the mainstream; it also makes them likely sites of anxiety for straight male spectators. It will

surprise no one that *Maurice*, a gay love story, offers the audience such a spectacle, but the idea that *A Room with a View* is simmering with feminine, queer and ambiguous sexualities will seem strange to many.[10]

The eroticised presentation of the male body is, indeed, a crucial component of heritage film and television fictions. Mr Darcy's sodden emergence from water in the BBC's adaptation of *Pride and Prejudice* (1995), wet clothes plastered to his skin, serves as an iconic example – and, indeed, was an image central to the marketing and promotion of the programme. In *Wilde*, the camera regularly lingers on beautiful men: the recumbent, naked form of the painter John Gray (Ioan Gruffudd) in bed with Oscar, for instance, or the lithe, nattily attired body of an unnamed male prostitute (Orlando Bloom), soliciting Wilde's gaze and custom.

Further aspects of the heritage film may contribute to the genre's appeal to gay male spectators. John Hill, for instance, has claimed that 'the heritage film . . . invests many of its male relationships with a clear homo-erotic dimension',[11] offering as example a persuasive analysis of the relationship dynamics in operation in *Where Angels Fear to Tread* (Sturridge, 1991). Hill also pays particular attention to the bathing sequence in *A Room with a View*, in which Freddy Honeychurch (Rupert Graves), George Emerson (Julian Sands) and the Reverend Mr Beebe (Simon Callow) lark about naked in an outdoor pool. As Hill argues:

> Judged in conventional terms, the bathing scene . . . lacks adequate integration with the rest of the film and sets up a certain disjunction of tone and meaning. However, at the same time, it is precisely the resulting 'awkwardness' around sexuality that makes the scene so interesting. [. . .] While this may not add up to an entirely coherent counter-discourse, it does at least open up a degree of ambivalence around sexuality.[12]

The existence of these aspects of heritage cinema – overt, prominently situated homosexual characterisation, a propensity towards campness, the eroticised spectacle of the male body, a homo-erotic charge between male characters – helps to explain the genre's appeal to a gay male audience. However, sweeping claims made in favour of the heritage genre and its accommodation of homosexuality need to be somewhat tempered. Three brief points are worth making here. Firstly, as Andrew Higson notes, despite the prevalence of gay and female characters in heritage films, 'we need to remember the extent to which films like *Howards End* are promoted and circulated within the culture precisely as heritage films, and not as woman's pictures or queer dramas'.[13] Secondly, although heritage cinema may feature lingering images of attractive male bodies, sexual activity is extremely rare in these films: when present, it is usually depicted in a muted, 'sensitive' fashion. In other words, the genre's representations of homosexuality will only go so far. Thirdly, as John Hill points out, the British heritage film of the 1980s circulated within a culture in which much more open and questioning representations of gender and sexuality . . . were possible. As such, in comparison with many contemporary British films, the representations of gender and sexuality which the heritage film provided were often timid and restrained.[14]

Indeed, heritage cinema's depictions of homosexuality operate within a very specific representational regime. To be precise, although the genre makes available some space for homosexual representations and audience pleasures, more disruptive, queer forms of sexuality are markedly absent. On the whole, heritage films, in their depictions of lesbian and gay characters, draw heavily on central tropes associated with the political rhetoric of the gay rights movement of the 1970s and 1980s. As Richard Dyer comments, these films are 'inclined to cherish in the past antecedents of the practices and beliefs of gay liberation: being yourself, coming out, heroism'.[15] As many of the most commercially and critically successful instances of the genre were produced during the 1980s, this is perhaps unsurprising. Liberal political arguments and opinions in circulation at the time were integrated into tales set in earlier (more homophobic) eras. This persisted into the 1990s – as Dyer observes of *Wilde*, the film features a 'gay liberation' 'narrative of realization': that is, Oscar's 'gradual acceptance of what [he] always knew about himself'.[16] And yet the film – as with the other attempts to cinematically render Wilde's life – is rather unsatisfactory.[17] This, I would argue, is due to heritage cinema's inability to adequately handle the full implications of Wilde's life and writings. In the remainder of this chapter, then, I want to explore two main concerns. Firstly, I wish to highlight how instances of *Wilde*'s imagery, narrative, and dialogue attempt to queerly trouble the heritage genre's limitations in handling homosexuality. And secondly, I will examine how a specific aspect of this film – the casting of particular actors in lead roles – contributes to its overall queerness.

Queer Oscar

Over the last decade or so, a variety of writers (many of whom could be categorised as queer theorists) have argued, retroactively, for Oscar Wilde's radicalism. Indeed, many of them have claimed that Wilde should be interpreted as proto-queer. Wayne Koestenbaum, for instance, in an article on *De Profundis*, the letter that Wilde wrote to Lord Alfred 'Bosie' Douglas while Wilde was incarcerated in Reading Gaol, describes the text as 'a liminal, revolutionary document'.[18] He also, flamboyantly and rather hyperbolically, calls its author 'a gay Satan': 'radically reversing the dominant logos', Koestenbaum writes, 'Wilde was precursor to such postmodernists as Andy Warhol'.[19] Similarly, in an essay on inversion and narcissism in the writings of Wilde, Gregory Bredbeck claims that 'we can read in Wilde a signifying dynamic that is an ur-form of contemporary gay male political Camp'.[20]

These are not isolated cases. To take just one more example, Jonathan Dollimore returns repeatedly to Wilde in his seminal text *Sexual Dissidence*. Dollimore assesses Wilde's 'political radicalism', especially as it is expressed in Wilde's 1891 essay 'The Soul of Man under Socialism': in this tract, Dollimore identifies an anti-humanist, anti-essentialist, radical socialist agenda. Connecting 'The Soul of Man' to other writings by Wilde, as well as Wilde's life, Dollimore argues that 'Wilde's notion of individualism is inseparable from transgressive desire and a transgressive aesthetic'.[21] (Several authors, in fact, have claimed that Wilde's first experiences of homosexuality with Robbie Ross occurred at the time that his period of major writing also began.) Having connected the realm of artistic production to 'transgressive desire', Dollimore outlines Wilde's agitational political programme, which aimed to disturb and unsettle:

> Wilde's experience of deviant desire . . ., leads him not to escape the repressive ordering of society, but to a reinscription within it, and an inversion of the binaries upon which that ordering depends; desire, and the transgressive aesthetic which it fashions, reacts against, disrupts, and displaces from within.[22]

The language Dollimore uses in this account is redolent of the writings of a number of authors associated with the fields of postmodernism and poststructuralism. Although he does not label Wilde 'queer' (his book was published in 1991, the year the phrase 'queer theory' was first coined by Teresa de Lauretis), Dollimore does draw connections between Wilde and postmodernism (a crucial influence on queer theory):

> Wilde's transgressive aesthetic suggests that certain aspects of what post/ modern theory finds so very contemporary about itself – anti-essentialism especially, and the critique of the depth model of identity and culture – are not so new, having been developed as subversive and defensive strategies in subcultures before more recent manifestations in the intellectual main stream.[23]

The numerous accounts of Wilde's radicalism – his sexual, artistic and political transgressions – raise a significant concern for films about Wilde. How can the format of the heritage film – respectable and middlebrow, willing to incorporate lesbian and gay characters within 'gay liberation' limits – accommodate Wilde's radicalism, his queerness? That is, if the queer theorists just discussed are correct in their interpretations of Wilde's politics, his anti-essentialist approach to subjectivity, and so on, then how can such a staid genre ever adequately depict his character?

Evidently, authors such as Bredbeck, Dollimore and Koestenbaum choose to place emphasis on specific aspects of Wilde's life and work. Wilde is a much more paradoxical figure than their arguments generally allow for. His radical status must surely be undermined or partially offset, for instance, by his class associations, and by the canonisation of his work as literature. Revivals of his best-known works continue to play to largely middle-class audiences in the theatre and cinema (see, for instance, the recent film versions of *An Ideal Husband* (Parker, 1999) and *The Importance of Being Earnest* (Parker, 2002)); widespread familiarity with their content may also have somewhat blunted their impact. Neil Bartlett, in his book on Oscar Wilde, *Who Was That Man?*, outlines some of the elements of Wilde's writings that could cause political problems for gay men and their relationship to Oscar:

> In what sense of the word was this most famous of homosexuals actually a homosexual? He was married. His best and most successful play, *The Importance of Being Earnest*, may be the most precious pearl of English camp, but it celebrates the triumph of marriage over all adversity, brings down its curtain on a trio of engagements, and was deliberately premiered on St Valentine's Day. [. . .] *An Ideal Husband* ends with its hero not only reunited with a meekly loving wife, but elected to the Cabinet – a combination of ideals warmly and publicly applauded by the Prince of Wales on the opening night. So much for the radical gay author of *The Soul of Man Under Socialism*.[24]

And yet clearly the reiterated comments regarding Wilde's radical proto-queer politics and aesthetics carry some weight. Do they have any bearing on the recent film of Wilde's life? That is, can we detect this radicalism anywhere within it? I would argue that there are minor hints and allusions – fleeting moments. For instance, an early, rather iconic shot has Oscar, clad in cream and dandyishly swinging a cane, walking against the tide of a group of men all dressed in black. The stark contrasts in the direction of their perambulatory movement, and in the colours of the clothing, enable the image to be read as a literal depiction of Wilde's radical queer programme of 'inversion'.

A longer sequence from around halfway through the film offers a second, more substantial example. Bosie (Jude Law) and Oscar are having lunch in a restaurant, when the Marquess of Queensbury (Tom Wilkinson), Bosie's father, coincidentally enters the venue. Bosie invites Queensbury to dine with them. Initially wary, the Marquess accepts and soon relaxes: Bosie leaves, and Wilde entertains Bosie's father with characteristically seductive wordplay, going so far as to suggest that the two men (that is, Wilde and Queensbury) have more in common with each other than Queensbury may have assumed: 'we are exactly alike'. In the next scene, which takes place at Queensbury's stables, Bosie attempts to heal the long-standing rift with his father caused by Bosie's relationship with Oscar, pointing out how long the Marquess's dinner date with Wilde lasted: 'You were there for ages . . . I knew you'd like him once you met him.' But Queensbury seems to have been left deeply unsettled by his encounter with Wilde: he describes Oscar as both 'charming' and 'evil'. 'Men shouldn't be charming', he says: 'Wilde's no fool. He talks wonder-fully, really wonderfully. That means nothing when what he says is such rot. Worse than rot – evil.' Wilde's queerly disruptive influence then begins to manifest itself in the Marquess's use of language. Attempting to judge the quality of horses, Queensbury spits that one of them 'isn't straight'. He also requests one 'troll' up and down – the word 'troll', of course, being queer slang for cruising. The scene ends with Queensbury yelling homophobic insults at Bosie – 'You filthy-minded sissy! You're nothing but a bumboy!' Syntax almost abandoned, red in the face, queer words spurt uncontrollably from his lips.

As this sequence suggests, perhaps the most obviously 'queer' or transgressive aspects of *Wilde* are those which draw on Wilde's writings, including his aphorisms – that give them voice, and record the reactions of the public to them. Andy Medhurst, in an article on *Wilde*, observes this in operation:

> Stephen Fry's Oscar strides through the film spewing out epigrams to a succession of adoring entourages, establishing fame and fortune on the back of his delicious felicity with language. This is the Queer Wit in full flow, the man who dares to say the unsayable, getting away with it through his dextrous skill in cloaking his critiques in humour.[25]

Language use, then, is the prime mode through which Oscar's radical political programme is enacted: as Bosie says to Wilde, on their first meeting in *Wilde*, 'You use your wit like a foil. You cut through all those starched shirtfronts. You draw blood.' Indeed, such is the power of this language use, that *Wilde* is unlike almost all other instances of heritage cinema. Although heritage films are usually wordy, as befits their close affiliation with canonical works of fiction, their language is often mellifluous and monotonous, bland and predictable, empty and redundant. With *Wilde*, in comparison, the construction and delivery of barbed sentences, the semantic charge of word arrangements, and the impact of utterances on those who hear them, all carry a queer potential – unfortunately, a potential that is rarely capitalised on.[26]

Ultimately, of course, Oscar Wilde's queer use of language became a central aspect of the court cases that he endured. As Dollimore identifies,

> In the first of the three trials involving Wilde in 1895, he was cross-examined on his *Phrases and Philosophies* . . ., the implication of opposing counsel being that its elegant binary inversions, along with *Dorian Gray*, were 'calculated to subvert morality and encourage unnatural vice'.[27]

His way with words, that is, and their challenge to dominant modes of thought, was linked to other – moral and sexual – forms of transgression. In *Wilde*, these accusations of the prosecution feature as part of the film's diegesis. As Oscar stands in the dock, throwing out pithy phrases, the audience in the court is seen acting inappropriately – that is, laughing – and hence disrupting the accepted register of the environment. However, with a swift bang of the gavel, seemliness is soon reasserted. In other words, as with the other examples of scenes discussed above, these are all-too-rare irruptions of disruptive queerness, and are swiftly contained.

Casting Wilde

A further eruption of queerness in *Wilde* is caused by the decision to cast specific actors in the lead roles. It is my contention that Stephen Fry and Jude Law bring with them a host of associations and connotations that serve to problematise the 'gay liberation' form of the homosexual heritage film. I will offer brief comments on these actors in turn.

Fry, like Wilde, is renowned for his ability with words. In addition to his autobiography, he has written several novels, and a collected volume of his journalism and other writings is also available. A formidable – and possibly rather intimidating – interviewee, Fry made his name in comedy, through associations with the Emma Thompson/Ben Elton/Kenneth Branagh crowd, his Radio 4 show *Saturday Night Fry*, regular slots on *Saturday Night Live* (UK), roles in *Blackadder*, and the TV series *A Bit of Fry and Laurie*. Mostly, Fry's sense of humour was (and

Figure 14.1 'Formidable – and possibly rather intimidating': Stephen Fry as Oscar in
           Wilde (1997).

Source: BFI Stills, Posters and Designs (Samuelson/BBC/Capitol/Pandora Films).

remains) caustic, punning and loquacious, centred around sophisticated wordplay. Skits and sketches performed by Fry and Laurie, their form often deconstructive of the conventions of comedy, frequently attacked the credibility and status of staid, dominant institutions: the civil service, doctors, psychiatry, spying, the army, and so on. Gay characters and references often appeared: one 'vox pop' moment in an episode of *Fry and Laurie*, for instance, featured Fry saying 'Oh yes. All of them. I've slept with every single one. Well every front-bencher anyway.' Prior to the making of *Wilde*, Fry had developed a reputation for unpredictability, boisterous largesse, and a threatening edge: he had a well-publicised criminal record (mostly for theft, although he was briefly imprisoned for fraud), and at one point absconded from the country to Belgium. This personal history impinges on Fry's portrayal of Wilde, with Fry's legal, sexual and intellectual profile – which I would label decidedly queer – dovetailing rather tidily with Wilde's.

And yet of course, like Wilde, Fry's 'radical' status is undercut by certain aspects of his biography. Raised in a financially well-off household (his father was an inventor), Fry attended a number of highly respected private boys' schools. His warm, mellifluous tones now appear regularly as the voiceover to a variety of advertisements, and he has been the genial host of the BAFTAs. His politics are unclear, although he has written regularly for the right-wing broadsheet the *Daily Telegraph*, and at one point nurtured a friendship with Prince Charles (a serendipitous connection back to the Prince of Wales). Fry has become, arguably, a 'respectable homosexual' – a queer wit, certainly, but one who rarely troubles the bounds of decency or propriety. In fact, it could be posited that Fry's transition into this patrician position occurred as a result of his playing Wilde.

In contrast, Jude Law is possibly the queerer figure in *Wilde*. From paparazzi photographs in weekly celebrity gossip magazines to official portraits for *Vanity Fair* by Mario Testino, Law is renowned for baring his trim, toned physique: his body is routinely offered up in still images as an erotic object of contemplation. This also occurs in his film roles – indeed, *Wilde* offers its audiences the spectacle of Law's sweaty, tensed torso as Bosie shudders to an orgasm astride Oscar, in addition to later, sustained shots of Law's buttocks. Jude Law's queerness, however, extends beyond the display of his body: extratextual, speculative gossip regarding his sexual orientation often circulates subculturally. In addition, several of the characters he has played – including those in *Gattaca* (Niccol, 1997) and *The Talented Mr Ripley* (Minghella, 1999) – are sexually ambiguous, open to queer interpretation and appropriation. Bosie, in *Wilde*, is not as queer as Oscar, primarily because he lacks Wilde's linguistic skill. However, the film does suggest that Bosie was the sexually more transgressive individual: he takes Oscar to visit a male brothel and openly gropes one of the men, Oscar's flowery utterances suddenly rather ineffectual and out-of-place; later in the film, Bosie fucks a 'renter' on a hotel bed as Wilde looks on, somewhat impassively.

Alternative versions

Neil Bartlett has expressed his exasperation at the conventional and predictable form that accounts of Oscar Wilde's life and work have taken – and his words can be seen to relate to the tidy 'gay lib' form almost wholly adopted by *Wilde*:

> The shape of the story was unconvincing, even though it was familiar. Everything I knew focused too neatly on one central event, apparently reflecting our own contemporary situation, in which everything can be described as being before or after 'coming out'. Even the texts in the *Complete Works* [*of Oscar Wilde*] seemed to be organized as either 'before' or 'after' the trials of 1895.[28]

As Bartlett complains, 'the picture wasn't complete. Bits were obviously and intriguingly missing. Some characters had been painted out, or rather had never been painted in.'[29] Wilde himself – especially in *De Profundis* – actually seems to have conceived of his own life narrative as having a conventional arc. However, the publication in recent years of a range of biographies of people whose lives touched Wilde's obliquely or fleetingly has highlighted the impossibility of 'fixing' his story in too neat a format.

Indeed, it would seem that the form of the heritage film, even with its generous incorporation of lesbian and gay characters, is too closely tied to a 'gay liberation' perspective to fully accommodate such paradoxical, potentially radically queer figures as Oscar Wilde. While I do not wish here to explicitly condemn *Wilde*, which is not without its pleasures, it may be that cinematic handlings of aspects of Wilde's life and work would be better suited by less conventional or generic formats. Because of this, it perhaps makes sense that Oscar appears in a more obviously 'queer' film like Todd Haynes' *Velvet Goldmine* (1998), a homage to the glam rock scene which plays with notions of authenticity and truth, surface and depth, and challenges conventional narrative structure. Haynes's movie opens in 1854 with the baby Oscar being deposited on his parents' doorstep in Dublin by a spaceship. Shortly after, as a young schoolboy, Oscar claims – brashly, anachronistically and queerly – that when he grows up he wants to be a pop idol.

Acknowledgements

The author would like to thank the audience at the *Screen* conference, July 2003, for their insightful suggestions and queries regarding a previous draft of this chapter.

Notes

1 Stephen Fry, *Moab is My Washpot* (London: Arrow Books, 1998), p.83.
2 Ibid., p.100.
3 Richard Dyer (2002) 'Homosexuality and Heritage', in *The Culture of Queers* (London and New York: Routledge), p.205.

4   Andrew Higson (1993) 'Re-presenting the National Past: Nostalgia and Pastiche in the Heritage Film', in Lester Friedman, ed., *British Cinema and Thatcherism: Fires Were Started* (London: UCL Press), p.114. See also: Cairns Craig (2001) 'Rooms Without A View', in Ginette Vincendeau, ed., *Film/Literature/Heritage: A Sight and Sound Reader* (London: BFI), pp.3–6; and Tana Wollen (1991) 'Over Our Shoulders: Nostalgic Screen Fictions for the 1980s', in John Corner and Sylvia Harvey, eds., *Enterprise and Heritage: Crosscurrents of National Culture* (London and New York: Routledge), pp.178–93.

5   Andrew Higson (2003) *English Heritage, English Cinema: Costume Drama since 1980* (Oxford: Oxford University Press).

6   Dyer, op. cit., p.204.

7   Ibid., p.206.

8   Andrew Higson, 'Re-presenting the National Past', op. cit., p.126.

9   Ibid., p.125.

10 Claire Monk, 'Sexuality and Heritage', in Vincendeau, ed., op. cit., p.9.

11 John Hill (1999) *British Cinema in the 1980s: Issues and Themes* (Oxford: Clarendon Press), p.94.

12 Ibid., p.96.

13 Andrew Higson (1996) 'The Heritage Film and British Cinema', in Higson, ed., *Dissolving Views: Key Writings on British Cinema* (London: Cassell), p.245.

14 Hill, op. cit., p.98.

15 Dyer, op. cit., p.207.

16 Ibid., p.207, p.208.

17 For a coruscating review of the film, see Tony Rayns, in Vincendeau, ed., op. cit., pp.186–8: he calls the film 'dull and superficial', lacking 'the courage to ditch its feeble aspirations to historiography' and displaying a 'dismal lack of wit'.

18 Wayne Koestenbaum (1990) 'Wilde's Hard Labour and the Birth of Gay Reading', in Joseph A. Boone and Michael Cadden, eds., *Engendering Men: The Question of Male Feminist Criticism* (New York and London: Routledge), p.181.

19 Ibid., p.177.

20 Gregory W. Bredbeck (1994) 'Narcissus in the Wilde: Textual Cathexis and the Historical Origins of Queer Camp', in Moe Meyer, ed., *The Politics and Poetics of Camp* (London and New York: Routledge), p.52. A similar argument is made by Michael Bronski (1984), in his book *Culture Clash: The Making of Gay Sensibility* (Boston: South End Press): see p.58.

21 Jonathan Dollimore (1991) *Sexual Dissidence: Augustine to Wilde, Freud to Foucault* (Oxford: Oxford University Press), p.8.

22 Ibid., p.14. For a critique of Dollimore's argument, and an alternative queer evaluation of Wilde, see Eve Kosofsky Sedgwick (1994) 'Tales of the Avunculate: Queer Tutelage in *The Importance of Being Earnest*', in *Tendencies* (London: Routledge), pp.52–72.

23 Dollimore, op. cit., p.25.

24 Neil Bartlett (1988) *Who Was That Man? A Present for Mr Oscar Wilde* (London: Serpent's Tail, 1988), p.34.

25 Andy Medhurst, 'Licensed to cheek', *Sight and Sound*, Vol. 7 No. 10 (New Series), October 1997, p.32.

26 In relation to this topic, it would also be worth assessing the use of language in the earlier film versions of Wilde's life. Unfortunately, I do not have room here to explore this avenue of investigation.

27 Dollimore, op. cit., p.67.

28 Bartlett, op. cit., p.29.

29 Ibid., pp.28–9.

15 An interview with Lisa Gornick

Reflections on a 'first draft' film about love and its labels

Ani Ritchie

At the world premiere of *Do I Love You?*, in a centrepiece screening at the London Lesbian and Gay Film Festival at the British Film Institute in April 2003, Lisa Gornick's debut DV feature was introduced as 'the first full-length film about UK lesbian life in more than a decade'.[1] As such, this film has attracted considerable attention both at home and abroad as has Gornick herself. *Do I Love You?* has toured worldwide over the last year, picking up several awards on the way including 'The Audience Award' at Cinnefable Festival Du Film (in Paris) and scooping Gornick the coveted 'Best New Director' at Seattle Lesbian and Gay Film Festival. The film was made on a shoestring budget of just £1,000 (pre grading and dubbing) with a tiny band of cast and crew. Gornick wrote, directed and starred in the piece which she has described as 'a thesis on love and its labels'; a film about questions not answers and a 'philosophical discourse on the notion of love'.

The film focuses on the life of thirty-something Marina (played by Lisa Gornick) as she searches for answers to the big questions in life. Marina's relationship with her girlfriend Romy (Raquel Cassidy) is on the rocks: 'there's something compulsive about the descent into cheating' she muses at one point in the film, as she explores the possibility of sex with ex and potential boyfriends. Her very identity as a lesbian is uncertain '. . . why in fact, am I a lesbian?' and she struggles with questions of gender. Marina turns to a range of the people we commonly seek answers from: her parents, her therapist, journalists and friends. Ultimately, she is left unsatisfied by all of these encounters, and although the relationship with Romy survives, the final scene shows Marina riding her bike along London streets, as Lisa Gornick suggests, 'still figuring it out'.

The following discussion, drawn from interview material and personal correspondence with Gornick, sets a context for *Do I Love You?*, exploring issues of production and philosophy with particular focus on the representation of lesbian sexuality and sexual activity in the film.

Ritchie: How does it feel to have made the first British lesbian film in over a decade?

Figure 15.1   'Still figuring it out': Marina (Lisa Gornick) contemplates her relationship
with Romy (Raquel Cassidy) in *Do I Love You?* (2003).

Source: Courtesy of Lisa Gornick (copyright Liane Harris/Valiant Doll).

Gornick: I wasn't aware when I made it that it was the first. I was aware that there
hadn't been many lesbian features coming out of Britain, but I wasn't aware
that there hadn't been any. I wasn't aware that I was making history when I was
doing it. I'm really pleased with the way the film's been taken on by Britain:
Millivres have bought the distribution rights, and Channel 4 took it on after the
London Lesbian and Gay Film Festival. The NFT have been really special in
their support of *Do I Love You?*, screening it during the film festival in 2003 and
also in a Valentines Day special in February 2004.

Ritchie: You made a short film with the same title in 2001, how related are the two
pieces?

Gornick: I wonder how related the short film is to it? I think it's more related in
name, well obviously in title; I kind of fell in love with the title when I was
working on the short, I got hooked on the title *Do I Love You?* and I wanted it
for the long film.

Ritchie: Can you tell me about the process of making the short film?

Gornick: With the short film I began by writing lots of little scenarios, but I didn't
quite know why I was doing it, I didn't have a whole film in mind. Mainly what
I was writing was dialogues or short scenes based on things that I would find
embarrassing. I think that I write in the same way that I used to improvise, I

love improvising. So I would be improvising with myself and writing the little dialogues up. I'm sure that's how most people write but because I come from acting first, when I wrote this film it felt very much like I was doing little improvisations with myself and writing it down very quickly. If an idea's come very strongly in the improvisation then I don't really edit it down and start crafting it.

It's a first draft film in a way. With screen-writing you go through fifteen drafts, and I think the ability of *Do I Love You?* is that there are hardly any drafts with this film. I didn't really change a lot of the first script. I like the *first-draftness* of it.

The short was very much an exploration of my early ideas. *Do I Love You?* the feature became much more about an investigation. In the feature I was able to write much more in the line of the narrator being in the thing, the author being in the thing.

When we came to shoot, we'd filmed about five scenes with other actors, and I didn't really feel part of it. I felt quite alien from it. I wonder if that was because I wasn't in it, and my desire was to jump in; I'm not saying I have to be in everything I film. My urge with *Do I Love You?* was to jump into the narrative. Maybe that is what I have to do with my films. People have said that I'm obviously influenced by Woody Allen, and I keep trying not to be, I keep saying that I'm not, but you know of course I am. One area where I do feel more influenced by Woody Allen is in the representation of the male characters though. I wanted to say a lot in the film about the idea of spectatorship – the watcher and the gaze. In terms of the ways in which men are used in the film, the roles were really a take on the way that I see a lot of men using women in films, you know they're in-out very quickly. I've been asked, 'why are the men in and out so quick', or criticised for having male characters that the audience can't get a real hold on. But that's actually done quite purposefully. You don't get to know the men because a lot of the time you don't know women in films. I meant it as a kind of joke. For example, Woody Allen has a lot of women and they come in and out, in and out. I suppose I wanted to say something about the male view of women as pretty little things. I think there's a gradation of men, I'm not sure if that's noticeable in the film, but I start off with a really nice man and then go down to the worst. I suppose the idea is that even nice men can be mean.

Ritchie: You have written that *Do I Love You?* (the feature) was intended as a 'thesis on love and its labels'. Can you tell me a bit more about how you view this theme operating in the film?

Gornick: I feel like I've had to back away from being philosophical because that doesn't sell. I learned a lot about what sells and what doesn't from the film festivals in America. If you use the word 'philosophy' or 'thesis', everyone just goes 'forget it' and they run a mile. I love those words; I want to make film punters not feel so scared of the word philosophy. There is this idea that you can't use that word, a misconception that although we might understand terms like philosophy, film audiences won't. But actually I think that film audiences will. There's this whole general fear that people are less intelligent than they are. People actually want to be complimented with intelligence, and I don't think all audiences do want to be fed everything with a really strong narrative – we need to credit audiences with a bit more intelligence than that.

I want to make philosophy films. In this film, I wanted to be like those men who go into cafés to talk and philosophise, but I wanted it to be women doing it. We don't see enough women doing that, we don't see enough women actively philosophising. It's ironic that some of the reviews that I've got have thought that the film is quite slight, and I feel they've misunderstood it. They don't understand those atavistic type philosophies; this film is not complete, it's about allowing the uncompleted thought, allowing the lack of answers. It's about allowing the doubt to be the philosophy.

I guess what I'm saying to my audiences is 'maybe you go and answer it, maybe my answer's going to be crap, maybe we all have to find our own answers'. A lot of the characters in the film are the kinds of people that you would go to for answers; the journalist, the therapist, the parents. But they don't give us the answers. I suppose at the end of the day, what I'm saying is 'you to yourself have to be true'. We go to all these gurus looking for answers, and what any guru will tell you is 'you know the truth'. And it's taken me such a long time to learn that. I hope that some of those beliefs come across in the film.

There's such demand for a strong conclusion at the end of films, and I always feel that pressure. In a way, the ending of this film *had* to be that they get back together. Had I been really brave I would have left them apart.

Ritchie: You tackle a lot of big questions around the issue of lesbian identity in *Do I Love You?* In particular, Marina seems to really struggle with questions of gender – in one scene in the film she suggests:

Maybe it's not wise to be away from men for so long, and maybe by avoiding them I was, in some strange way, turning myself into one. You see, all my sexual fantasies, in fact in order just to be sexual, I had to imagine I was this huge, burly, macho man.

Marina describes this *inner man* again when she is describing lesbian sex to her father, and later her mother asks '*you don't want to be a man, do you?*' We've spoken before about your desire to move away from autobiographical readings of the film, were you worried about including any of these issues?

Gornick: I was scared about including the men thing in case women didn't like it. I thought quite a lot about the gender stuff, but I think the one real fear I had was how women would respond to the male sex scenes. Luckily the women in the audience at the London Lesbian and Gay Film Festival screening laughed at those scenes, they didn't seem to get put off.

Ritchie: Did you feel any pressure to include such a range of issues? *Do I Love You?* tackles a lot of stereotypes and clichés about lesbian identity, did you ever worry about the way you represented these?

Gornick: I didn't feel like I forced anything in there. I really like philosophy books that are very quick and they cover a wide cornucopia; books where the writer is just floating around lots of different ideas. I really wanted to create a film that looked like that. So there was purposefulness in 'they could be this, they could be that . . .'. But it wasn't meant to be like ticking down a list of clichés or stereotypes.

I suppose that there was one pressure I felt on the film, with it going out to lesbian and gay audiences. I wanted hope for the film; I wanted to say a hopeful thing about love. I think sometimes I've said that and people have been like 'yey, love wins the day' and I think I did fall into a bit of narrative filmmaking there, wanting a happy ending. I suppose I did want a love story. I thought, okay, if anything I'll make a love story out of this and I won't be really philosophic and existential like 'well there's no answer' because that was going to be my last voice-over, in one of my edits 'there's no answer, on to the next?' I used to do that but I felt that people would have hated me even more then. Audiences would feel like they'd invested in my film only to come out with that at the end, with something bleak instead of something hopeful.

At the end of the film in the final edit I still say I'm figuring it out. The film doesn't tie up all the ends; I'm not simply saying 'we're great and guess what, I love her'. It's more about finishing with the realisation 'you know what, I'm still figuring it out'. I hope I've managed to allow enough of a question there. I hope that it's still a film about searching.

Ritchie: As you know, my research interests are fairly specifically focused on the representation of lesbian sex on screen, an issue debated at length during the panel discussion *Getcha Getcha Ya-Yas: Putting Lesbian Sex on Screen* which ran during the film festival at which *Do I Love You?* premiered. You've worked with sexual representation in the past – for example, the installation piece you made in 2002 (*A Graphic Love Story*). What I find interesting in *Do I Love You?* is that you've chosen to include heterosexual sex scenes but not lesbian sex scenes. How did you arrive at that decision?

Gornick: During the editing process I was sometimes criticised for not having enough sex in the film. People said that I needed to have more sex in it to make it sell. I didn't want to though; I didn't want to have to put more sex in it just to make it sell. The film does talk about sex, but in an intellectual way.

Ritchie: Scenes of sexual activity between women in the film seem often to be about sexual desire which is unconsummated. Marina rebuffs the attentions of her ex-girlfriend in the dinner party scene, she is unsure of how to respond to the therapist's flirtations. There is also the bedroom scene between Lois and Alice, where Alice rejects Lois's advances. It seems to me that there are several opportunities for sex scenes in the film and yet none are followed through?

Gornick: I think I shied away from the sex in that particular scene, with Lois and Alice. When I was working with male editors they loved that bit. I suppose it's like the heterosexual male view of lesbianism; sexy woman [Lois] comes in, does a dance, slides up the bed . . . I could have shown more of that in the final cut, but I wanted to focus on Alice's reaction to Lois, her rejection of this beautiful woman.

Ritchie: There's an interesting scene in the film where Romy and Marina are watching heterosexual pornography. Marina claims that Romy is becoming '*increasingly addicted to porn*' in the context of their relationship which has become asexual.

Gornick: I think in this scene, as in many scenes of the film, my intentions in the writing may have been different from what they became in the edit when I was able to reassess the scenes and give new meanings to them in their placement in the film, or the voice-over that accompanies them. This scene in my writing was about the passivity of the audience member in the face of the performance of sex on the screen. How we sit and are gorged at by the noise and passion of the television. It came from a picture I drew about a couple who aren't particularly presently sexual watching porn. It's about the banging noise and the silence of their relationship, a sad sexual moment. It was always meant to imply this, and I think it still shows a bad time in the relationship. But there are other layers to this scene as well. It's heavy heterosexual sex and perhaps alludes to Marina's fantasy about being a big daddy herself. It is also a scene where the audience knows more than Romy, because Marina is already embarking on her investigations into men and infidelity. I am interested in the audience aspect of our lives and I think this was an idea, connecting to the way that we accept what journalists say 'the wise people, the people who make money . . .'; the therapists, the parents. The television is just another place where we as audience members give up our power. Romy is stuck as an audience member, desperate to know the conclusion to a sex scene – '*I want to see what happens*'. This desperation for narrative is taken to the extreme of needing to know what happens in a porn scene. Her line now makes me smile, whereas I wonder, did I write it with a joke in mind?

Once a film becomes a 'lesbian film' it is required to have at least one sex scene. I would be really interested to try and shoot such a scene, but I didn't in this film, it didn't feel right at the time. I happen to love films without sex in them, but I am also intrigued about what a 'sex scene' is. This film was very much about 'what is sex?' But I did it without showing it. I didn't want to say too much.

Ritchie: Do you see *Do I Love You?* as a 'lesbian film'?

Gornick: Well it's interesting because I wonder if I do. Because I'm so struggling with labels would I want to label it? Would I just want it to be labelled how it wants to be labelled? And most people do label it as a lesbian film. I'm not saying it's not a lesbian film, but I was thinking of it more as a philosophical film. I started calling it a romantic comedy about breaking up, and not mentioning the word lesbian. I was told not to mention the word lesbian – by a lesbian – in order to sell it.

Ritchie: The character Marina in the film tackles this issue:

> *Louise seemed to base all her arguments on these huge definitions, this huge labelling. And I don't know if I particularly want to be branded in one big group, I've always found definitions very embarrassing. I don't know, I was probably in the midst of some huge branding crisis.*

You've frequently alluded to the autobiographical element of Marina's character; in the above quotation we see her questioning the labelling that Louise is so bound up in, and we've spoken about your reluctance to call *Do I Love You?* a 'lesbian' film. Are we all, as lesbians, in the midst of 'some huge branding crisis'?

Gornick: I think the film looks a lot about labels, and I think I use the term 'lesbian label' as a more universal thing about labelling being destructive. I mean I know it's been very important for lesbians to be able to say 'I'm a lesbian, I'm here I'm queer this is my label'. But I don't want to feel hemmed in by something. But I find the whole notion of 'lesbian' really exciting. Because it could be, or should be, something that is quite label-less. I think a lot of lesbians do like the branding, they do want the labels and maybe it's out of fear but they need to do that. Because they have to be butch or femme or at least make up their mind, they have to feel safe in their brand. But I haven't been brought up to do that. And I think it's important that some of us do reject the branding. I wonder if I did enough about that in the film?

I only avoid calling myself lesbian out of a fear of labels. I go, well maybe I am bisexual, and I might be that. But going around festivals has made me feel more strongly lesbian. I sometimes feel very British when I'm taking the film around festivals: I feel like a British filmmaker lesbian. I hear my accent a lot when I'm in these other places.

The film has been showing in lesbian and gay film festivals and I can see that lesbians are supporting the film. If the film is seen to stand up for all lesbians then some will see it and feel upset and say 'but this isn't me'. If it's seen as a 'lesbian film' then some lesbians will feel like 'well this doesn't say anything to me'. They might feel frustrated by the film, and that's okay, that's allowed. It's asking too much of the film to be the community voice, it shouldn't have to have this pressure, it should just be a film. I don't want to be the mouthpiece for UK lesbians. I really don't want to speak for all UK lesbians.

Ritchie: *Do I Love you* has been marketed very strongly as a British film. I know that you've toured with the film worldwide this year, have there been differences in the way that the film has been received outside of the UK?

Gornick: I think Britain is very different from America. The Americans are more worried about it. The British are like 'we're supporting our UK film' and I just felt 'I am British'. I suddenly felt really British. And I thought 'good for Britain'. This is the place to be. I feel a real hope for British Film actually. I just felt that America was so worried about it, and I felt like they'd take it if I was a man. If this was a man doing it, you know, if it had been a gay man doing it, they would have taken it; but I just felt like they were scared of lesbians. The distributors are just scared. The thing about American film festivals is that they're run by gay men, and I think gay men are scared of lesbian films, they're scared that they won't sell. And that's a great big misogyny that's still there for lesbians. I feel there is still a lot of feminism to be done.

Notes

1   Seventeenth London Lesbian and Gay Film Festival programme: p.8.

Selective filmography

This filmography alphabetically lists British and Irish feature-length films and television programmes which, as discussed in the introduction, can either be termed queer – in that they directly deal with lesbian, gay, bisexual, transgender themes and/or identities (e.g. *Beautiful Thing, Oranges Are Not the Only Fruit* or *The Crying Game*) – or in some sense or another lend themselves to, or openly solicit, a queer mode of interpretation – through sub-textual mechanisms or extra-textual perceptions of the orientations of the actors/directors/writers involved in their production (e.g. readings of 'the Glueman' in *A Canterbury Tale*, reinterpretations of Noel Coward's screenplay for *Brief Encounter* or the 'straight' roles of Dirk Bogarde or Kenneth Williams). This compilation is in no way exhaustive, and some films/television programmes may well have been omitted for one reason or another, but overall it is representative of the films discussed in this volume and those generally perceived to warrant special appreciative consideration by contemporary queer audiences.

As previous editors in this series have discussed at length, the criteria for classifying films as British are highly problematic in such a historically co-productive and international context. This is especially pertinent here when the majority of the films involved deal with themes that place them more than any other at odds with the limited funding resources and strategic commercial agendas of the British film 'industry'. International co-production/funding has therefore been a very real necessity in order to circumvent such heterocentric, prescriptive and commercially driven practices. Primarily then, this filmography lists films and television productions which are either British or Irish in origin and/or funding or, whilst funded or produced through non-British/non-Irish means, are still perceivably 'British' or 'Irish' in terms of their subject matter and/or location.

Data for each entry are presented in the following order

1. Entries are listed alphabetically by title
2. Film titles are indicated in capitals (e.g. AKA)

3. Titles of television programmes/series or feature-length television dramas/films are indicated in upper and lower case (e.g. *Dafydd*)
4. Year of first UK release/broadcast
5. Production company/ies
6. Country/ies of origin

Abbreviations used

BBC	British Broadcasting Corporation
BFI	British Film Institute
Cast	Main leading Actors
Dir	Director
Prod	Producer
Sc	Author of Screenplay
S4C	Channel 4 Wales
STV	Scottish Television
TV	Programme/film/series produced for television
UK	United Kingdom
USA	United States of America

This is by no means the definitive list of 'British Queer Cinema', but my aim here is more to illustrate the breadth of 'queerness' in British Cinema across a diverse range of genres and historical periods.

AKA (2002)

UK Film Council/Third Rock Films. UK. *Dir/Prod/Sc*: Duncan Roy.

Prod: Julian Hayward, Margaret Matheson, Richard West. *Cast*: Matthew Leitch, Lindsey Coulson, George Asprey, Peter Youngblood Hills.

Moving story of a young East End working-class lad, who escapes his abusive family life by assuming a new identity and infiltrating the very queer high society of late 1970s West London.

ALIVE AND KICKING (1996)

First Look Pictures. UK/USA. *Dir*: Nancy Meckler.

Prod: Lorraine Goodman, Martin Pope. *Sc*: Martin Sherman. *Cast*: Jason Flemyng, Anthony Sher, Dorothy Tutin, Anthony Higgins.

Poignant AIDS drama, charting the rocky relationship between a narcissistic young dancer and a middle-aged psychotherapist set in contemporary 'Swinging London'.

THE ANGELIC CONVERSATION (1985)

BFI. UK. *Dir/Sc*: Derek Jarman.

Prod: James Mackay. *Cast*: Dave Baby, Timothy Burke, Simon Costin, Judy Dench.

Dreamlike, surreal exploration of the hauntingly homoerotic nature of Shakespeare's sonnets.

ANOTHER COUNTRY (1984)

Goldcrest. UK. *Dir*: Marek Kanievska.

Prod: Alan Marshall. *Sc*: Julian Mitchell, from his stage play. *Cast*: Rupert Everett, Colin Firth, Michael Jenn, Robert Addie.

1930s public school memoirs of homosexuality and betrayal, based on the life of infamous spy Guy Burgess.

BEAUTIFUL THING (1996)

Film Four. UK. *Dir*: Hettie Macdonald.

Prod: Tony Garnett, Bill Shapter. *Sc*: Jonathan Harvey, based on his play. *Cast*: Glen Berry, Scott Neal, Linda Henry, Tameka Empson.

Teenage 'coming-out' love story set on a working-class council estate in south-east London.

BEDROOMS AND HALLWAYS (1998)

BBC Films/ARP/Pandora Film. UK. *Dir*: Rose Troche.

Prod: Ceci Dempsey, Dorothy Berwin. *Cast*: Tom Hollander, Hugo Weaving, Kevin McKidd, Simon Callow.

Unconventional romantic comedy about friendship, sexual experimentation and male bonding in 1990s London.

BENT (1997)

Film Four. UK. *Dir*: Sean Mathias.

Prod: Hisami Kuroiwa, Sarah Radclyffe. *Sc*: Martin Sherman, from his play. *Cast*: Clive Owen, Lothaire Bluteau, Ian MacKellen, Mick Jagger.

Intensely moving gay love story set in a Nazi concentration camp during the Second World War.

BILITIS (1982)

Films 21. UK/France. *Dir*: David Hamilton.

Prod: David Hamilton, Sylvio Tabet. *Sc*: Catherine Breillat, from Pierre Louys' novel. *Cast*: Patti D'Arbanville, Mona Kristensen, Bernard Giraudeau, Mathieu Carriére.

Erotic 'coming-of-age' lesbian melodrama, about a 16-year-old girl's relationship with an older woman.

BILLY ELLIOT (2000)

Working Title/BBC Films/Arts Council of England/Tiger Aspect. UK. *Dir*: Stephen Daldry.

Prod: Greg Brenman, Jon Finn. *Sc*: Lee Hall. *Cast*: Jamie Bell, Gary Lewis, Julie Walters, Jamie Draven.

Unrequited gay love in a heart-warming tale of an 11-year-old boy's desire to escape his poor working-class home life to become a ballet dancer in London.

BITTER MOON (1992)

R.P. Productions. France/UK. *Dir*: Roman Polanski.

Prod: Robert Benmussa, Roman Polanski, Alain Sarde, Timothy Burrill. *Sc*: Roman Polanski, Gérard Brach, John Brownjohn, from Pascal Bruckner's novel. *Cast*: Peter Coyote, Emmanuelle Seigner, Hugh Grant, Kristin Scott Thomas.

Satirical melodrama charting the complex sexual adventures of two couples aboard a cruise ship to Istanbul.

BORSTAL BOY (2000)

Hell's Kitchen/BSkyB/RTE/Irish Film Board. UK/Ireland. *Dir*: Peter Sheridan.

Prod: Jim Sheridan, Paul Myler. Sc: Nye Heron, Peter Sheridan, from Brendan Behan's book. *Cast*: Shawn Hatosy, Danny Dyer, Eva Birthistle, Michael York.

Semi-autobiographical drama exploring Irish poet Brendan Behan's experiences of life and love in a British borstal during the 1940s.

THE BOSTONIANS (1984)

Merchant Ivory Productions. UK/USA. *Dir*: James Ivory.

Prod: Connie Kaiserman, Michael S. Landes, Ismail Merchant, Albert Schwartz. *Sc*: Ruth Prawer Jhabvala, from Henry James' novel. *Cast*: Vanessa Redgrave, Christopher Reeve, Madeleine Potter, Jessica Tandy.

Nineteenth-century story of a love triangle between a repressed lesbian, a reactionary Southern lawyer and a young girl.

BOYFRIENDS (1997)

Essex Features. UK. *Dir/Sc/Prod*: Neil Hunter, Tom Hunsinger.

Cast: James Dreyfuss, Mark Sands, Michael Urwin, Andrew Ableson.

Witty exploration of the pitfalls of gay relationships in the 1990s.

BRIEF ENCOUNTER (1945)

Cineguild. UK. *Dir*: David Lean.

Prod: Noel Coward, Anthony Havelock-Allan, Ronald Neame. *Sc*: Noel Coward, Anthony Havelock-Allan, David Lean, Ronald Neame, from Noel Coward's play. *Cast*: Celia Johnson, Trevor Howard, Cyril Raymond, Valentine Dyall.

Post-war romantic classic exploring the passionate complexities of social responsibility and extra-marital infidelity.

BUTTERFLY KISS (1995)

Dan Films. UK. *Dir*: Michael Winterbottom.

Prod: Julie Baines, Sarah Daniel. *Sc*: Frank Cottrell Boyce, Michael Winterbottom. *Cast*: Amanda Plummer, Saskia Reeves, Kathy Jamieson, Des McAleer.

Disturbing psychodrama that puts an innovative spin on the 'killer lesbian' cliché.

A CANTERBURY TALE (1944)

Archers Film Productions. UK. *Dir/Sc/Prod*: Michael Powell, Emeric Pressburger. *Cast*: Eric Portman, Sheila Sim, Dennis Price, Freda Jackson.

Visionary war-time melodrama, about a journey of self-discovery that ensues as a rebellious young Land Girl and two soldiers attempt to solve the mystery of 'the Glueman'.

CARAVAGGIO (1986)

BFI. UK. *Dir/Sc*: Derek Jarman.

Prod: Sarah Radclyffe, Colin MacCabe. *Cast*: Nigel Terry, Sean Bean, Dexter Fletcher, Tilda Swinton.

Spectacularly elegant, homoerotic portrait of the bisexual Renaissance painter.

CARRINGTON (1995)

Polygram/Le Studio Canal Plus/Gramercy Pictures. UK/France. *Dir/Sc*: Christopher Hampton.

Prod: Francis Boespflug, Philippe Carcassonne, John McGrath, Fabienne Vonier. *Cast*: Emma Thompson, Jonathan Pryce, Jeremy Northam, Samuel West.

Unconventional love story about artist Dora Carrington's 'relationship' with flamboyant gay Bloomsbury Group writer Lytton Strachey.

CLOSING NUMBERS (1993)

Channel 4/Film Four.UK. *Dir*: Marc Jenny, Stephen Whittaker.

Prod: Jennifer Howarth. *Sc*: David Cook. *Cast*: Jane Asher, Nigel Charnock, Tim Woodward, Patrick Pearson.

Moving AIDS drama exploring the painful aftermath of a wife's discovery of her husband's secret homosexuality.

COWBOYS AND ANGELS (2003)

Wide Eye Films/Irish Film Board/Octagon Films. Ireland/UK/Germany. *Dir/Sc*: David Gleeson.

Prod: James Flynn, Nathalie Lichtenthaeler, Peter Stockhaus. *Cast*: Michael Legge, Allen Leech, Amy Shiels, David Murray.

Coming-of-age comedy drama about two mismatched Irish lads – one gay and one straight – who decide to share a flat together in the very cosmopolitan city of Limerick.

THE CRYING GAME (1992)

Palace Pictures/Channel 4. UK/Ireland. *Dir/Sc*: Neil Jordan.

Prod: Nik Powell, Stephen Woolley. *Cast*: Stephen Rea, Jaye Davidson, Miranda Richardson, Forest Whitaker.

Controversial political thriller exploring the 'unconventional' relationship between an ex-IRA assassin and a trans-gendered East End hairdresser.

Dafydd (TV) (1993)

Channel 4/S4C Wales. UK. *Dir*: Ceri Sherlock.

Cast: Richard Harrington, William 'Birdman' Thomas.

Ground-breaking Welsh-language film charting the troubled life of a young Welsh 'rent boy' living in Amsterdam.

DARLING (1965)

Vic Films/Appia Films. UK. *Dir*: John Schlesinger.

Prod: Joseph Janni, Victor Lyndon. Sc: Frederic Raphael. *Cast*: Julie Christie, Laurence Harvey, Dirk Bogarde, José Luis De Villalonga.

1960s classic about a young model's hedonistic experiences of 'Swinging London'.

DIFFERENT FOR GIRLS (1996)

BBC Films/CiBy Sales Ltd/Great Guns/X Pictures. UK. *Dir*: Richard Spence.

Prod: John Chapman. Sc: Tony Marchant. *Cast*: Rupert Graves, Steven Mackintosh, Miriam Margoyles, Saskia Reeves.

Romantic 'trannie' comedy about the mismatched relationship between two old school friends coming to terms with the fact that one of them has had a sex change.

DISTANT VOICES, STILL LIVES (1988)

BFI/Channel 4/Zweites Deutsches Fernsehen. UK. *Dir/Sc*: Terence Davies.

Prod: Jennifer Howarth, Colin McCabe. *Cast*: Pete Postlethwaite, Angela Walsh, Andrew Schofield, Dean William.

Haunting autobiographical portrait of a family's struggle with domestic abuse, set against the backdrop of war-time Britain.

DO I LOVE YOU? (2003)

Valiant Doll. UK. *Dir/Prod/Sc*: Lisa Gornick.

Cast: Lisa Gornick, Ruth Posner, Raquel Cassidy, Sarah Patterson.

Lesbian life, love and labels in contemporary London.

THE DRESSER (1983)

Goldcrest Films. UK. *Dir*: Peter Yates.

Prod: Ronald Harwood, Nigel Wooll, Peter Yates. Sc: Ronald Harwood, from his play. *Cast*: Albert Finney, Tom Courtenay, Edward Fox, Zena Walker.

Moving and humorous study of the interdependent relationship between a gay theatrical dresser and an ageing actor.

DR. JEKYLL AND SISTER HYDE (1971)

Hammer Film Productions/EMI Films Ltd. UK. *Dir*: Roy Ward Baker.

Prod: Brian Clemens, Albert Fennell. *Sc*: Brian Clemens. *Cast*: Ralph Bates, Martine Beswick, Gerald Sim, Lewis Fiander.

Unusual transsexual twist on the camp horror classic.

EAT THE RICH (1987)

Channel 4 Films/Iron Fist Motion Pictures. UK. *Dir*: Peter Richardson.

Prod: Michael White, Tim Van Rellim. *Sc*: Peter Richardson, Peter Richens. *Cast*: Nosher Powell, Ronald Allen, Lanah Pellay, Peter Richardson.

Outrageous attack on 1980s Thatcherite Britain, featuring an anti-establishment revolution led by a transsexual waiter.

EDWARD II (1991)

Working Title/BBC/British Screen. UK. *Dir*: Derek Jarman.

Prod: Steve Clark-Hall, Anthony Root. Sc: Derek Jarman, from Christopher Marlowe's play. *Cast*: Steve Waddington, Andrew Tiernan, Tilda Swinton, Nigel Terry.

Under-rated British contribution to the 'New Queer Cinema' movement, based on the life of England's most tragic and controversial King.

EMPIRE STATE (1987)

Four Corners/Team Pictures. UK. *Dir*: Ron Peck.

Prod: Norma Heyman. *Sc*: Mark Ayres, Ron Peck. *Cast*: Ray McAnally, Martin Landau, Lee Drysdale, Sadie Frost.

Homoerotic gangland thriller set in an East London gay club.

ENDGAME (2001)

Evolution Films/Various Films. UK. *Dir/Sc*: Gary Wicks.

Prod: Keith Dearling, Richard Hallows, Simon A. Maudsley, Andrew Tate. *Cast*: Mark McGann, Daniel Newman, Corey Johnson, Toni Barry.

Lurid gangland thriller about the sadomasochistic relationship between an East End crime boss and a teenage rentboy.

An Englishman Abroad (TV) (1985)

BBC. UK. *Dir*: John Schlesinger.

Prod: Innes Lloyd. Sc: Alan Bennett. *Cast*: Alan Bates, Coral Browne, Peter Chelsom, Vernon Dobtcheff.

Made-for-television drama, based on events in the life of notorious homosexual spy Guy Burgess.

ENTERTAINING MR SLOANE (1970)

Canterbury Film Productions. UK/Austria. *Dir*: Douglas Hickox.

Prod: Douglas Kentish. Sc: Clive Exton, from Joe Orton's play. *Cast*: Beryl Reid, Harry Andrews, Peter McEnery, Alan Webb.

Witty adaptation of Orton's controversial 1960s play, about a sexually ambivalent young man's manipulation of the bourgeois brother and sister with whom he lodges.

Forgive and Forget (TV) (2000)

STV.UK. *Dir*: Aisling Walsh.

Prod: Philip Hinchcliffe, Carmel Maloney. *Sc*: Mark Burt. *Cast*: Steve John Shepherd, John Simm, Laura Fraser, Meera Syal.

Touching contemporary social drama exploring the unrequited love between a closeted gay builder and his straight best friend.

FOUR WEDDINGS AND A FUNERAL (1994)

Working Title/Channel 4 Films.UK. *Dir*: Mike Newell.

Prod: Tim Bevan, Richard Curtis, Eric Fellner, Duncan Kenworthy. *Sc*: Richard Curtis. *Cast*: Hugh Grant, Andie MacDowell, Simon Callow, John Hannah.

Witty ensemble romantic comedy about love and loss amongst a group of friends in contemporary London.

THE FRUIT MACHINE (1988)

Granada Films. UK. *Dir*: Philip Saville.

Prod: Steve Morrison. *Sc*: Frank Clarke. *Cast*: Emile Charles, Tony Forsyth, Clare Higgins, Robbie Coltrane.

Romantic thriller about two Liverpudlian teenagers who go on the run after witnessing the murder of a transvestite at their local gay bar.

THE FULL MONTY (1997)

Channel 4 Films/Redwave Films. UK. *Dir*: Peter Cattaneo.

Prod: Paul Bucknor, Polly Leys, Uberto Pasolini, Lesley Stewart. *Sc*: Simon Beaufoy. *Cast*: Robert Carlyle, Mark Addy, William Snape, Hugo Speer.

'There's nowt as queer as folk' in this engaging 'masculinity-in-crisis' story of a group of unemployed Sheffield steel workers who become rather unconventional male strippers.

THE GARDEN (1990)

Channel 4/British Screen/Basilisk Productions. UK/Germany. *Dir/Sc*: Derek Jarman.

Prod: James Mackay. *Cast*: Tilda Swinton, Johnny Mills, Philip MacDonald, Spencer Leigh.

Surreal and poetic AIDS allegory, exploring images of homosexual love against a backdrop of homophobia and persecution.

GET REAL (1998)

Graphite Films/Get Real Ltd. UK. *Dir*: Simon Shore.

Prod: Anant Singh, Helena Spring. *Sc*: Patrick Wilde, from his play. *Cast*: Ben Silverstone, Brad Gorton, Charlotte Brittain, Kate McEnery.

Humorous but sensitive exploration of the complexities of teen sexuality and 'coming out' in 1990s Britain.

THE HAUNTING (1963)

Argyle Enterprises. UK. *Dir*: Robert Wise.

Prod: Denis Johnson, Robert Wise. *Sc*: Nelson Gidding, from Shirley Jackson's novel *The Haunting of Hill House*. Cast: Julie Harris, Claire Bloom, Richard Johnson, Russ Tamblyn.

A neurotic spinster and a ground-breakingly confident young lesbian are amongst a group of parapsychologists trapped in a haunted house in this classic 1960s horror story.

HOLLOW REED (1996)
Scala Productions/Senator Films/Iberoamericana. UK/Germany/Spain. *Dir*: Angela Pope.
Prod: Nik Powell, Stephen Woolley. *Sc*: Neville Bolt, Paula Milne. *Cast*: Martin Donovan, Ian Hart, Joely Richardson, Jason Flemyng.

Contemporary family melodrama about the bitter custody battle that ensues between a latent gay doctor and his ex-wife.

I WANT WHAT I WANT (1971)
Cinerama Releasing/Marayan Productions/Orion Pictures. UK. *Dir*: John Dexter.
Prod: Raymond Stross. *Sc*: Gillian Freeman, from Geoff Brown's novel. *Cast*: Anne Haywood, Harry Andrews, Jill Bennett, Paul Rogers.

Ground-breaking exploration of a young man's desire to live his life as a woman.

IF . . . (1968)
Memorial Enterprises/Paramount. UK. *Dir*: Lindsay Anderson.
Prod: Lindsay Anderson, Michael Medwin. Sc: David Sherwin, John Howlett. *Cast*: Malcolm McDowell, David Wood, Richard Warwick, Christine Noonan.

Unapologetically homoerotic allegory set in a repressive boarding school on the brink of anti-establishment rebellion.

JUBILEE (1978)
Whaley-Malin/Megalovision. UK. *Dir/Sc*: Derek Jarman.
Prod: Howard Malin, James Whaley. *Cast*: Jenny Runacre, Toyah Wilcox, Jordan, Little Nell.

Controversial queer punk fantasy set in a post-apocalyptic future England.

JUST LIKE A WOMAN (1992)
Zenith/Rank/British Screen/LWT. UK. *Dir*: Christopher Monger.
Prod: Nick Elliott, Nick Evans, Archie Tait, Fred Turner. *Sc*: Nick Evans, from Monica Jay's novel. *Cast*: Julie Walters, Adrian Pasdar, Paul Freeman, Susan Wooldridge.

Witty romantic comedy about heterosexual transvestitism.

THE KILLING OF SISTER GEORGE (1968)
Associates and Aldrich/Cinerama/Palomar Pictures. USA. *Dir*: Robert Aldrich.
Prod: Robert Aldrich, Walter Blake, Edgar J. Scherick. *Sc*: Lukas Heller, from Frank Marcus' play. *Cast*: Beryl Reid, Susannah York, Coral Browne, Ronald Fraser.

Blackly comic story of an ageing lesbian actress's struggle to keep both her relationship with her child-like lover and her job on a popular television soap opera.

THE L-SHAPED ROOM (1962)

Romulus Films/British Lion. UK. *Dir*: Bryan Forbes.

Prod: Richard Attenborough, James Woolf. *Sc*: Bryan Forbes, from Lynne Reid Banks' book. *Cast*: Leslie Caron, Anthony Booth, Avis Bunnage, Patricia Phoenix.

1960s social drama about a pregnant young woman's depressing experience of life in a London boarding house.

THE LAST OF ENGLAND (1988)

Channel 4/British Screen/ZDF/Anglo International. UK/Germany. *Dir/Sc*: Derek Jarman.

Prod: Don Boyd, Yvonne Little, James Mackay, Mayo Thompson. *Cast*: 'Spring' Rupert Audley, Gay Gaynor, Matthew Hawkins, Tilda Swinton.

Surreal, dream-like 'state of the nation' critique of 1980s Thatcherite Britain.

THE LAWLESS HEART (2001)

Martin Pope Productions Ltd. UK. *Dir/Sc*: Tom Hunsinger, Neil Hunter.

Prod: Francesca Barra, Steve Christian, Jim Reeve, Roger Shannon. *Cast*: Tom Hollander, Bill Nighy, Douglas Henshall, Stuart Laing.

Modern story of love, lust and death, told from three very different points of view.

THE LEATHER BOYS (1963)

British Lion/Garrick/Raymond Stross Productions. UK. *Dir*: Sidney J. Furie.

Prod: Raymond Stross. *Sc*: Gillian Freeman, from Eliot George's book. *Cast*: Dudley Sutton, Colin Campbell, Rita Tushingham, Gladys Henson.

Unrequited but sympathetically portrayed story of the homoerotic buddy relationship between a gay motorcyclist and a disillusioned but married young mechanic.

LIKE IT IS (1998)

Channel 4 Films. UK. *Dir*: Paul Oremland.

Prod: Tracey Gardiner, Martin Long. *Sc*: Robert Gray. *Cast*: Roger Daltrey, Dani Behr, Ian Rose, Steve Bell.

Unconventional contemporary romance between a closeted northern bare-knuckle boxer and a narcissistic London record producer.

A Little Bit of Lippy (TV) (1992)
BBC. UK. *Dir*: Chris Bernard.
Prod: George Faber, Howard Kingston. *Sc*: Martyn Hesford. *Cast*: Alison Swann,
   Danny Cunningham, Rachel Davies, Kenneth Cranham.

Cross-dressing northern comedy drama about a working-class heterosexual
couple's experimentation with transvestitism to spice up their dull sex life.

LOOK BACK IN ANGER (1959)
Woodfall Films. UK. *Dir*: Tony Richardson.
Prod: Harry Saltzman. *Sc*: Nigel Kneale, with additional dialogue by John Osborne,
   based on his stage play. *Cast*: Richard Burton, Claire Bloom, Mary Ure, Gary
   Raymond.

Classic 'New Wave' film based on John Osborne's controversial 'kitchen sink'
play.

THE LONELINESS OF THE LONG DISTANCE RUNNER (1962)
British Lion/Bryanston Films. UK. *Dir/Prod*: Tony Richardson.
Sc: Alan Sillitoe, based on his short story. *Cast*: Tom Courtenay, Michael Redgrave,
   Avis Bunnage, Alec McCowan.

Lyrical story of teen rebellion, set in the prototypically homoerotic confines of
an all-male borstal.

THE LONG DAY CLOSES (1992)
BFI/FilmFour. UK. *Dir/Sc*: Terence Davies.
Prod: Ben Gibson, Colin McCabe, Maureen McCue, Angela Topping. *Cast*: Marjorie
   Yates, Leigh McCormack, Anthony Watson, Nicholas Lamont.

Touching portrayal of working-class family life in 1950s Liverpool, as a young
boy comes to terms with his sexuality.

The Lost Language of Cranes (TV) (1992)
BBC. UK. *Dir*: Nigel Finch.
Prod: Ruth Caleb, Kimberly Myers, Mark Shivas. *Sc*: Sean Mathias, from David
   Leavitt's book. *Cast*: Brian Cox, Eileen Atkins, Angus MacFadyen, Corey Parker.

Moving drama about a young gay man's discovery of his father's hidden
homosexuality.

LOVE AND DEATH ON LONG ISLAND (1997)
BBC Films/Arts Council of England/British Screen.UK/Canada. *Dir*: Richard
Kwietniowski.

Prod: Steve Clark-Hall, Brian Donovan, Christopher Zimmer. *Sc*: Richard Kwietniowski, from Gilbert Adair's book. *Cast*: John Hurt, Jason Priestley, Fiona Loewi, Sheila Hancock.

Poignant study of an ageing writer's unrequited obsession with a young American actor.

LOVE IS THE DEVIL (1998)

BBC Films/BFI/Arts Council of England. UK/France/Japan. *Dir/Sc*: John Maybury.

Prod: Takashi Asai, Ben Gibson, Patrice Haddad, Frances-Anne Solomon. *Cast*: Derek Jacobi, Daniel Craig, Tilda Swinton, Anne Lambton.

Disturbing and surreal portrait of controversial British painter Frances Bacon.

MADAGASCAR SKIN (1994)

BFI/Channel 4. UK. *Dir/Sc*: Christopher Newby

Prod: Julie Baines, Sarah Daniel, Ben Gibson. Cast: John Hannah, Bernard Hill, Mark Anthony, Mark Pettit.

Offbeat love story between a disillusioned young gay man who finds romance with a petty thief at the seaside.

THE MAN WHO FELL TO EARTH (1976)

British Lion Film Corporation. UK. *Dir*: Nicolas Roeg.

Prod: Michael Deeley, Si Litvinoff, John Peverall, Barry Spikings. *Sc*: Paul Mayersberg, from Walter Tevis' novel. *Cast*: David Bowie, Candy Clark, Rip Torn, Buck Henry.

Unique study of 1970s alienation as a young gay lawyer helps a mysterious 'spaceman' establish a new life on Earth.

MAURICE (1987)

Merchant Ivory Productions. UK. *Dir*: James Ivory.

Prod: Ismail Merchant. *Sc*: Kit Hesketh-Harvey, James Ivory, from E.M. Forster's novel. *Cast*: James Wilby, Hugh Grant, Rupert Graves, Billie Whitelaw.

Classic gay love story that explores social repression and homosexuality in pre-First World War England.

MERCI DOCTEUR REY (2002)

Merchant Ivory Productions. UK/France. *Dir/Sc*: Andrew Litvak.

Prod: Ismail Merchant, Nathalie Gastaldo, Paul Bradley, Rahila Bootwala. *Cast*: Dianne Wiest, Jane Birkin, Stanislas Merhar, Simon Callow.

Humorous murder mystery about a lonely opera diva's gay son who witnesses the murder of his estranged gay father.

Metrosexuality (TV) (2001)

Channel 4. UK. *Dir/Sc*: Rikki Beadle Blair.

Prod: Laurence Bowen, Carol Harding. *Cast*: Rikki Beadle Blair, Noel Clarke, Rebecca Varney, Paul Keating.

Vibrant made-for-television comedy drama about polyracial and polysexual lifestyles in new millennial queer London.

MONA LISA (1986)

Handmade Films. UK. *Dir*: Neil Jordan.

Prod: George Harrison, Stephen Woolley, Denis O'Brien, Nik Powell. *Sc*: Neil Jordan and David Leland. Cast: Bob Hoskins, Cathy Tyson, Michael Caine, Robbie Coltrane.

Stylish underworld thriller in which a high-class prostitute hires an ex-con to help find her missing lesbian lover.

MONIQUE (1969)

Tigon. UK. *Dir/Sc*: John Bown.

Prod: Michael Style, Tony Tenser. *Cast*: David Sumner, Joan Alcorn, Sibylla Kay, Nicola Bown.

Low-budget 1960s comedy drama in which a bisexual French au pair spices up the marriage and sex life of a bored young couple.

THE MUSIC LOVERS (1971)

United Artists/Russfilms. UK. *Dir*: Ken Russell.

Prod: Roy Baird, Ken Russell. Sc: Melvyn Bragg, from Catherine Drinker Bowen and Barbara von Meck's book. *Cast*: Richard Chamberlain, Glenda Jackson, Max Adrian, Christopher Gable.

Controversial and flamboyant biography of Tchaikovsky, charting his disastrous relationships with women and confusion over his homosexuality.

MY BEAUTIFUL LAUNDRETTE (1985)

Channel 4/Working Title Films. UK. *Dir*: Stephen Frears.

Prod: Tim Bevan, Sarah Radclyffe. *Sc*: Hanif Kureishi. *Cast*: Gordon Warnecke, Daniel Day-Lewis, Saeed Jaffrey, Roshan Seth.

Provocative study of race relations and social economics in 1980s Britain told through the relationship between a young English-born Pakistani and his white racist gay lover.

The Naked Civil Servant (TV) (1975)
Thames Television. UK. *Dir*: Jack Gold.
Prod: Verity Lambert. *Sc*: Philip Mackie, from Quentin Crisp's book. *Cast*: John
  Hurt, Liz Gebhardt, Patricia Hodge, Stanley Lebor.

Witty biographical study of the dramatic life and flamboyant times of Quentin
Crisp.

NERVOUS ENERGY (1995)
BBC Scotland. UK. *Dir*: Jean Stewart.
Prod: Ann Scott. *Sc*: Howard Schuman. *Cast*: Alfred Molina, Cal MacAninch, John
  McGlynn, Siobhan Redmond.

Tragi-comic AIDS drama involving a Glaswegian man's nightmarish attempts to
gain acceptance from his estranged family.

NIGHTHAWKS (1979)
Four Corners/Team Pictures.UK. *Dir/Sc/Prod*: Ron Peck, Paul Hallam.
Cast: Ken Robertson, Tony Westrope, Rachel Nicholas James, Maureen Dolan.

Britain's first independent gay-themed film, exploring the double-life of a
closeted schoolteacher as he experiences the evolving gay nightlife of 1970s
London.

NINE DEAD GAY GUYS (2002)
Little Wing Films/9 Films. UK. *Dir/Sc*: Lab Ky Mo.
Prod: Amit Barooah, Robert Bevan, Amanda Coombes, Andrew Melmore. *Cast*:
  Glen Mulhern, Brendan Mackey, Steven Berkoff, Michael Praed.

Politically incorrect black comedy about the experiences of two penniless
straight Irish lads prostituting themselves on the contemporary London gay
scene.

NOCTURNE (1990)
Maya Vision. UK. *Dir*: Joy Chamberlain.
Sc: Trish Fairbanks. *Cast*: Lisa Eichhorn, Caroline Patterson, Karen Jones, Helena
  McCarthy.

Moving tale of self-discovery, as a middle-aged woman is forced to reflect upon
her repressive past after meeting two young lesbians.

Oranges Are Not The Only Fruit (TV) (1990)
BBC. UK. *Dir*: Beeban Kidron.
Sc: Jeanette Winterson, from her book. *Cast*: Charlotte Coleman, Geraldine
  McEwan, Kenneth Cranham, Pam Ferris.

Ground-breaking made-for-television 'coming-of-age' drama about the volatile relationship between a teenage lesbian and her oppressively evangelistic mother.

ORLANDO (1992)

Adventure Pictures/Lenfilm/Rio/Mikado/Sigma. UK/Russia/France/Italy/Netherlands. *Dir*: Sally Potter.

Prod: Christopher Sheppard. *Sc*: Sally Potter, from Virginia Woolf's novel. *Cast*: Tilda Swinton, John Wood, Lothaire Bluteau, Quentin Crisp.

Inventive and visually stunning adaptation of Virginia Woolf's controversial gender-bending novel.

PERFORMANCE (1970)

Goodtimes Enterprises/Warner Bros. UK. *Dir*: Nicolas Roeg, Donald Cammell.

Prod: David Cammell, Sanford Lieberson. *Sc*: Donald Cammell. *Cast*: James Fox, Mick Jagger, Anita Pallenberg, Ann Sidney.

Shocking and surreal story about a sexually repressed London gangster's experiences whilst hiding out in the hallucinogenic, gender-bending environment of a reclusive, androgynous rock star.

PETER'S FRIENDS (1992)

Renaissance Films/Channel 4/Goldwyn/BBC. UK. *Dir*: Kenneth Branagh.

Prod: Martin Bergmann, Kenneth Branagh, Stephen Evans, David Parfitt. *Sc*: Martin Bergmann, Rita Rudner. *Cast*: Stephen Fry, Emma Thompson, Kenneth Branagh, Hugh Laurie.

Touching comedy drama about a group of quarrelsome university friends who meet up on New Year's Eve and discover the tragic secret of their host.

THE PILLOW BOOK (1995)

Channel 4 Films/Studio Canal Plus/Kassander & Wigman/Alpha Films. France/UK/Netherlands. *Dir*: Peter Greenaway.

Prod: Terry Glinwood, Jean-Louis Piel, Tom Reeve, Denis Wigman. *Cast*: Vivian Wu, Ewan MacGregor, Yoshi Oida, Ken Ogata.

Beautiful, erotic avant-garde story of a bisexual Englishman's ménage-à-trois relationship with a vengeful young woman and a middle-aged publisher, set in post-modern contemporary Japan.

THE PLEASURE PRINCIPLE (1991)

Psychology News. UK. *Dir/Sc*: David Cohen.

Prod: David Cohen, Joe McAllister. *Cast*: Peter Firth, Lynsey Baxter, Haydn Gwynne, Lysette Anthony.

Low-budget sex comedy about a womanising freelance journalist and his lesbian ex-wife.

Portrait of a Marriage (TV) (1990)

BBC. UK/New Zealand. *Dir*: Stephen Whittaker.

Prod: Anna Kalnars, Colin Tucker. *Sc*: Penelope Mortimer, from Nigel Nicolson's novel. *Cast*: Janet McTeer, David Haig, Cathryn Harrison, Diana Fairfax.

Passionate made-for-television drama charting the tempestuous lesbian affair between writers Vita Sackville-West and Violet Trefusis-Keppel.

PREACHING TO THE PERVERTED (1997)

Cyclops Vision. UK. *Dir/Sc*: Stuart Urban.

Prod: Keith Hayley, Daniel Unger, Stuart Urban. *Cast*: Guinevere Turner, Christien Anholt, Tom Bell, Julie Graham.

Under-rated 1990s sex comedy about a young Christian conservative's sexual awakening whilst on an undercover assignment in the 'polymorphously perverse' House of Thwax fetish club.

PRICK UP YOUR EARS (1987)

Zenith/Civilhand. UK. *Dir*: Stephen Frears.

Prod: Andrew Brown. *Sc*: Alan Bennett. *Cast*: Gary Oldman, Alfred Molina, Vanessa Redgrave, Wallace Shawn.

Biographical account of cult playwright Joe Orton's turbulent relationship with, and subsequent murder by, his obsessive gay lover Kenneth Halliwell.

PRIEST (1994)

BBC/Electric Pictures/Miramax. UK. *Dir*: Antonia Bird.

Prod: George Faber, Joanna Newbery, Mark Shivas, Josephine Ward. *Sc*: Jimmy McGovern. *Cast*: Robert Carlyle, Linus Roache, Tom Wilkinson, Cathy Tyson.

Acclaimed controversial story of a closeted catholic priest's struggle with his double-life, and the aftermath of being publicly 'outed'.

PRIVATES ON PARADE (1982)

Handmade Films. UK. *Dir*: Michael Blakemore.

Prod: George Harrison, Denis O'Brien, Simon Relph. *Sc*: Peter Nichols. *Cast*: Patrick Pearson, Michael Elphick, Joe Melia, Denis Quilley.

Hilariously camp comedy about the adventures of a British army theatrical troupe's cross-dressing antics whilst entertaining the troops in the Malayan Jungle during the Second World War.

Queer As Folk (TV) (1999)
Channel 4. UK. *Dir*: Sarah Harding, Charles McDougall.
Prod: Russell T. Davies, Nicola Shindler. *Sc*: Russell T. Davies. Cast: Aidan Gillen,
   Craig Kelly, Charlie Hunnam, Denise Black.

Ground-breaking and highly controversial television drama exploring the
sexually promiscuous adventures of a diverse group of friends set in modern-day
Manchester's Gay Village.

A Question of Attribution (TV) (1992)
BBC. UK. *Dir*: John Schlesinger.
Prod: Innes Lloyd, Martin Pope. *Sc*: Alan Bennett. *Cast*: James Fox, David Calder,
   Geoffrey Palmer, Prunella Scales.

Biographical account of homosexual art dealer Anthony Blunt's exposure as the
'Fourth Man' in the notorious Cambridge spy ring.

THE RAINBOW (1989)
Vestron Pictures. UK. *Dir*: Ken Russell.
Prod: Dan Ireland, William J. Quigley, Ronaldo Vasconcellos, Ken Russell. *Sc*: Ken
   Russell, Vivian Russell, from D.H. Lawrence's novel. *Cast*: Sammi Davis, Paul
   McGann, Amanda Donohoe, Christopher Gable.

Sensual adaptation of D.H. Lawrence's classic novel about a bohemian lesbian
gym instructor's seduction of a sexually inquisitive young woman.

RICHARD'S THINGS (1980)
Southern Pictures. UK. *Dir*: Anthony Harvey.
Prod: Al Burgess, Mark Shivas. *Sc*: Frederic Raphael, from his novel. *Cast*: Liv
   Ullmann, Amanda Redman, Tim Pigott-Smith, Peter Burton.

Sombre made-for-television drama about the surprise lesbian affair that develops
between a middle-aged widow and her late husband's mistress.

THE ROCKY HORROR PICTURE SHOW (1975)
Twentieth Century Fox. UK/USA. *Dir*: Jim Sharman.
Prod: Michael White. *Sc*: Richard O'Brien, from his play. *Cast*: Tim Curry, Susan
   Sarandon, Barry Bostwick, Richard O'Brien.

High camp sci-fi spoof about the corruption of a clean-cut All-American young
couple at the hands of a group of bisexual alien transvestites.

SALOME'S LAST DANCE (1988)
Jolly Russell Productions. UK. *Dir*: Ken Russell.

Prod: Penny Corke, Dan Ireland, William J. Quigley, Ronaldo Vasconcellos. *Sc*: Ken Russell, Vivian Russell, from Oscar Wilde's play. *Cast*: Glenda Jackson, Stratford Johns, Nickolas Grace, Douglas Hodge.

Stylish and erotic fantasy in which Oscar Wilde and lover Lord Alfred 'Bosie' Douglas are entertained by an illegal performance of his banned play 'Salome' whilst visiting a gay brothel.

SCRUBBERS (1983)
Handmade Films. UK. *Dir*: Mai Zetterling.

Prod: Don Boyd, George Harrison, Denis O'Brien. *Sc*: Susannah Buxton, Roy Minton, Jeremy Watt, Mai Zetterling. *Cast*: Amanda York, Chrissie Cotterill, Debby Bishop, Elizabeth Edmonds.

Stark and disturbing drama set in the violent and erotic world of a women's prison.

SCUM (1979)
BBC. UK. *Dir*: Alan Clarke.

Prod: Don Boyd, Martin Campbell, Clive Parsons, Michael Relph. *Sc*: Roy Minton. *Cast*: Ray Winstone, Mick Ford, Martin Philips, John Blundell.

'Who's the Daddy?' in this highly controversial drama set in an intensely homoerotic and violent London borstal.

SEBASTIANE (1976)
Cinegate Ltd. UK. *Dir*: Derek Jarman.

Prod: Howard Malin, James Whaley. *Sc*: Paul Humfress, Derek Jarman, James Whaley. *Cast*: Barney James, Neil Kennedy, Leonardo Treviglio, Richard Warwick.

Innovative psycho-sexual exploration of the legend of St Sebastian.

SECRET CEREMONY (1968)
Universal Pictures. UK. *Dir*: Joseph Losey.

Prod: John Heyman, Norman Priggen. *Sc*: George Tabori, from Marco Denevi's short story. *Cast*: Elizabeth Taylor, Mia Farrow, Robert Mitchum, Pamela Brown.

Erotically charged story of the strange mother–daughter relationship that develops between a wealthy young woman and an ageing prostitute.

THE SERVANT (1963)
Springbok Films. UK. *Dir*: Joseph Losey.

Prod: Joseph Losey, Norman Priggen. *Sc*: Harold Pinter, from Robin Maugham's book. *Cast*: Dirk Bogarde, James Fox, Sarah Miles, Wendy Craig.

Cult 1960s psycho-drama about the homoerotic power games that ensue between an emotionally unbalanced upper-class young man and his manipulative working-class servant.

SHADEY (1987)

Larkspur Films/Channel 4. UK. *Dir*: Philip Saville.

Prod: Otto Plaschkes. *Sc*: Snoo Wilson. *Cast*: Antony Sher, Billie Whitelaw, Patrick Macnee, Katherine Helmond.

Off-beat spy spoof about a supernaturally gifted garage mechanic's attempts to find money for a sex change operation whilst pursued by a sinister lesbian British government agent.

SISTER MY SISTER (1994)

NFH Productions. UK/USA. *Dir*: Nancy Meckler.

Prod: Joyce Herlihy, Norma Heyman. *Sc*: Wendy Kesselman, from her play. *Cast*: Julie Walters, Joely Richardson, Jodhi May, Sophie Thursfield.

Harrowing true-life story of the incestuous relationship between two young maids employed in a 1930s French bourgeois household, who conspire to brutally murder their tyrannical Madam.

STONEWALL (1995)

BBC/Arena New York. UK/USA. *Dir*: Nigel Finch.

Prod: Ruth Caleb, George Faber, Anthony Wall, Christine Vachon. *Sc*: Rikki Beadle Blair, from Martin Duberman's novel. *Cast*: Guillermo Diaz, Fred Weller, Brendan Corbalis, Duane Boutte.

British-made fictional account of the historic events that led up to the Stonewall riots in New York in 1969.

SUNDAY, BLOODY SUNDAY (1971)

United Artists/Vectia Films Ltd. UK. *Dir*: John Schlesinger.

Prod: Joseph Janni, Edward Joseph. *Sc*: Penelope Gilliatt. *Cast*: Glenda Jackson, Peter Finch, Murray Head, Peggy Ashcroft.

Absorbing study of the love triangle between a separated career woman, a middle-aged gay Jewish doctor, and a young bisexual designer in 1970s London.

A TASTE OF HONEY (1961)

Woodfall Films. UK. *Dir/Prod*: Tony Richardson.

Sc: Shelagh Delaney, Tony Richardson, from Shelagh Delaney's play. *Cast*: Rita Tushingham, Murray Melvin, Dora Bryan, Robert Stephens.

Ground-breaking 'New Wave' classic based on the controversial stage play.

THE TERENCE DAVIES TRILOGY (1984)
BFI. UK. *Dir/Sc*: Terence Davies.
Cast: Terry O'Sullivan, Wilfrid Brambell, Sheila Raynor.

Poetic, partly autobiographical, three-part story of a Liverpudlian gay man's life from victimised schoolboy to repressed middle-age and subsequent death.

THIN ICE (1994)
Thin Ice Productions. UK. *Dir/Prod*: Fiona Cunningham-Reid.
Sc: Fiona Cunningham-Reid, Geraldine Sherman. *Cast*: Charlotte Avery, Sabra Williams, James Dreyfuss, Clare Higgins.

Low-budget lesbian romantic drama about the relationship that develops between an 'out and proud' black photographer and a sexually confused white middle-class amateur ice skater, as they team up to enter the figure-skating competition in the 1994 Gay Games.

THIS SPORTING LIFE (1963)
Independent Artists Production/Rank Organisation. UK. *Dir*: Lindsay Anderson.
Prod: Karel Reisz. *Sc*: David Storey, from his novel. *Cast*: Richard Harris, Rachel Roberts, Alan Badel, William Hartnell.

Tragic 'kitchen sink' drama about the doomed love affair between an aggressive professional rugby player and his widowed, sexually repressed, landlady.

Tipping the Velvet (TV) (2002)
BBC. UK. *Dir*: Geoffrey Sax.
Prod: Sally Head, Georgina Lowe, Gareth Neame, Sally Woodward Gentle. *Sc*: Andrew Davies, from Sarah Waters' novel. *Cast*: Rachael Stirling, Keeley Hawes, Anna Chancellor, Jodhi May.

Daring and passionate story of lesbian awakenings, set in the exciting world of the 1890s music hall.

TO DIE FOR (1994)
Victor/British Screen. UK. *Dir*: Peter Mackenzie Litten.
Sc: Johnny Byrne, Peter Mackenzie Litten, Paul McEvoy. *Cast*: Ian Williams, Thomas Arklie, Tony Slattery, Dillie Keane.

Supernatural romantic comedy about a Drag Queen who dies of AIDS, but later returns from the dead to haunt his former lover.

TOTAL ECLIPSE (1995)

Capital Films/FIT Productions/Fine Line Features/K2 Film. UK/France/Belgium/Italy. *Dir*: Agnieszka Holland.

Prod: Staffan Ahrenberg, Jean-Yves Asselin, Pascale Faubert, Philip Hinchcliffe. *Sc*: Christopher Hampton, from his play. *Cast*: David Thewlis, Leonardo DiCaprio, Romane Bohringer, Dominique Blanc.

Tempestuous exploration of nineteenth-century French poet Arthur Rimbaud's doomed, violent affair with fellow poet Paul Verlaine.

THE TRIALS OF OSCAR WILDE (1960)

Foreign Film. UK. *Dir*: Ken Hughes.

Prod: Irving Allen, Albert R. Broccoli, Harold Huth. *Sc*: Ken Hughes, from John Furnell's play and Montgomery Hyde's book. *Cast*: Peter Finch, Yvonne Mitchell, James Mason, Lionel Jeffries.

Moving courtroom drama charting Oscar Wilde's doomed libel case against the Marquis of Queensbury, during which he was accused and found guilty of sodomy.

TRIPLE ECHO (1973)

Senta/Hemdale. UK. *Dir*: Michael Apted.

Prod: Graham Cottle. *Sc*: Robin Chapman, from H.E. Bates' novel. *Cast*: Glenda Jackson, Oliver Reed, Brian Deacon, Anthony May.

Unusual cross-dressing drama about a young soldier, AWOL from the army during the Second World War, who disguises himself as a woman whilst hiding out at a remote farmhouse.

TWINS OF EVIL (1972)

Hammer Film Productions. UK. *Dir*: John Hough.

Prod: Harry Fine, Michael Style. *Sc*: Tudor Gates, Sheridan Le Fanu. *Cast*: Peter Cushing, Dennis Price, Mary Collinson, Madeleine Collinson.

Horror 'sexploitation' about twin vampires with an uncanny taste for biting their female victims on the breast.

Two of Us (TV) (1987)

BBC. UK. *Dir/Prod*: Roger Tonge.

Sc: Leslie Stewart. *Cast*: Jason Rush, Lee Whitlock, Jenny Jay, Kathy Burke.

Controversial made-for-television 'coming-out' drama about two teenage working-class boys who fall in love, but have to run away to the seaside to escape the homophobic social pressures of family and friends.

VALENTINO (1977)

United Artists/Aperture Films/Chartoff-Winkler Productions.UK/USA. *Dir*: Ken Russell.

Prod: Harry Benn, Robert Chartoff, Irwin Winkler. *Sc*: Mardik Martin, Ken Russell, from Brad Steiger's book. *Cast*: Rudolf Nureyev, Leslie Caron, Michelle Phillips, Felicity Kendal.

Surreal exposé of the sexually ambiguous life of silent screen legend Rudolph Valentino.

THE VAMPIRE LOVERS (1970)

Hammer Films/American International Pictures. UK. *Dir*: Roy Ward Baker.

Prod: Harry Fine, Michael Style. *Sc*: Sheridan Le Fanu, Harry Fine, Tudor Gates, Michael Style. *Cast*: Ingrid Pitt, George Cole, Kate O'Mara, Peter Cushing.

Camply humorous Hammer Horror classic, adapted from Sheridan Le Fanu's 'Carmilla', about an ageing lesbian vampire.

VAMPYRES (1974)

Essay Films/Lurco Films. UK. *Dir*: Joseph Larraz.

Prod: Brian Smedley-Aston. *Sc*: D. Daubeney, Thomas Owen. *Cast*: Marianne Morris, Anulka Dziubinska, Murray Brown, Brian Deacon.

Luridly exploitative erotic horror story about two lesbian vampires living in a decaying mansion.

VELVET GOLDMINE (1998)

Channel 4 Films/Miramax. UK/USA. *Dir/Sc*: Todd Haynes.

Prod: Christine Vachon. *Cast*: Jonathan Rhys Meyers, Ewan McGregor, Christian Bale, Toni Collette.

Postmodern pastiche of the 1970s glam rock scene, charting the volatile queer love affair between two very different rock stars.

VICTIM (1961)

Allied Filmmakers/Parkway/Rank Organisation. UK. *Dir*: Basil Dearden.

Prod: Michael Relph, Basil Dearden. *Sc*: Janet Green, John McCormick. *Cast*: Dirk Bogarde, Sylvia Syms, Dennis Price, Peter McEnery.

Historic 'social problem' drama about blackmail and homosexuality in the criminalised environment of early 1960s London.

VILLAIN (1971)

Anglo-EMI/Kastner/Ladd/Kanter. UK. *Dir*: Michael Tuchner.

Prod: Jay Kanter, Elliot Kastner, Alan Ladd Jnr. *Sc*: Dick Clement, Ian La Frenais. *Cast*: Richard Burton, Ian McShane, Nigel Davenport, Donald Sinden.

Violent East End gangland thriller about a sadistic homosexual crime boss.

WILDE (1997)
Samuelson/BBC/Capitol Films/Dove International/Pandora Films. UK/Germany/Japan. *Dir*: Brian Gilbert.
Prod: Alex Graham, Alan Howden, Deborah Raffin, Michiyo Yoshizaki. *Sc*: Julian Mitchell, from Richard Ellmann's book. *Cast*: Stephen Fry, Jude Law, Vanessa Redgrave, Jennifer Ehle.

Historical biopic of the iconic gay writer, charting his latent realisation of his homosexuality, and the stormy relationships that ultimately led to scandal and incarceration.

WILD FLOWERS (1989)
Front Room Productions. UK. *Dir*: Robert Smith.
Prod: Chris Harvey. *Sc*: Sharman MacDonald. *Cast*: Beatie Edney, Colette O'Neil, Stevan Rimkus, Sheila Keith.

Drama about a repressed young woman's fascination with her boyfriend's bisexual mother.

WITHNAIL AND I (1987)
Handmade Films. UK. *Dir/Sc*: Bruce Robinson.
Prod: George Harrison, Paul M. Heller, Denis O'Brien, David Wimbury. *Cast*: Richard E. Grant, Paul McGann, Richard Griffiths, Ralph Brown.

Witty and intelligent film that documents the lives of two out-of-work actors who flee their Swinging London flat for an idyllic weekend in the country at a gay relative's cottage.

WITTGENSTEIN (1993)
BFI/Channel 4/Uplink Co./Bandung. UK. *Dir*: Derek Jarman.
Prod: Tariq Ali, Takashi Asai, Ben Gibson. *Sc*: Ken Butler, Terry Eagleton, Derek Jarman. *Cast*: Clancy Chassay, Jill Balcon, Sally Dexter, Gina Marsh.

Avant-garde and highly intelligent study of the life of the alienated homosexual philosopher.

THE WOLVES OF KROMER (1998)
Disco Dog Productions. UK. *Dir*: Will Gould.
Prod: Charles Lambert. *Sc*: Charles Lambert, Matthew Read, from Charles Lambert's play. *Cast*: Lee Williams, James Leyton, Angharad Rees, Kevin Moore.

Unusual allegorical fantasy about the tragic gay love affair between two werewolves.

WOMEN IN LOVE (1969)
UA/Brandywine. UK. *Dir*: Ken Russell.
Prod: Larry Kramer. *Sc*: Larry Kramer, from D.H. Lawrence's novel. *Cast*: Glenda Jackson, Alan Bates, Oliver Reed, Jennie Linden.

Intensely homoerotic adaptation of D.H. Lawrence's classic novel.

YOUNG SOUL REBELS (1991)
BFI/Film Four. UK/France/Spain/Germany. *Dir*: Isaac Julien.
Prod: Nadine Marsh-Edwards. *Sc*: Paul Hallam, Isaac Julien, Derek Saldaan McClintock. *Cast*: Valentine Nonyela, Mo Sesay, Dorian Healey, Frances Barber.

Nostalgic and vibrant inter-racial gay love story set during the Queen's Jubilee in 1977.

ZEE AND COMPANY (1971)
Zee Films. UK. *Dir*: Brian G. Hutton.
Prod: Jay Kanter, Elliot Kastner, Alan Ladd Jnr. *Sc*: Edna O'Brien. *Cast*: Elizabeth Taylor, Michael Caine, Susannah York.

Complex drama about the love triangle between an estranged couple, and the philandering husband's bisexual lover.

Index

Page numbers in *italics* denotes illustrations

Aaron, Michele 121, 124
Accident 61, 65
Ackland, Rodney 38, 42
AIDS 14–15, 171–81; backlash against gay men and lesbians 172; bad gay scene in *Nervous Energy* 178–9; and bisexuals 15, 172, 173, 178; and 'gay positivity' 14, 172–3; and good gay man in *Closing Numbers* 15, 173–8; and myth of gay male vampire 171; and *Peter's Friends* 180–1; safer sex education and gay men 176–7
AKA 16, 216
Aldrich, Robert 11, 91, 92–3, 94, 110
Aliens 49
Alive and Kicking 216
Allen, Woody 209
Allsop, Kenneth 102
Altman, Dennis 4–5
Anderson, Lindsay 77, 83; *If . . .* 31, 224; *This Sporting Life* 10, 78, 81–3, *82*, 235
Angelic Conversation, The 145, 217
Another Country 13, 61, *62*, 197, 217
Araki, Gregg 121
Armstrong, Raymond 14, 145–56
As Good as it Gets 49
Asher, Jane 15, 173, *175*
Asquith, Anthony 3, 6, 8–9, 35–41, *36*, 44
Asquith, Lord Herbert 37
Astonished Heart, The 28
Atkins, Eileen 101
Austen, Jane 196

Australian cinema 184–5

Babuscio, Jack: *Gay News, The Importance of Being Earnest* 39
Bad Lord Byron, The 64
Badel, Alan 81
Barber, Felix 94
Barrios, Richard 36
Bartlett, Neil: *Who Was That Man?* 201, 205
Bates, Alan 78
BBC: and *Edward II* 154–5
Beautiful Thing 3, 15–16, 113, 183–93, *185*, *191*, 217
Bedrooms and Hallways 217
Behind the Mask 42
Bennett, Alan 128
Bent 62, 217
Bergman, Ingrid 37
Berkowitz, Richard 176–7
Berry, Glen 183, *185*
Betts, Ernest 57
Biches, Les 93
Bilitis 217–18
Billy Elliot 218
Billy Liar 83
bisexuality: and AIDS 15, 172, 173, 178
Bitter Moon 218
Black Tent, The 8, 42–3
Blair, Tony 173
Bloom, Orlando 198
Bloomsbury Group 111
Blue 145

boarding school 31
Bogarde, Dirk 3, 8, 38, 62, 64–7, 84; and
    aborted *Lawrence of Arabia* 41, 61; in
    Once a Jolly Swagman 26, 28, 65; *A
    Perfect Relationship* 67; in *The Servant* 64;
    television documentaries on 66; in
    Victim 22, 64, 66
Borstal Boy 13, 218
Bostonians, The 218
Bourne, Stephen 8–9, 35–44; *Brief
    Encounters* 23
Boyfriends 218
Branagh, Kenneth 180
'branding' crisis 17
Bredbeck, Gregory 199
Breton, Michéle 72
Bridge on the River Kwai, The 64
Brief Encounter 29, 219
British Cinema: Past and Present 1
Broadbent, Jim 163
Browne, Coral 94, *99*
Browning Version, The 8, 37, 40–1, 61, 63
Bryan, Dora 79
Burston, Paul 15–16, 188
Burton, Richard 78
Butler, Judith 71, 122
Butler, Ken 146
Butterfly Kiss 16, 219
Byrnes, Paul 68

Callan, Michael 176–7
Callow, Simon 8, 62, 110, 198
Cammell, Donald 71, 86
Canterbury Tale, A 3, 9, 47–60, *48*, *53*, 219
Captive Heart, The 63
Caravaggio 13, 145, 219
Caravan 29
Carpenter, Edward 107–8
Carrington 13, 197, 219
Carry on Cabby 26
Carry on Constable 7
Carry On films 6, 99
Cashman, Michael 181
Cassidy, Raquel 207, *208*
casting: significance of 8, 12, 28–9
Cavani, Liliana 65
childhood, gay: and Davies' home movies
    13–14, 133–42
Children 134, 136

Children's Hour, The 93
Christie, Julie 84
Christmas Carol, A 42
classical framework: and representation of
    homosexuality 11–12, 105–13
Clayton, Jack 78
closet bisexual 15
Closing Numbers 3, 15, 173–8, *175*,
    179–80, 219–20
Collins, Kevin 150
Collinson, Peter 23
Company of Wolves 160
Cook, Pam 35
Coward, Noel 6, 28, 44, 64
Cowboys and Angels 220
Crawford, Joan 153
Crossman, Richard 37
Crying Game, The 3, 5, 14, 157–68, *158*,
    166, 220
Cukor, George 40
Curram, Roland 84

Dafydd 220
Dahlman, Carl 159
Dance with a Stranger 67
Dangerous Exile 42
Dangerous Moonlight 42
Daniels, Ben 187
Danks, Adrian 72
Danquah, Paul 80
Darling 65, 83–5, 220
Davidson, Jaye 157, *158*, 163, *166*
Davies, Russell T. 16, 181
Davies, Terence 3, 13–14, 133–42;
    Distant Voices, Still Lives 13, 134, 135–8,
    135, 139, 142, 221; *The Long Day Closes*
    13, 134, 138–42, *140*, 226; *The Terence
    Davies Trilogy* 134, 136, 142, 235;
Davis, Fred 112
Davis, Glyn 11, 12, 195–206
Davis, Oscar 195–205
Day-Lewis, Daniel *123*
Dead of Night 40, 62
Deadly Affair, The 150
Dearden, Basil 9, 44
Death & Transfiguration 134
Death in Venice 65
Dehn, Paul 38
Delaney, Shelagh 79

Demobbed 33
Denison, Michael 39
Desert Hearts 188
Different for Girls 220
Distant Voices, Still Lives 13, 134, 135–8, *135*, 139, 142, 221
Do I Love You? 16–17, 207–14, *208*, 221
Dollimore, Jonathan: *Sexual Dissidence* 200, 202
Dors, Diana 43
Doty, Alexander 6, 9, 47–60, 122
Dover, K.J. 113
Dowling, Linda 107
Dr. Jekyll and Sister Hyde 221
Dresser, The 221
Dunbar, Adrian 159
DuttaAhmad, Shantanu 163
Dyer, Richard 5, 11, 12, 36, 79, 105, 116, 196, 197, 199

Eastenders 181
Eat the Rich 221
Edelman, Lee 171
Educating Archie 100
Edward II 14, 121, 145–55, *146*, 221
Ellis, Jim 13, 133–42
Elsaesser, Thomas 134
Empire State 222
Empson, Tameka 187, *191*
Endgame 222
Englishman Abroad, An 222
Entertaining Mr Sloane 222
Evans, Edith 39
Everett, Rupert 8, 61, 62, *62*, 67–8, 69
Everett, Wendy 139

Forbes, Bryan 11, 43
Farmer, Brett 5
Farrar, David 32
Father Brown 64
female homosexuality *see* lesbianism
Finch, Peter 195
Ford, John 42
Forgive and Forget 222
Forster, E.M. 107–8, 110, 111, 115, 196
Forwood, Tony 65
Foucault, Michel 122
Four Weddings and a Funeral 180, 222–3
Fox, James 73

Frears, Stephen 13, 122; *My Beautiful Launderette* 12, 111, 115, 122–4, *123*, 228; *Prick Up Your Ears* 13, 124–31, *125*, 231
Fruit Machine, The 223
Fry and Laurie 204
Fry, Stephen: personal history 12, 203–4; in *Peter's Friends* 180; in *Wilde* 12–13, 181, 195, 202, 203–4, *203*
Full Monty, The 223
Fuller, Graham 49, 50, 57

Gainsborough melodramas 6, 29
Garber, Marjorie 163
Garbo, Greta 153
Garden, The 145, 223
Garnett, Tony 186
Gateways 93, 96–7, 188–9
Gattaca 204
Gay Men's Health Crisis (GHMC) 177
'gay positivity': and AIDS 14, 172–3
gay rights movement 12
Get Real 12, 105, 111–12, 113–15, *114*, 223
Gibbs, Patrick 100
Gibson, Joy Leslie 68, 69
Gielgud, John 6, 44, 66
Gilbert, Brian 12, 181
Gillen, Aidan 181
Glamorous Night 42
Godfrey, Patrick 109
Gods and Monsters 61
Goring, Marius 32
Gornick, Lisa 16, 207–14, *208*
Gorton, Brad 112, *114*
Goulding, Edmund 40
Grant, Hugh *108*, 109
Graves, Rupert 198
Great Expectations 64
Greece: and cinematic representation of homosexuality 105–11
Greenwood, Joan 39
Griffith, Kenneth 8, 29, 30–1, *30*
Griffiths, Robin 71–87
Gruffudd, Ioan 198
Guinness, Alec 6, 8, 23, 62, 63, 64

Hales, Garry 181
Hallam, Paul 87

Halliwell, Kenneth 13, 124–31
Handler, Kristin 167
Hanson, Ellis 171
Hardy, Thomas 196
Harris, Richard 81, *82*
Hartnell, William 81
Harvey, Laurence 84
Haunting, The 223
Hawtrey, Charles 7, 100
Haynes, Todd 205
Heavenly Creatures 124
Helpmann, Robert 29
Henry, Linda 184, *191*
Henson, Basil 84
Hepburn, Audrey 93, 153
heritage films 11–12, 13, 116, 195–9,
    205; characteristics of 196; and
    homosexuality 11, 197–9; language of
    202; limitations in handling
    homosexuality as depicted in *Wilde*
    199–203
High Treason 27, 28, 29–31, *30*
Higson, Andrew 1, 106, 196, 198;
    English Heritage, English Cinema 196,
    197
Hill, John 10, 11, 76, 83, 198, 198–9
Hiller, Wendy 39
Hinson, Hal 128
Hird, Thora 78
HMS Defiant 61, 67
Hobbs, Christopher 134
Hollinghurst, Alan 111
Hollow Reed 224
Hollywood 92–3
homosexuality: de-criminalisation of
    (1967) 80, 95; shift in social
    perceptions of in 1960s 85
Horrabin, Winifred 57
Hours and the Times, The 121
Howard, Leslie 38
Howards End 196, 198
Howerd, Frankie 33, 100
Howes, Keith 1, 24, 61–9; *Brief Encounters:
    Lesbians and Gays in British Cinema* 35
Hungry Hill 42, 63
Hunn, Deborah 122
Hurst, Brian Desmond 8–9, 35, 41–4
Hutchings, Peter 10, 76
Hutchinson, Tom 116

I Know Where I'm Going! 35
I Want What I Want 224
Ideal Husband, An 68, 201
If . . . 31, 224
Importance of Being Earnest, The 8, 38, 39,
    61, 63, 201
Interview with a Vampire 160
Ireland 160–1
Italian Job, The 64

Jackson, Freda 9
Jagger, Mick 72, 73–4
Jagose, Annamarie 4
James, Henry 196
Jarman, Derek 87, 152, 172, 181, 183;
    Dancing Ledge 152; and *Edward II* 14,
    121, 145–55, *146*, 221; films directed
    by 145
Jenkins, H.: *What Made Pistachio Nuts* 101
Jennings, Ros 15, 183–93
Johnson, Celia 29
Jordan, Neil: *Crying Game, The* 3, 5, 14,
    157–68
Jubilee 2, 145, 149, 154, 224
Julien, Isaac 183
Just Like a Woman 224

Kalin, Tom 121
Killing Fields, The 66–7
Killing of Sister George, The 3, 11, 91–102,
    92, *96*, *99*, 189, 224–5
Kind Hearts and Coronets 63
Kind of Loving, A 10, 78, 83
King, Justine 106
Kinsey Reports 172
Kirk, Kris 24
'Kitchen Sink' film 106
Koestenbaum, Wayne 199
Kramer, Larry 172
Kureishi, Hanif 124

L-Shaped Room, The 11, 225
Lab Ky Mo 16
Lang, Fritz 63
Last of England, The 145, 149, 154, 225
Last Romantic, The 44
Laughton, Charles 61
Lauretis, Teresa de 200
Law, Jude 12, 13, 181, 201, 203, 204

Lawless Heart, The 225
Lawrence of Arabia 41, 61, 64
Lay, Samantha 76
Lean, David 41
Leather Boys, The 225
Lejeune, C.A. 35
lesbianism: and *Do I Love You?* 16–17, 207–14, *208*, 221; and heritage films 197; and *The Killing of Sister George* 11, 91–102; public invisibility of 10–11, 95, 96
Levine, June Perry 109
Like It Is 12, 115, 225
Lipman, Maureen 101
Little Bit of Lippy, A 226
Living End, The 121
Lloyd Pack, Charles 28
Lodger, The 33
London Lesbian and Gay Film Festival 207
Loneliness of the Long Distance Runner, The 78, 226
Long Day Closes, The 13, 134, 138–42, *140*, 226
Longtime Companion 176
Look Back in Anger 10, 77–8, 226
Lord of the Rings, The 61, 69
Losey, Joseph 64, 65
Lost 25–6
Lost Language of Cranes, The 226
Love and Death on Long Island 226–7
Love is the Devil 13, 227
Lovell, Alan 1
Lowenthal, David: *The Past is a Foreign Country* 106
Luckett, Moya 83–4
Lynd, Laurie 121

McBride, Stephen 146
MacCabe, Colin 71, 74, 75
McCall, Cathal 161
McCormack, Leigh *140*
Macdonald, Hettie 15, 183
MacGinnis, Niall 40
McKee, Alan 189, 192
McKellen, Ian 8, 61, 62, 68–9, 172
MacKinnon, Kenneth 13, 121–31
MacLaine, Shirley 93
MacQuitty, William 43
McVay, Douglas 54

Madagascar Skin 227
Madonna & Child 134
Major, John 172
Man of the Moment 24
Man Who Fell to Earth, The 227
Mandy 23
Mansfield Park 197
Marcus, Frank 92, 93
Marlowe, Christopher 146, 148
Maurice 11, 105, 106, 107–11, *108*, 112, 114, 197, 198, 227
Meckler, Nancy 16
Medhurst, Andy 7–8, 12, 21–33, 77, 80, 202
Melvin, Murray 79
Merci Docteur Rey 227–8
Metrosexuality 228
Mills, John 40, 63
Minney, R.J. 41
Modesty Blaise 67
Molina, Alfred 126, 179
Mona Lisa 228
Monique 228
Monk, Claire 197–8
Montgomery, Douglass 38
Morley, Robert 195
Morris, Mary 6
Morris, Meaghan 184–5
Mr Perrin and Mr Traill 31–2
Mrs Doubtfire 49
Munch, Christopher 121
Murphy, Robert: *The British Cinema Book* 1
Music Lovers, The 228
My Beautiful Laundrette 12, 111, 116, 122–4, *123*, 228

Naked Civil Servant, The 13, 229
Naked Truth, The 63
Neal, Scott 183, *185*
Nervous Energy 178–9, 229
New Labour government 16
New Queer Cinema 14, 121, 122
New Wave 3, 8, 9–10, *10*, 75, 76–83, 80 *see also* Anderson, Lindsay; Richardson, Tony; Schlesinger, John
Nicholls, Anthony 28
Nicholson, John Gambril 113
Night Porter, The 65
Nighthawks 86, 87, 229

1960s 71–87
Nine Dead Gay Guys 16, *17*, 229
No Love for Johnnie 63
Nocturne 229
Novello, Ivor 44

Old Dark House, The 61
Oldman, Gary *125*, 126
Once A Jolly Swagman 26–7, *28*, 31, *65*
Oranges Are Not the Only Fruit 229–30
Orders to Kill 38
O'Regan, Tom 185–6
Oremland, Paul 12
Orlando 5, 230
Orton, Joe 13, 124, 125–31, *128*
Osborne, John 77, 78
Oscar Wilde 195
Our Man in Havana 64

Pacey, Ann 94
Pallenberg, Anita *72*
Parker, Oliver 68
Parmar, Pratibha 121, 183
Pascal, Gabriel 38
Payn, Graham 28
Peck, Ron 87
Percy, Esme 39
Performance 71–5, *72*, 86–7, 230
Peron, Evita 153
Peter's Friends 180–1, 230
Pidduck, Julianne 188
Pillow Book, The 230
Pinter, Harold 64
Playboy of the Western World 44
Pleasure Principle, The 230–1
Portman, Eric 9, 38, 40, 48
Portrait of a Marriage 13, 231
positive unoriginality 184–6
Postlethwaite, Peter *135*
postmodernism 200
Potter, Sally 5
Powell, Michael 9, 35, 47, 55
Praed, Michael *17*
pre-gay British film: looking for queers in
   7–8, 21–33
Preaching to the Perverted 231
Pressburger, Emeric 9, 35, 47, 55
Price, Dennis 9, 29, 38, *53*, 61, 62, 63–4
Prick Up Your Ears 13, 124–31, *125*, 231

Pride and Prejudice 198
Priest 231
Prisoner, The 23–4
Privates on Parade 231
production code (US) 94
Providence 66
Puttnam, David 66
Pygmalion 8, 38–9

Qcinema 121
Quaker View of Sex, A 95
Queen Is Dead, The 149
queer: and gay 121–2
'queer', usage of term 4
queer cultural criticism 188
queer film studies 5
Queer as Folk 16, 181, 232
'queer gaze' 124
Queer Theory 4, 5, 122, 188, 200
Question of Attribution, A 232
Quiet American, The 63
Quinn, Vincent 28

Rainbow, The 232
Rank, J. Arthur 44
ratings system 94
Rattigan, Terence 38, 40, 41, 61
Rea, Stephen 157, *158*
Red Shoes, The 9, 55
Redgrave, Michael 6, 8, 9, 38, 62–3; in
   The Browning Version 61; in *Dead of Night*
   62; in *The Importance of Being Earnest* 39,
   63; in *The Way to the Stars* 40
Redgrave, Vanessa 42, 126, 130
Reed, Carol 41
Reid, Beryl 3, 11, 91, *92*, 94–5, 97,
   99–102
Reid, Fiona Cunningham 16
Reisz, Karel 78
Relph, Michael 44, 61
Remains of the Day, The 196
Remembrance of Things Fast 62
Reynolds, Robert 188
Rich, B. Ruby 14, 121
Richards, Dick 94
Richards, Jeffrey 1
Richard's Things 232
Richardson, Colin 15–16
Richardson, Miranda 159, 165, *166*

Richardson, Tony 77–8, 79, 188; *Look Back in Anger* 10, 77–8, 226; *A Taste of Honey* 79–80, *79*, 234–5;
Ritchie, Ani 16, 207–14
Ritchie, Guy 16
Ritchie, June 78
Roberts, Rachel 78, 81
Robertson, Ken *86*
Robinson, David 42
Rocky Horror Picture Show, The 232
Roeg, Nicolas 71, 86
Room at the Top 78
Room with a View, A 11, 105, 106–7, 109, 110, 111, 112–13, 116, 196, 198
Round the Horne 29
Roy, Duncan 16
Rozema, Patricia 197
R.S.V.P. 121
Russo, Vito 5, 36
Rutherford, Margaret 39

safer sex education 176–7
Salome's Last Dance 232–3
Salon, The 33
Sands, Julian 198
Sapphire 32–3
Saturday Night and Sunday Morning 78
Sayle, Alexie 101
Schlesinger, John 77, 83–5; *Darling* 65, 83–5, 220; *A Kind of Loving* 10, 78, 83
Schuman, Howard 178
Scrooge 42
Scrubbers 233
Scum 233
Sebastiane 145, 154, 233
Secret Beyond the Door, The 63
Secret Ceremony 233
Section 28 150–1, 173
Sedgwick, Eve Kosofsky 122
Seekers, The 28–9
Servant, The 61, 64–5, 67, 233–4
Sexual Offences Act (1967) 43, 95
Shadey 234
Shaw, George Bernard 38, 39
Shawn, Wallace 126
She'll Be Wearing Pink Pajamas 106
Sher, Antony 62
Shilts, Randy: *And the Band Played On* 171–2

Shirley Valentine 106
Shore, Simon 12, 113
Silence of the Lambs 49
Silverstone, Ben 112, *114*
Sim, Sheila *48*
Simba 42
Simon and Laura 33
Simpson, Mark 121–2, 167
Sinden, Donald 42
Sister My Sister 16, 234
Six Degrees of Separation 61
Some Like It Hot 153
South Kensington 62
Spanish Gardener, The 61
Spicer, Andrew 75
Steel, Anthony 42
Stevenson, Jack 84
Stewart, Jean 178
Stonewall 234
Street, Sarah 86
Sunday, Bloody Sunday 83, 234
Sunset Boulevard 73
Sweet, Sergeant John 57
Swinging London 10, 75, 83–4, *84*, 86
Swinton, Tilda 8, 147
Swoon 121
Syal, Meera 183
Syms, Sylvia 64

Tale of Two Cities, A 61
Talented Mr Ripley, The 204
Taste of Honey, A 79–80, *79*, 234–5
Tchaikovsky, Piotr Ilyich 154
Tempest, The 145
Terence Davies Trilogy, The 134, 136, 142, 235
Terrence Higgins Trust 177, 178
Terry, Nigel 147
Theirs is the Glory 42
Therese and Isabelle 93
Thin Ice 16, 235
Third Man, The 64
This Sporting Life 10, 78, 81–3, *82*, 235
Thynne, Lizzie 10, 11, 91–102
Tiernan, Andrew *146*, 147, 148
Tipping the Velvet 17, 235
To Die For 235
Total Eclipse 236
transvestism 163

Trials of Oscar Wilde, The 63, 195, 236
Triple Echo 236
Trottie True 42
Trouble in Store 24
Tuke, Henry Scott 112
Tushingham, Rita 79
Tutin, Dorothy 39
Twins of Evil 236
Two of Us 236

Valentino 237
Vampire Lovers, The 237
Vampyres 237
Velvet Goldmine 205, 237
Vertigo 165
Victim 9, *22*, 23, 28, 44, 61, 63, 64, 66, 77, 79, 97, 237
Victoria, Queen 10
Villain 237–8
Visconti, Luchino 44, 65

Waddington, Steven 146, *146*, 148
Walbrook, Anton 42
Walker, Alexander 113
Walker, Stephen 15, 173
Walters, Julie 129
War Requiem 145
Ward, Michael 3, 8, 24–7, *25*, 33
Warnecke, Gordon *123*
Warner, David 150
Waters, Sarah 197
Watney, Simon 177
Waugh, Thomas 113
Way to the Stars, The 40, 63
We Dive at Dawn 40
Wells, H.G. 38
Whale, James 6, 61
Wharton, Edith 196

Where Angels Fear to Tread 198
White, Armond 134
White, Chris 105
Whitehead, Tony 177
Whitman, Walt 113
Whittaker, Forest 159
Wilby, James *108*
Wild Flowers 238
Wilde 12–13, 181, 195, 197, 198, 199, 201–4, *203*, 205, 238
Wilde, Oscar 12, 39, 113, 195, 199–201, 202, 205
Wilder, Billy 153
Wilkinson, Tom 181, 201
Williams, Christopher 134
Williams, Kenneth 6, 7, 26, 28–9, 100, 127
Williams, Michael 11, 12, 105–16
Wilson, Elizabeth 95
Winslow Boy, The 37
Winterbottom, Michael 16
Wisdom, Norman 24
Withnail and I 238
Wittgenstein 145, 238
Wolfenden Report (1957) 10–11, 77, 95
Wolves of Kromer, The 238–9
Women in Love 239
Women, The 49
Woods, Gregory 14, 15, 171–81
Woodward, Tim *175*
Woollen, Peter 1
Wyler, William 93

York, Susannah 94, 96, *96*
Young Lovers, The 38
Young Soul Rebels 239

Zee and Company 239

Related titles from Routledge

Queer Cinema, the *Film* Reader
Harry Benshoff and Sean Griffin (eds.)

Queer Cinema, the Film Reader brings together key writings that use queer theory to explore cinematic sexualities, especially those historically designated as gay, lesbian, bisexual and/or transgendered. The collection examines the relationship between cinematic representations of sexuality and their social, historical, and industrial contexts. Sections include:

- Auteurs – examining the ways in which sexuality figures in the work of queer filmmakers;
- Forms – looking at queer cinematic spaces in film noir, the musical, and animated and horror films;
- Camp – looking at how this reception strategy and mode of textual production retains its critical charge in contemporary mainstream culture;
- Reception – three historical case studies of queer fans interacting with media texts.

Contributors include: Jack Babuscio, Richard Dyer, Sean Griffin, Harry Benshoff, Brett Farmer, Moe Meyer, Andrea Weiss.

Hb: 0–415–31986–2
Pb: 0–415–31987–0

Available at all good bookshops
For ordering and further information please visit:
www.routledge.com